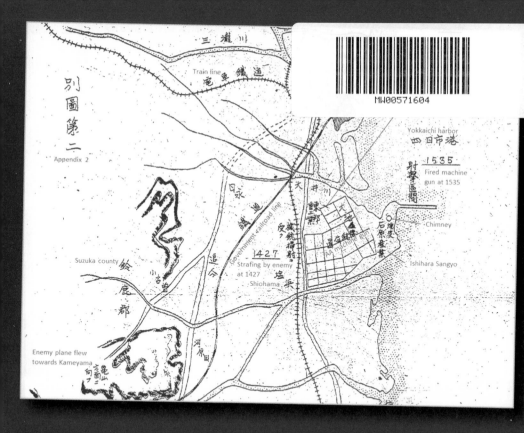

三瀧川
Appendix 2
別圖第二

Train line 電車鐵道
Yokkaichi harbor 四日市港

1535
Fired machine gun at 1535
射撃區間

Government railroad line
天井川

Chimney

Suzuka county
鈴鹿郡

1427
Strafing by enemy at 1427
塩浜
Shiohama

Ishihara Sangyo
石原産業

AA machine gun
高射機銃

Enemy plane flew towards Kameyama
亀山

# The New York Times.

NEW YORK, THURSDAY, APRIL 22, 1943.

LATE CITY EDITION

THREE CENTS

## JAPANESE EXECUTE OUR AIRMEN; U. S. WILL PUNISH ALL RESPONSIBLE; 8TH ARMY CAPTURES ENFIDAVILLE

PLANE OUTPUT
ELSON SAYS.
ILL GAINING

Secret Polish Radio
Asks Aid, Cut Off

BRITISH DRIVE ON

Eastern Anchor of Foe's
Southern Line Taken
in Encirclement

ADVANCE IN MOUNTAINS

Troops Push Past Djebel Garci
as First Army Takes Point
Above Medjez-el-Bab

By FRANK L. KLUCKHOHN

### Britain Warns Nazis on Gas; Hears They Plan to Use It

'Several Sources' Report Hitler Is Ready to
Employ Lethal Fumes in Russia—
Instant Reprisals Promised

By MILTON BRACKER

### PRESIDENT AGHAST

He Says Civilized People
Will Share Horror at
Act of Japanese

DOOLITTLE FLIERS VICTIMS

Some of 8 Captured Men Slain
as Bombers of Civilians—
Congress Members Angry

By BERTRAM D. HULEN

NAVY CALLED SLOW
IN SUBMARINE WAR

# VANISHING
# ACT

# VANISHING
# ACT

## THE ENDURING MYSTERY
## BEHIND THE LEGENDARY
## DOOLITTLE RAID
## OVER TOKYO

# DAN HAMPTON

ST. MARTIN'S PRESS
NEW YORK

First published in the United States by St. Martin's Press, an imprint of
St. Martin's Publishing Group

VANISHING ACT. Copyright © 2024 by Ascalon, LLC. All rights reserved.
Printed in the United States of America. For information, address
St. Martin's Publishing Group, 120 Broadway, New York, NY 10271.

www.stmartins.com

Design by Meryl Sussman Levavi

Library of Congress Cataloging-in-Publication Data

Names: Hampton, Dan, author.
Title: Vanishing act : the enduring mystery behind the legendary Doolittle
    raid over Tokyo / Dan Hampton.
Description: First edition. | New York : St. Martin's Press, 2024. | Includes
    bibliographical references.
Identifiers: LCCN 2023058453 | ISBN 9781250283245 (hardcover) |
    ISBN 9781250283252 (ebook)
Subjects: LCSH: Tokyo (Japan)—History—Bombardment, 1942. | World
    War, 1939–1945—Campaigns—Japan. | World War, 1939–1945—
    Aerial operations, American. | World War, 1939–1945—Soviet Union. |
    Emmens, Robert G., 1914–1992. | York, Edward J., 1912–1984. | Doolittle,
    James Harold, 1896–1993. | Arnold, Henry Harley, 1886–1950. | World
    War, 1939–1945—Prisoners and prisons, Russian. | Lend-lease operations
    (1941–1945)
Classification: LCC D767.25.T6 H36 2024 | DDC 940.54/4973—dc23/
    eng/20240122
LC record available at https://lccn.loc.gov/2023058453

Our books may be purchased in bulk for promotional, educational,
or business use. Please contact your local bookseller or the Macmillan
Corporate and Premium Sales Department at 1-800-221-7945, extension
5442, or by email at MacmillanSpecialMarkets@macmillan.com.

First Edition: 2024

10  9  8  7  6  5  4  3  2  1

*These are the times that try men's souls.*

*The summer soldier and the sunshine patriot will, in this crisis,*

*shrink from the service of their country; but he that stands by it*

*now, deserves the love and thanks of man and woman.*

*Tyranny, like hell, is not easily conquered.*

—Thomas Paine
December 23, 1776

# CONTENTS

# AUTHOR'S NOTE

Following the December 1941 Pearl Harbor disaster and the subsequent losses of Guam and Wake Island to the Japanese, the United States had its back against the wall in the spring of 1942. Washington desperately needed two things: time to rearm its military as much as possible and a gesture of defiance that would show the enemy, and also a fence-sitting Soviet Union, that America was still in the fight.

Attacking the Japanese homeland seemed to fulfill both needs.

Such an affront could derail Tokyo's offensive actions and curtail imperial momentum in the Pacific. This would buy some time for the United States, while undeniably demonstrating to Japan and her Axis partners in Berlin and Rome that the Second World War was far from over. A daring plan to raid Japan from the air was passed to Major General Henry Harley "Hap" Arnold, chief of the U.S. Army Air Forces, who chose Lieutenant Colonel James Doolittle to lead the mission. "Daring" because success hinged on doing what the Japanese considered impossible: Doolittle and his pilots would fly Army land-based bombers from an aircraft carrier far beyond the range of any expected attack.

Unfortunately, the carrier task force was detected by Japanese ships, and Doolittle was forced to launch from nearly twice the planned distance away from their targets. Fuel would be critical, if not impossible, but the Army pilots never hesitated. Sixteen B-25 Mitchells swept in from the Pacific east of Japan and caught the Japanese completely by surprise. Fifteen of those bombers hit objectives around Tokyo and other cities before roaring off at rooftop altitude toward China, where they hoped to land safely.

One Mitchell did not.

Plane 8, piloted by Captain Edward J. York, never made it to Tokyo. Instead, after crossing the Japanese coast, York and his copilot, Lieutenant Robert G. Emmens, headed northwest across Honshu and then across the Sea of Japan for the Soviet Union, where they landed and were interned for over a year. Reasons given for this extraordinary deviation range from the dubious to the ridiculous, yet the myths cloaking the only Doolittle bomber that actually landed after crossing Japan have endured for over eight decades.

This is not another account of the Doolittle Raid, but rather a close examination of the last enduring mystery connected to it: the flight of the raid's eighth bomber to Russia. In order to provide, at long last, a realistic explanation for this flight, this book analyzes the raid and examines its historical context, which is crucial to understanding why one of the Mitchell bombers flew to the Soviet Union rather than China.

For over eighty years the reason given was lack of fuel, which is technically true but contrived, and only a fraction of the story. Why was that aircraft, B-25 #42-2242, the only aircraft to fly off the USS *Hornet* with unmodified carburetors that caused such a problem? Why were Ed York and Bob Emmens the only pilots on the raid to have maps of Russia? Some published accounts of the Doolittle Raid put Plane 8 over Tokyo before it diverted to Russia, but that, like so much official accounting of the raid, is not true.

Plane 8 never flew within fifty miles of downtown Tokyo—and never intended to do so.

Courtesy of a Mr. Makoto Morimoto, an extraordinarily talented Japanese researcher, I have also included the actual bomb impacts for most of the Doolittle Raiders in this book. This evidence shows that, contrary to official after-action reports and colorful, but fictional, accounts of the mission, most of these detonated nowhere close to the planned or reported locations. In no way does this detract from the courage of those sixteen bomber crews; I have flown combat missions deep inside enemy territory, and even in modern warfare, with high-quality digital maps, GPS targeting, and amazingly accurate weapon systems, there is always a mist from the fog of war. How much foggier was it, then, for these men who *did not* have updated maps or targeting photos, men who had been navigating with marginal magnetic compasses at low altitude for hours over the open ocean, men who then attempted to hit targets they'd never seen and with only seconds to find them?

It was not possible to conduct accurate battle-damage assessment because no American aircraft would be over Tokyo again for two more years. The raid occurred during a very dark time in the history of the United States, and people needed heroes, which these men were. In fact, no one was especially interested in the actual results of the mission. It served its original psychological purpose against a determined, ruthless foe and, as you will read, purposes beyond that. If the primary targets were missed, the bombs still fell on Japan, and barely four months after Pearl Harbor this was just fine with the America of 1942.

Whenever possible, I quote first-person dialogue directly from primary sources and consult contemporary eyewitness accounts. I include plausible and verifiable accounts regardless of the observer's country of origin to give a balanced picture of the events, rather than one slanted from a purely American angle. My purpose, as in many of my other works, is to simply set the record straight and make the truth known to the reader. History told inaccurately is not history—it is fiction or, worse, propaganda.

In the case of Plane 8's vanishing act, there is no smoking gun. Doolittle himself had no written orders for the raid, nor did Ed York for his mission to the Soviet Union. There wasn't the time or the need. America was engaged in a literal life-and-death struggle, with a fanatical enemy at her throat, and a few quietly spoken sentences were all that was required to initiate the raid. However, as you will discover, when the circumstantial evidence is combined with post-mission intelligence debriefings and examined through a combat pilot's eyes, holes in the official story begin to show. Small ones, to be sure, but when taken together they grow large enough to strip away the façade and reveal the purposes behind Plane 8's extraordinary deviation to Russia.

I encountered many inconsistencies with both the official records and debriefs, as well as in Robert Emmens's book *Guests of the Kremlin*. Some authors accepted these accounts at face value, dug no further, and produced wildly inaccurate accounts of both missions. Other authors admirably strove to relate the truth, and did so to the extent this was possible. I discovered many of these inconsistencies were due to the elapsed time between the event and the writings, but others were deliberate obfuscation by officers who had sworn to keep a secret. Secrets, and a man's word, were taken more seriously than they generally are now, and Ed York and Bob Emmens were professionals who had given their word not to disclose the purpose behind their flight to Russia.

Robert Arnold, General Hap Arnold's grandson, told me his father once said, "someday, I'll tell you about Ski York and your grandfather." Unfortunately, the elder Arnold passed away before he could do so, and both Emmens and York carried the secrets to their graves, insisting there was no "mission" to the Soviet Union.

But there was.

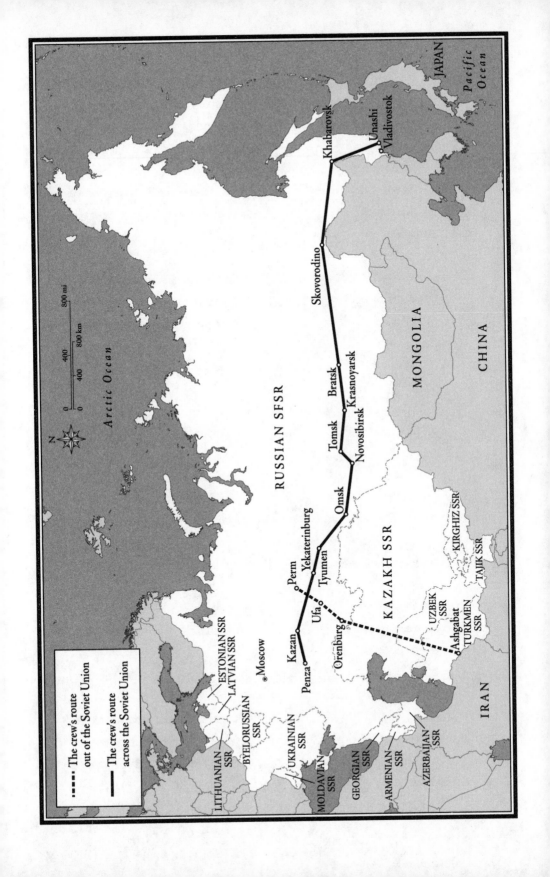

# PROLOGUE

APRIL 18, 1942

THE WESTERN PACIFIC OCEAN,

824 STATUTE MILES EAST OF TOKYO

Madness.

It was absolute madness, but he was going to do it anyway.

The pilot's hands were sweaty and his mouth was dry. Sitting in a bomber cockpit fifteen feet above the wooden flight deck and sixty-five feet over a pitching, churning sea, the twenty-nine-year-old Army Air Forces captain commanded the eighth plane in line for takeoff.

Watching the horizon pitch as the USS *Hornet*, America's newest aircraft carrier, swung into the wind, he reached over to three pairs of sliding levers mounted on a pedestal between the two cockpit seats. The left-hand pair were the throttles, and these were all the way back. He left these alone. Nudging the middle two black knobs fully forward, Ed York locked the propellers into position. The red-topped levers on the far right controlled the mixture of fuel and air into the carburetors, and the pilot tapped these all the way forward as well, since he would need all the power possible for this takeoff. Through the rudder pedals, the pilot felt a deep rumble as the warship's four massive Babcock & Wilcox steam turbines muscled the 26,000-ton carrier through angry seas at twenty knots. In company with the carrier *Enterprise* and four cruisers, the tiny task force was now less than five hours' flying time off the enemy coast; it was terribly vulnerable and exposed.

Like wet shields, ninety-six gleaming propeller blades from sixteen B-25 Mitchell medium bombers whirled in the heavy salt air. Two pilots in each cockpit stared at the twin tails of each preceding plane, the white-flecked ocean, and a Navy lieutenant named Edgar Osborne who, with a checkered flag, was leaning into the wind forward of the clustered bombers. Feeling the great carrier dip and rise a few times, the Signal Officer, as he was called, waited until the ship began to drop into a trough, then twirled his flag. When *Hornet* hit the bottom, the lieutenant lunged forward and pointed at the bow, flag extended like a fencer's foil. Immediately, the lead B-25 lurched ahead, agonizingly slow, as the carrier's bow slowly rose under the wave. Everyone watching had the same thought: *he'll never make it.*

But Lieutenant Colonel Jimmy Doolittle did just that. Famed aviator and racing pilot with a doctorate from the Massachusetts Institute of Technology, Doolittle represented the best that occurred when formal education was combined with practical experience and natural skill. A born leader and skillful organizer, he had the unique abilities and unimpeachable reputation necessary to make Arnold's basic plan an operational reality in the minimum amount of time.

And time was critical.

Just 131 days after the Imperial Japanese Navy attacked the American fleet at Pearl Harbor, the United States, reeling from a string of defeats, had finally turned to fight. Although two carriers, four cruisers, eight destroyers, and two oilers hardly constituted an armada, it

did constitute the bulk of American naval power remaining in the Pacific.*

The fifteen ships were also a dagger, albeit a thin one, aimed directly at the heart of the Japanese Empire.

None of the waiting pilots believed a handful of medium bombers would strike much of a blow, at least not a physical one, against the enemy. Sixteen aircraft with four bombs apiece were simply were not enough, but there were other types of wounds they fully intended to inflict—a psychological one, for instance, pricking the thin skin of Japanese national pride, which might provoke Tokyo into a rash act of some sort. This approach had merit against a foe obsessed with "saving face," and such an affront would be a figurative gauntlet slapped across the Empire's collective cheek. It would also show Japan, and the world, that the United States was able and willing to fight back, all propaganda to the contrary, and that she would not capitulate as had the moldy colonial empires Tokyo had defeated so easily over the past four months.

Of course, the mission could also backfire. To exact revenge, Japan might deploy its army from China into the Pacific. Even a fraction of this million-man force would render any near-term American counteroffensive problematic. Such an attack on the Home Islands could also trigger an invasion of Hawaii, which was unlikely, or genocidal retribution in China, which was very likely. On the other hand, such an insult might goad an enraged enemy into vengeance based more on emotion than on strategic or tactical logic—and an angry foe sometimes makes mistakes. Much must be chanced in war, and for Doolittle and his men this calculated risk was worth taking, which was why eighty brave Americans in a handful of land-based bombers found themselves on a pitching carrier deck 750 nautical miles off the Japanese coast.

---

* USS *Hornet* and *Enterprise*; heavy cruisers *Salt Lake City*, *Vincennes*, *Northampton*; light cruiser *Nashville*; destroyers *Balch*, *Fanning*, *Benham*, *Ellet*, *Gwin*, *Meredith*, *Grayson*, *Monssen*; fleet oilers *Sabine* and *Cimarron*.

Charging into twenty-knot gusts, *Hornet* now had forty-five miles per hour of wind over her flight deck. Doolittle, piloting the lead bomber, needed only another twenty miles per hour to get airborne and avoid sliding off the deck, clipping the carrier's island with his wingtip, or stalling. Like every other Army pilot behind him, Doolittle had never taken off at sea, but he wobbled into the air with distance to spare, and immediately commenced America's first offensive action against the Japanese Home Islands. The plan *had* been to close another 250 miles before launching the Mitchells, but as with most plans, this one had changed. Sighted by a seventy-ton Japanese patrol craft an hour earlier, the element of surprise was lost, and the decision was made to launch immediately. This meant flying 824 statute miles to the imperial capital and arriving over Japan in broad daylight. It also very likely meant not having enough fuel to reach the dubiously friendly Chinese coast after the attack.

Watching from the cockpit of the eighth plane, Captain Edward "Ski" York realized he was holding his breath and exhaled slowly. Staring through the salt-streaked windscreen, he swallowed hard as Doolittle's bomber seemed to hang motionless over the carrier's bow, silhouetted against the gray overcast as the big ship began to drop again. But Jimmy made it, and one after another, the next five B-25s clawed their way airborne, circled the carrier, then turned west. York watched the seventh plane, *Ruptured Duck*, crawl forward and then turn to line up on the broad white stripe running down the middle of the deck.

The Mitchell was a land-based medium bomber and was not designed to take off at sea from a carrier deck. But there it was, waddling into the air just as the six before it had done on this wet, overcast morning on April 18, 1942. Ski didn't really think the takeoff was going to be difficult, but as he watched, the *Duck* pitched up drastically, nose-high, and nearly stalled. At thirty feet over the deck this would have certainly been fatal, but the pilot, Captain Ted Lawson, managed to recover and waffle out over the waves. Flaps, York

thought. He forgot to lower his flaps for takeoff. Reaching down between the seats, barely above the floor, he checked his own flaps in the ten-degree down position.

Wiping his right hand on his pants, Ski leaned forward so he could see the man standing below the carrier's wing bridge holding a blackboard. It was Lieutenant Hank Miller, the naval aviator who'd taught the fine points of carrier takeoffs during premission training in Florida to the Army pilots—to all but York's copilot, Lieutenant Bob Emmens. Ski had done a few with Miller, though no one else knew but Colonel Doolittle. Plane 8 was added to the raid, seemingly at the last minute, and it was important that the other crews believed that. It was important that York's own crew, except Emmens, believed it as well. Squinting at the blackboard, Ski read the big block letters:

STABILIZER IN NEUTRAL!

Made sense.

With headwind generated by nature and the charging carrier, plus ten degrees of flaps and the carrier's upward pitch, there was no need to yank back on the controls as Lawson had done. Doolittle and the others had literally been tossed into the air, so York knew to resist the instinctive urge to pull back on the big yoke. Lining up on the white stripe, Ski peered around Emmens to ensure the right wingtip was clear of the carrier's island. It was, by a scant six feet, so there was no margin for error. Satisfied, he peered at the copilot's panel, then ran his eyes over the engine gages one last time. Manifold and oil pressure; main fuel tanks; oil and cylinder head pressure . . . they were all "in the green" range and operating perfectly. Glancing at Bob Emmens, both pilots nodded to each other, and the copilot stuck his fist out the side window, thumb up.

With practiced rhythm, the signal officer began whirling his flag as the carrier dropped. Straightening his legs, York pushed the rudder pedals to the floor to hold the brakes and smoothly shoved both throttles forward to their stops. Throbbing with raw power, the B-25 strained against the power of thirty-four-hundred horses, roaring filled the cockpit, and the entire plane vibrated. "Make damned sure those throttles don't slip back," York yelled, and he felt Bob's hand brace below his on the control quadrant. If the throttles were jarred back during the takeoff, they'd never get airborne, and, with no room to stop, the Mitchell would end up in the frothy ocean.

There!

Miller lunged forward when the carrier bottomed out in the trough, and as his checkered flag leveled, York's feet came off the brakes. Plane 8 weaved, and Ski's stomach tightened as the wheels slid sideways on the wet deck. Eyes locked on both white lines, the pilot controlled the rudders with his feet, fighting to keep the nose straight as the bomber gathered speed. From the corner of his right eye, Ski saw the carrier's island pass and the waving sailors vanished behind his wingtip. Amazingly, after a hundred feet, he felt the Mitchell's nose lift. Eyes flickering between the painted lines and *Hornet*'s rising bow, he managed a glimpse of the airspeed indicator: sixty-two miles per hour.

Now . . . now!

As the carrier's bow stopped pitching up, he felt that sweet spot every pilot knows when the wheels leave the ground, or in this case the deck, and the plane begins to *fly*. Swallowing hard again, he ignored a bead of sweat running over his left cheekbone and concentrated completely on keeping Plane 8 pointed at the gray sky between the clouds and sea. Blurred seconds passed . . . the sweat ran into his mouth . . . and then they were off! No deck beneath their belly, just tossing white caps.

Seventy-five miles per hour.

He felt Emmens shift and then heard the electric whirring as the flaps came up. The Mitchell's nose dropped with the loss of lift, but both big Wright Cyclones overcame that with pure power. Eyes locked on the fuzzy horizon, York began to breathe again as the nose lifted slightly and the plane again gathered speed. At one hundred miles per hour he eased the yoke over with a bit of right rudder and leveled off just fifty feet over the water. Truly flying now, Ski stole a glance back toward the *Hornet* but couldn't see her. A smaller warship, a destroyer he thought, made a magnificent sight clawing through the big waves with white spray feathering back from her bows.

One hundred and twenty miles per hour.

Reaching down, the pilot pulled the big green gear handle up and heard the hydraulics lift his three wheels. When the gear doors clanked shut, Ed exhaled, wiped his hands on his pants again one at a time, then headed west for the Japanese coast. It was 0846.

"Nice takeoff, Ski!" Bob Emmens shouted over the roaring engines. "How was it compared to your practice takeoffs back in Florida?"

York's eyes flickered to the bulkhead-mounted interphone box next to his left thigh. It was set to INTER, so the crew could listen to each other, and he needed them to hear this. "How the hell should I know?" York yelled back, and flashed a grin at the copilot, who grinned back. "I never made one."

# PART I

To every man upon this earth
Death cometh soon or late.
And how can man die better
Than facing fearful odds,
For the ashes of his fathers,
And the temples of his gods.

—Thomas Macaulay

# 1

## CLIMB MOUNT NIITAKA

One hundred and thirty-two days earlier, December 7, 1941, all six of the Imperial Japanese Navy's fleet carriers swung into the wind 230 miles north off the Hawaiian island of Oahu.* Less than a week before, Admiral Chūichi Nagumo had received a coded message stating, "Climb Mount Niitaka." He was now free to open his sealed orders confirming that the Empire of Japan was going to war against Britain and Holland—and the United States of America.

Lieutenant Commander Shigeru Itaya of the *Akagi* led the first of forty-three A6M Zero fighters into the air, followed by dive-bombers, torpedo bombers, and more fighters. All told, 353 aircraft struck the U.S. Pacific Fleet base at Pearl Harbor, and in less than two hours 18 warships were destroyed and 2,403 Americans killed in action. At 12:30 on December 8, 1941, President Franklin Roosevelt addressed a joint session of Congress to "ask that . . . since the unprovoked and dastardly attack by Japan on Sunday, December 7, 1941, a state of war has existed between the United States and the Japanese Empire." Petty differences forgotten, legislators absorbed

---

* *Akagi, Kaga, Sōryū, Hiryū, Zuikaku,* and *Shōkaku.*

the seven-minute speech, and by 13:10 the declaration passed both houses; America was once again at war.

The Japanese armada of thirty-two ships that steamed from freezing, fog-wreathed Hitokappu Bay twelve days before the attack was the military solution to a perceived strategic emergency: Japan, Hideki Tojo declared, was being strangled by the West—specifically the United States. Bereft of essential minerals such as copper, iron ore for steel production, and bauxite for aluminum, Japan was forced to import almost everything required for heavy industry and military manufacturing. For a nation bent on imperial expansion, this was a critical and unacceptable weakness.

China had been the immediate solution for many of these resource issues, and conquest of that country served as a convenient foil for surging Japanese nationalism arising during the global depression of the 1930s. However, control of China brought Japan directly into conflict with Imperial Russia, then later the Soviet Union, and both nations were wary of the other. Through concessions granted by the Chinese Qing dynasty, the Russian empire built a single-track rail line through Inner Mongolia to the port of Vladivostok. Following its 1902 completion, Russia then constructed a 600-mile spur line from Harbin in the Heilongjiang Province and then south to Port Arthur on the Yellow Sea, an ice-free, deepwater harbor and burgeoning naval base. Later termed the South Manchurian Railway, this spur line and the threat it posed to Japanese ambitions in China was a major catalyst for the 1904 Russo-Japanese War.

Following the 1905 Japanese victory in this conflict, rights to the South Manchuria Railway system and its surrounding zones of control were granted to Tokyo as a prize. Rail transport was vital for transporting the riches from the Manchurian interior to Port Arthur, so Tokyo constructed hospitals, schools, power plants, and spur lines all along the six-hundred-mile main railroad. Protesting Japan's widening encroachment, nationalist leader Chiang Kai-shek and Chang Hsüeh-liang, the "young marshal" of Manchuria, agreed to temporarily cooperate with each other to assert Chinese sovereignty over the contested areas.

Without orders from Tokyo, a small group of Japanese Kwantung Army officers decided to provide the Empire with an excuse for war. During the late evening of September 18, 1931, Lieutenant Suemori Kawamoto of the 29th Infantry Regiment detonated a small bomb near the railway tracks at Mukden, some 250 miles north of Port Arthur. The tiny blast did no physical damage, and despite a train passing safely through the area six minutes later, Japanese officers claimed that Chinese troops were responsible for the "attack." The Kwantung Army had its pretext for invasion. Promptly occupying the rest of Manchuria, the Empire eventually created the resource-rich puppet state of Manchukuo, which also provided vital access to China's interior and created a buffer zone against the Soviet Union. Japan answered swift global condemnation by withdrawing from the League of Nations in 1933 and, three years later, by signing the Anti-Communist International (Comintern) Pact with Nazi Germany.

On the night of July 27, 1937, a Japanese private named Shimura Kikujiro was on maneuvers with his unit north of Beijing when he supposedly went missing. His commander demanded permission from the Chinese garrison to enter and search the nearby town of Wanping, which was refused. A Chinese soldier panicked, firing a shot, and fighting immediately erupted. Tokyo, now firmly under nationalistic military control, had an ideal pretext for a full-scale invasion, and by mid-December 1937, Shanghai had fallen and Japanese soldiers were marching in a victory parade through Nanking, the former capital of the Republic of China.

Nearly three years later, during September 1940, following Germany's defeat of France, Tokyo joined the Axis and sent units of their 22nd Army into French Indochina. At the end of the month there were imperial troops stationed in Hanoi and Haiphong Harbor, as the Vichy government "allowed" Japanese combat troops to transit its territory. By April 1941, over 140,000 imperial soldiers were massed in southern Indochina, poised to strike into Malaya and the Dutch East Indies.

To date, Washington had reacted to the steadily worsening situation through a series of weak diplomatic protests and ad hoc actions intended to economically pressure Japan into acquiescence. Clawing itself out of the Great Depression, the United States was overwhelmingly isolationist regarding war—at least a war in Europe. Following Hitler's march into Poland in September 1939, fully 84 percent of Americans were against military intervention, though most supported contributing war materiel to fight the Axis. Becoming ensnared in another "European war" was an unpopular notion, and a majority agreed with Charles Lindbergh's statement that Americans should not "fight everybody in the world who prefers some other system of life to ours." Lindbergh, incidentally, *did* earnestly believe that the United States should fight in self-defense of the Western Hemisphere and itself.

However, by April 1941, American public opinion was changing. During the first twenty months of the Second World War, Hitler swallowed up western Europe and occupied the continental Atlantic coast from the Norwegian fjords to the Pyrenees. Italy had invaded Egypt, and Rommel was running wild in North Africa. Washington had passed the National Defense Act, initiated the nation's first peacetime draft, and sold Lend-Lease to the public. Sales of many resources to Japan, including scrap iron, aluminum, and any aviation gas over 87 octane, were curtailed or eliminated. Not oil, however—not yet. President Roosevelt believed, probably correctly, that any such move would provoke a rapid Japanese invasion of the Dutch East Indies, and America desperately needed time to build up its withered military.

But April 1941 was the final straw.

There was no way to ignore Tokyo's hubris, nor was there any ambiguity about such a troop buildup in southern Indochina. Congress passed H.R. 1776, "An Act to Promote the Defense of the United States," better known as Lend-Lease, in March, which permitted the president to transfer arms as he saw fit to any nations he deemed necessary for American security. Fully convinced now that Tokyo would not respond to anything but force, and having very little physical force at his disposal, Roosevelt flexed his economic muscles accordingly. All Japanese assets within the United States were frozen on July 26 by Executive Order 8832, which "was designed among other things to prevent the use of the financial facilities of the United States and trade between Japan and the United States, in ways harmful to national defense and American interests."

Japan outwardly protested, but her military leaders were largely nonplussed—they'd already decided to go to war, notwithstanding some drastic move for peace by the United States, so if anything, the embargo accelerated their timetable. The only obstacle to an imperial invasion of the Dutch East Indies and control over most of the South Pacific was the United States Pacific Fleet based in Oahu, Hawaii. Admiral Isoroku Yamamoto, commander of the Imperial Navy's Combined Fleet, had been formally planning an attack on Pearl Harbor since January 1941 but had been thinking of it much longer. He had also painstakingly analyzed Colonel Billy Mitchell's 1925 report, titled "Winged Defense," which detailed the harbor's weaknesses. Sixteen years before the Japanese attack, Mitchell wrote, "Bombardment, attack to be made on Ford Island (Hawaii) at 7:30 A.M. . . . . Attack to be made on Clark Field [Philippines] at 10:40 A.M." He also predicted such an attack would be made on a Sunday morning, which it was.*

Yamamoto knew the Americans had conducted several war games against Pearl Harbor during the 1930s, including Grand Joint Exercise Number 4 in 1932, where Rear Admiral Harry Yarnell's

---

* The Japanese did exactly that, at 07:55 on Sunday, December 7, 1941. Clark Field was hit at 12:35.

carrier aircraft suddenly appeared over Ford Island on February 7, 1932—a Sunday morning. Two additional Fleet Problems in 1933 and 1938 conclusively proved Hawaii's vulnerability, and the efficacy of attacks by carrier-based aviation. Many American naval officers were well aware of this threat and opposed Roosevelt's 1940 relocation of the fleet from Long Beach and San Diego to Hawaii. The president believed a base 2,500 miles closer to the Japanese would be a deterrent, but the professionals, particularly Admiral James O. Richardson, the Navy's preeminent Asiatic expert, disagreed. Suffering from budget cuts and the Depression, the Navy was in no position to fight in 1940, and they were certain that moving the fleet away from the protection of the American mainland only made it a more attractive target.

They were correct.

Yamamoto had taken a keen interest in the British Royal Navy's November 11, 1940, assault on the Italian battle fleet at Taranto. It was a large, relatively shallow, and well-defended anchorage similar to Pearl Harbor, and in the span of several hours obsolete British Fairey Swordfish had disabled half the enemy fleet. The Japanese admiral dispatched Lieutenant Commander Takeshi Naito from Berlin to make a personal survey, and this reaffirmed the viability of a surprise attack on the Hawaiian base. Though the Japanese considered the Soviet Union its greatest land-based threat, the American fleet had long been in the Imperial Navy's crosshairs.

In fact, Yamamoto had a hypothetical assault on Oahu added to the Imperial Naval Academy syllabus in 1936, the same year the Type 91 torpedo was modified with *kyoban*, wooden stabilizers that permitted aerial operations against shallow water targets— like Pearl Harbor. By 1938 a heavier warhead was added, along with improved, detachable wooden stabilizers, and by August 1941 an experienced pilot could ensure the Type 91 dove no deeper than thirty feet during an attack. Nazi Germany was so impressed with the torpedo that a technology transfer—torpedoes for radar—was proposed.*

While the summer and fall of 1941 was an anxious time for the United States, it was a heady period for the Axis and a doctrinal vindication of German national socialism, Italian fascism, and Japanese imperialism. Rommel's Afrika Korps controlled the Gulf of Sirte as far west as El Agheila, and he crossed Libya's eastern border heading toward Cairo and the Suez Canal. But the Axis suffered setbacks as well, which should have been a warning that, although surprised and often routed, the Allies were not as weak as expected and were capable of fighting back. Hermann Göring's vaunted Luftwaffe had been unable to destroy the Royal Air Force, and with increased American aid, Britain was hanging on. Then, during May, the Royal Navy succeeded in the impossible by sinking the *Bismarck*, pride of the German Kriegsmarine.

But the Paris Protocols had been signed that same month, which gave the Nazis access to all French military facilities in Syria. If Rommel could join through North Africa, this would effectively trap the British forces in Egypt in a vise and cost the Allies the Suez Canal. Hard-pressed though they were, the British responded in early June with an offensive aimed at neutralizing the threat from turncoat Vichy forces. Having surrendered thirteen months before to the Germans, the French commander of the Army of the Levant had no qualms about surrendering again, asked for an armistice, and signed the Convention of Acre on July 14, 1941. Yet Greece, Yugoslavia, and Crete had fallen to the Germans, and on June 22 Hitler invaded the Soviet Union. By late July his legions had swept through the Balkans and charged past Kiev in the south toward the

---

* *I-30* left Japan for Germany in late 1942, and the Type 91 was modified and designated *Lufttorpedo LT 850* by the Germans. In October 1942, loaded with blueprints and equipment for the Wurzburg air defense radar, *I-30* returned via Singapore. Fortunately for the Allies, it struck a British mine three miles into the Keppel Channel and the game-changing radar technology never reached Tokyo.

Black Sea. Smolensk had fallen, with some three hundred thousand Russians taken prisoner, and Fedor von Bock's Army Group Center was now less than four hundred miles west of Moscow.

Tokyo watched this particular offensive with great satisfaction and noted that with Moscow reeling from the heavy, multipronged German assault, the Russians were suddenly much less of a threat to Japanese actions in China and the Pacific. Well aware that Washington was at last rearming its emasculated military, Tokyo judged there would never be a better time to attack the United States. The oil embargo clenched it. Eighty percent of Japan's oil came from America, and without this incoming supply, Tokyo had only a three-year reserve stockpiled, which would be reduced to eighteen months or less under wartime conditions. Also, during the fall of 1941, German U-boats had torpedoed three neutral U.S. Navy destroyers, and American public opinion was swinging toward war.*

The Japanese had to move soon.

While the December 7 attack was successful, it was not the crushing blow Yamamoto planned. True, in addition to 2,403 lives lost there were four American battleships resting in the mud at the bottom of Pearl Harbor, and four others were damaged—but no aircraft carriers.† In 1941 the United States had only seven carriers in commission, and four were assigned to the Atlantic Fleet.‡ In the Pacific, the *Saratoga* (CV-3) was preparing to embark her air group from Naval Air Station San Diego just as Pearl Harbor was attacked. Task Force 8, centered on the *Enterprise*, lay 215 miles west of Hawaii that Sunday morning, while the *Lexington* and Task Force 12 were another eight hundred miles to the northwest. Both

---

* USS *Greer* (DD-145) by U-652, *Kearny* (DD-432) by U-568, and the *Reuben James* (DD-245) by U-552.

† The Japanese would count five battleships; however, the aged USS *Utah* (BB-31) was a target ship.

‡ USS *Ranger* (CV-4), *Yorktown* (CV-5), *Wasp* (CV-7), and *Hornet* (CV-8). The latter had been commissioned in October and not yet undergone her shakedown cruise.

carriers had ferried Marine aircraft to Wake Island and Midway Atoll, respectively, and were steaming home to Oahu.

Representing the bulk of America's remaining striking strength in the Pacific, the three carriers were irreplaceable targets, both strategic and tactical, and failing to destroy them would directly contribute to Japan's reversals during the battles of Coral Sea and Midway. Yet most of the Imperial Navy's battleship admirals, Yamamoto excluded, largely failed to grasp this. In their haste to declare victory, they also overlooked the disastrous error made by leaving the Pearl Harbor Navy Yard's vital infrastructure generally intact. Machine and repair shops, some two hundred thousand square feet of hangar space on Ford Island, and the coaling station were all unscathed. If the Japanese had bothered to hit the nearby 4.5-million-gallon fuel farm, not only would the Pearl Harbor Submarine Base and its four fleet boats have been destroyed, but also Pacific Fleet Headquarters, which was only a quarter mile to the west on Quarry Loch.*

There were also five hundred thousand barrels of cement, stockpiled during 1940 in preparation for naval expansion, that were immediately put to use. Companies like Utah Construction and Pacific Bridge leapt into the cleanup by repairing the drydocks, and within a few weeks two new runways were laid out on Ford Island. Of the four sunken battleships, two would be raised and refitted to see action, with the *West Virginia* (BB-48) eventually steaming into Tokyo Bay for Japan's 1945 surrender. The remaining battleships would be back at sea by the end of 1944, along with all the heavy cruisers damaged during the attack.

Prescient imperial officers were aware of the risks incurred from not finishing their December 7 attack, but "victory fever" brought on by Japan's string of easy victories mocked their concerns. Why did it really matter, the argument surged through

---

* USS *Narwal* (SS-167), *Tautog* (SS-199), *Dolphin* (SS-161), and *Cachalot* (SS-170). All four boats survived the war and, between them, earned twenty-nine battle stars by sinking thirty-three Japanese ships, totaling 86,435 tons.

wardrooms, officer's billets, and staff headquarters? Hideki Tojo, Japan's prime minister and minister of war, believed that America would certainly sue for peace after her defeat at Pearl Harbor and that, if she didn't, the Imperial Navy would lure the Pacific Fleet into open water and rapidly crush them. A humorless, unimaginative man, Tojo was a fervent ethnocentric who absolutely believed in the racial superiority of his people and in America's soft, decadent weakness. This underestimation of American tenacity, ability, and national rage would eventually prove fatal for the Japanese.

Yet for the weeks following Pearl Harbor and the early months of 1942, the United States faced several crucial, overarching challenges—namely, how to survive against Japan's onslaught while hastily mobilizing for total war. As of December 11, 1941, America faced not only the Japanese but also now Germany and Italy. Hitler's declaration of war was read aloud to Leland Morris, the U.S. chargé d'affaires in Berlin. "Your President has wanted this war," Joachim von Ribbentrop, Hitler's foreign minister screamed. "Now he has it!"

Indeed he did.

December 8, 1941, saw elements of the Japanese 25th Army come ashore below the Thai border on the northern Malay Peninsula and begin thrusting south toward Singapore. That afternoon, Sir Tom Phillips sortied from Keppel Harbor commanding Task Force Z. With his flagship, HMS *Prince of Wales*; the battle cruiser *Repulse*; and four destroyers, Phillips steamed north to intercept and annihilate the imperial invasion fleet in the South China Sea. Unfortunately, the British were sighted by a Japanese submarine and, on the morning of December 10, were attacked by over eighty aircraft operating from Japan and Korea. Riddled with bombs and pierced by torpedoes, both big warships went down by early afternoon. Stunned by the defeat, Prime Minister Winston Churchill stated: "In all the war, I never received a more direct shock . . . as I turned over and twisted in bed the full horror of the news sank in upon me. There were no British or American ships in the Indian Ocean . . . across this vast expanse of waters, Japan was supreme, and we everywhere were weak and naked."

Twenty-four hundred miles northwest of the stricken warships, 504 American defenders stranded on a wretched flyspeck watched the horizon beyond the Marianas Islands. They did not wait long. Within an hour of the Pearl Harbor attack, Japanese land-based bombers from Saipan rolled in to attack Guam, and before dawn on December 10, a thirty-ship enemy armada appeared off the coast and landed 5,900 imperial troops at various points on the island. Equipped with Great War vintage Lewis guns and 1903 Spring-field rifles, the 153 Marines, 271 sailors, and 80 natives of the Insular Guard Force were quickly overwhelmed. George J. McMillin, naval governor of Guam, surrendered the island that morning.

Thirteen hundred nautical miles northeast of Guam lay a heart-shaped coral atoll surrounding a pristine turquoise lagoon ringed with palms and tan beaches. Idyllic as it appeared, Wake Island was destined to crack the myth of Japan's invincibility and demonstrate quite clearly that the Empire could bleed. Wake had belonged to the United States for forty-two years and was used regularly by Pan American Airways clippers as they transited the Pacific. In De-cember 1941, its five-thousand-foot crushed coral runway and two adjoining islets were defended by Marines of the 1st Defense Bat-talion, a handful of sailors, and a detachment of Army Air Corps communications personnel. Also, ferried in three days before Pearl Harbor were twelve Grumman F4F-3 Wildcat fighters of VMF-211. All told, the atoll counted thirty-eight officers and 485 enlisted men, of which 449 were combat trained, plus 1,145 Morris-Knudsen Corporation civilians of the Contractors, Pacific Naval Bases (CP-NAB) detailed to Wake for various construction projects.

On Monday, December 8, Pan Am's *Philippine Clipper* lifted off from the lagoon bound for Guam, but was recalled twenty minutes later by Major James P. S. Devereux, commander of the 1st Marine

Defense Battalion detachment, who had just learned of the attack on Oahu. Commander Winfield Scott Cunningham, the senior officer on the island, put Wake on full alert while Major Paul Putnam, VMF-211's commanding officer, ordered all his planes dispersed and his pilots ready to launch. Four fighters were fueled, armed, and ordered off to sweep the sky around Wake. When the clipper splashed down, her pilot, Captain John Hamilton, immediately volunteered to conduct a long-range air search. Putnam agreed, and takeoff was set for early afternoon.

They were too late.

Just before noon, thirty-four G3M Nell land-based naval bombers from Kwajalein's Twenty-Fourth Air Flotilla arrived overhead. With no radar, and with the engine noise drowned out by crashing waves, the Marine anti-aircraft guns had little warning, and bombs, glittering in the bright sunlight, tumbled down on Wake. Their first target was the airfield, and this initial attack mauled seven of the parked Wildcats, destroyed both 25,000-gallon fuel tanks, and killed or wounded thirty-three men from VMF-211. The fighter squadron, and Wake's best defense, was tactically emasculated, but the defenders were determined to hold on. Most of the civilians volunteered to help in any manner required: they transported ammunition and the wounded and repaired fortifications, and many chose to fight. For two days Japanese bombers ravaged the island, pocking the runway, destroying communications, and leveling the hospital. To a man, the defenders kept faith that they would not be deserted, that reinforcements were on the way from Pearl Harbor, and that these would arrive before the Japanese attempted a seaborne assault.

They were wrong on all counts.

During the night of December 10, the fleet submarine USS *Triton* picked up flashing surface lights south of Wake, as did the Marine lookouts on nearby Wilkes Island, and as the sun rose on December 11, three imperial cruisers with six destroyers appeared to the south.

There were also two armed transports for the 450 men Rear Admiral Sadamichi Kajioka believed could subdue Wake, in addition to a pair of old patrol boats for close escort. Eight thousand yards off Wake's south shore, the light cruiser *Yūbari* ran parallel to the beach receiving no fire and observing no movement. Watched all the way by the concealed Marines, at 0615 when she reversed and moved into 3,500 yards, the American five-inch shore batteries opened up. Kajioka's flagship took four solid hits at the waterline, sending *Yūbari* limping away listing heavily to port. From Wilke's Island, three salvos from Battery L's guns slammed into the destroyer *Hayate*, which promptly blew up and sank with her entire 167-man crew. Another destroyer was damaged, and both transports put about then, hastily headed out to sea in the face of Wake's fire.

At twenty thousand feet overhead, Major Putnam and the three remaining Wildcats waited until the enemy ships were beyond the range of the shore batteries, then pounced. Captain Henry Elrod put a hundred-pound bomb into the destroyer *Kisaragi*, which slewed to a stop, afire and covered by black smoke. Shocked by the vicious American defense, Kajioka broke off the action by 0700 and retreated toward Kwajalein. The forty-five-minute battle cost the Imperial Navy two destroyers sunk and three damaged along with a transport. All three cruisers were mangled by Wake's shore batteries. Battered but still fighting, the atoll's defenders gave the Imperial Navy its first bloody nose and unequivocally punctured the aura of Japanese invincibility. Heartened by the victory, Cunningham, Devereaux, and Putnam believed they could, in fact, survive until reinforcements arrived.

So they might have, if the current commander in chief, Pacific Fleet (CincPac) at Pearl Harbor had acted immediately and decisively. Still reeling from the Pearl Harbor disaster, and correctly expecting to be relieved of command, Admiral Husband Kimmel dithered. The seaplane tender *Tangier* (AV-8) was readied to evacuate the atoll's civilian personnel, but Kimmel was rightly hesitant to send her out to Wake unprotected. The carriers *Lexington* (CV-2) the *Saratoga* (CV-3) were patrolling in a triangle formed by Oahu and Johnston and Palmyra Atolls southwest of Hawaii. They could make a run to Wake in less than four days by refueling at sea, but Kimmel, shaken and timid, recalled both carriers. While this occurred, Vice Admiral Shigeyoshi Inoue, Commander of the Fourth Fleet's South Seas Force, realized he had underestimated American tenacity and requested reinforcements to reattack Wake.

On December 16, Yamamoto dispatched the carriers *Hiryū* and *Sōryū*, which were accompanied by two heavy cruisers and several destroyers to the atoll. The same day (December 15 at Pearl) the *Saratoga*, flying Rear Admiral Frank Jack Fletcher's flag, sortied for Wake from Oahu leading Task Force 14. Three days later, Kimmel was relieved, and Vice Admiral William S. Pye took over temporarily while the Pacific Fleet awaited its new commander: Admiral Chester Nimitz.

As the warships steamed toward the beleaguered atoll, the Japanese continued to attack from the air and steadily weaken Wake's defenses. By December 20, Putnam's fighter squadron was down to a single F4F and morale, especially among the civilians, was ebbing as most of the defenders realized that a reinforcing action, or an evacuation, should have occurred by now. So the sight of a Navy PBY Catalina landing in the lagoon that very afternoon was welcome to all. Word quickly spread that ships were en route to Wake with medical supplies, ammunition, and a pair of radars: an SCR-270 for long range and early warning and a SCR-268 for fire control. Most of the civilians would be taken off, and the Marine Fourth Defense Battalion would land to strengthen the garrison. *Saratoga*, now less than a thousand miles east, would also bring in Major Verne McCaul's VMF-221, so Wake would again have air cover. The atoll's defenders watched the PBY lift off at dawn the following morning bearing dispatches and bound for Midway, followed by Pearl Harbor. Two days. They only had to hold on another two days, and hopes were high.

But not for long.

At 0700 on December 21, near the time the PBY lifted off, *Hiryū* and *Sōryū* swung into the wind and launched every available aircraft toward Wake. The new Japanese plan called for two days of concentrated air attacks to more effectively "soften" the American defenses, followed by a much heavier amphibious assault. This same morning, Admiral Kajioka put out from Kwajalein steaming north for the two-day run up to Wake. This time he brought six heavy cruisers, six destroyers, and one thousand men of the Maizaru Special Naval Landing Force (SNLF) to breach the American defenses.* Additionally, four destroyers with augmented crews would, if necessary, beach themselves to provide additional manpower.

Escorted by eighteen Mitsubishi A6M Zero fighters, twenty-nine Aichi D3A Val dive-bombers from both carriers appeared over Wake at 0850 and concentrated on the anti-aircraft batteries. This attack was followed several hours later by thirty-three land-based bombers from Roi and another thirty-nine-plane carrier strike the next morning. This last attack permanently claimed the last two Marine Wildcat fighters, and the remnants of VMF-211 dispersed among the ground combat units. The arrival of enemy naval aircraft ominously foretold Wake's future, and both Cunningham and Devereaux correctly deduced that if Japanese carriers were prowling nearby, then another invasion attempt was imminent. At 1320 that afternoon Cunningham radioed the joint land-based and carrier-based attacks to Admiral Pye, who had now reviewed the reports

---

* SNLF troops were drawn from, and named for, the four Japanese naval districts: Maizuru, Sasebo, Kure, and Yokosuka. These men are sometimes, and quite incorrectly, labeled "Japanese marines." They were not. The SNLF was composed of sailors with very basic infantry training, unlike U.S. Marines, who specialize in combined arms amphibious assaults.

brought to Pearl by the PBY and, to his credit, stated "the situation at Wake seemed to warrant taking a greater chance to effect its reinforcement, even at the sacrifice of the *Tangier* and possible damage to some major ships of Task Force 14."

Nimitz agreed and ordered Halsey to assist Task Force 14. Given the urgency, it was assumed that *Saratoga* would press in with all haste, yet Fletcher, ever obsessed with fuel, insisted on refueling, which cost an entire day to complete. Wary of submarines, he was also zigzagging. This was arguably ineffective given his paltry twelve-knot steaming speed to accommodate the oiler *Neches*. With hindsight, it is far too easy to second-guess tactical decisions, yet the hard fact remains that Americans were fighting and dying, and had been desperately holding on for fourteen days with no help from Pearl Harbor.

A more aggressive commander might have pressed in to save these men. With the heavy cruisers *Minneapolis*, *San Francisco*, and *Astoria*, plus eight destroyers, Fletcher could have left suitable escorts for the slower *Neches* and seaplane tender *Tangiers*, then lunged ahead with the balance of his force to close on Wake and launch the Marine Wildcats. Better still, another admiral could have used the tactical situation to ambush the Japanese. What would seventy-odd unexpected American carrier aircraft have done to surprise *Hiryū* or *Sōryū*? Or, at the very least, Fletcher's task force could have evacuated Wake if he'd arrived several days earlier. One wonders how history could have changed for the atoll's surviving defenders if Kimmel had reacted decisively, or if Halsey's carrier had been the closer task force to Wake.

But it was not to be.

At 0235 Gun Number 10, a .50-caliber Marine machine gun on Wilkes, opened fire toward the sound of engines in the crashing surf, and its sixty-inch searchlight slashed through the darkness, catching a Japanese landing craft grinding onto the coral. Also illuminated in the glare were the two old destroyer transports, now designated as Patrol Boats 32 and 33, aground south of Wake's beach with assault troops swarming ashore. Just before 0300 Cunningham radioed Pearl Harbor "island under gunfire. Enemy apparently landing."

Admiral Pye was now faced with the type of decision that makes or breaks careers, and that can haunt a commander for the rest of his life. "The real question at issue," Pye later wrote, "is, shall we take the chance of the loss of a carrier group to attempt to attack the enemy forces in the vicinity of Wake." With enemy forces landing, the atoll appeared to be past saving, but to his credit the admiral considered offensive action even with the potential destruction of Task Force 14 worth the risk. Admiral Harold Stark, chief of naval operations (CNO), did not. Two weeks after Pearl Harbor, *any* carrier loss would critically weaken an already weakened Pacific Fleet. As of yet, there was no clear picture of where the Japanese would next strike; Hawaii, and even the U.S. West Coast, were not beyond the realm of possibilities. Stark made the decision that Wake was now a "liability" and recalled Task Force 14. From the Main Navy Building in Washington, D.C., this seemed quite logical. Yet 6,700 miles west, those isolated on a lonely atoll in a vast ocean facing death or a long, brutal captivity did not face such an abandonment quite so objectively.

The next few hours on Wake were punctuated by enemy landings, and the confusion of the battle was worsened by loss of communications. Japanese flags appeared across the middle of the atoll, and at least a dozen warships were now visible beyond the shoreline. On Wilkes, a handful of Marines under Lieutenant John McAllister were assaulted by one hundred SNLF troops of the *Takano* Unit. After several hours of hard fighting, there were no more Japanese, and the lieutenant counted ninety-four enemy bodies—the enemy unit had been killed to the last man. But even victories like this could not prevent Wake's conquest, and by early afternoon it was apparent to the bloodied defenders that the island must fall. Cunningham surrendered, and

1,622 brave Americans began, in some cases, a nearly four-year fight for survival in captivity.*

Staggering from bad news on every front, America clung to Wake's heroic defense and tragic end with desperate pride. George Gallup's latest poll found fully 97 percent of the country favored all-out war with Japan, and he added "although the particular time and place of the outbreak of hostilities came as a surprise, war with Japan was not unexpected by the public." Thomas Holcomb, commandant of the Marine Corps, would write:

"Wake Island began the war magnificently for the Marine Corps, and America found that the old soldierly virtues are still embodied in its fighting men. . . . Out of such actions as this a people's strength and ultimate victory must come. America remembers Wake Island and is proud. The enemy remembers Wake Island and is uneasy."

Tokyo should have taken the surprising resistance on Wake and in the Philippines as a warning, but did not. The worst strategic scenario imagined by the American chiefs of staff would be a concentrated Japanese thrust between New Guinea and Wake Island. Though the Japanese realized invading Australia was beyond its current military capabilities, neither Washington nor Melbourne knew that in early 1942. Tokyo did understand the desirability, but not the urgency, of isolating the continent from American seaborne support. Had Japan immediately slashed southwest into the Solomons from its bases in the Marshalls and Gilberts, imperial forces could have fanned out and quite likely taken American Samoa and the Fijis. This would cut the vital U.S. supply line between the U.S. West Coast and Australia and complete the outer defensive arc pro-

---

* Bonita Gilbert's *Building for War: The Epic Saga of the Civilian Contractors and Marines of Wake Island in World War II* lists those captured as four hundred Marines; sixty-seven members of the Navy; six members of the Army Air Corps; thirty-eight civilians, largely from Pan Am Airways; and 1,111 civilian CPNAB contractors. Ninety-five defenders were killed in action, and 135 of those captured would later die in prisoner of war camps. Five men were beheaded by the Japanese after the surrender, and ninety-eight civilian contractors were executed on Wake in 1943.

tecting the Japanese Home Islands. Such a move would also leave America with no real base in the Pacific except Hawaii. This done, the resource-rich Dutch East Indies, New Guinea, and the Solomons could be subdued at will with little Allied interference. Such a plan, Operation FS, did exist, but believing the Pacific Fleet was permanently crippled by Pearl Harbor, the Imperial General Staff did not consider it a priority.

A coup de grâce would then be to successfully neutralize the Panama Canal. This would delay U.S. naval reinforcements, specifically aircraft carriers from the Atlantic Fleet or East Coast shipyards, from reaching the Pacific.* Initiated by the French La Compagnie Universelle du Canal Interoceanique in 1880 to bypass the lengthy, dangerous, and expensive voyage around South America via Cape Horn, the canal was to link the Atlantic and Pacific Oceans by a fifty-mile passage through Panama's isthmus. After expending one billion francs and losing some twenty-two thousand workers, the bankrupt French concluded it was impossible and abandoned the project. The Americans, recognizing its strategic importance, bought out French interests and began construction in 1907, from both ends, and completed the "impossible" canal in 1914.† The roughly 13,000-nautical-mile voyage from New York to California via the Straits of Magellan or Drake's Passage was now only five thousand miles through the canal. Steaming time had been shaved from thirty-six to about fourteen days—this was a critical advantage in wartime, especially during 1942, when American assets were scarce and thinly spread.

---

* All twenty-three of the *Essex*-class carriers and four *Iowa*-class battleships were eventually launched from the East Coast yards of Newport News, Virginia; Fore River, Quincy, Massachusetts; Brooklyn Navy Yard, New York; and the Philadelphia Shipyard, Pennsylvania.

† The Americans had the advantages of qualified engineers, government backing via a private consortium, and a plan based on using a series of locks instead of attempting to cut a sea-level canal through the Panamanian jungle. The Americans also understood that malaria and yellow fever were transmitted by mosquitoes and took precautions accordingly.

Aware of all this, the Japanese *could* have dispatched a half dozen submarines equipped with floatplanes to bomb the canal—specifically, the Gatun Dam. If this was destroyed, there would be no hydroelectric power and the locks would be useless, thus putting the canal out of commission. Variants of the imperial A-, B-, and J-class submarines all carried E14Y Glen floatplanes that were launched from a deck catapult. In fact, the only fixed-wing aerial attack on the United States mainland was executed by *I-25*, a B1 scout submarine, against a pair of targets in Oregon.* With a 475-nautical-mile range, the Glen was certainly capable of hitting Gatun Dam from a launch point in the Gulf of Panama. Of course, the Americans would find a way to repair any damage, but this would take valuable resources and time, which would give the Japanese a relatively free hand for a bit longer in the Pacific.

American military strategists, and President Roosevelt, were also quite aware of this possibility, but they were facing critical decisions on all fronts at the moment. First and foremost was the challenge to overcome two decades of political and financial neglect and rebuild the armed forces as quickly as possible. A $58 billion budget was rapidly approved by the Seventy-Seventh Congress, and within six weeks of Pearl Harbor the newly created War Production Board would cover 25,000 prime contractors and 120,000 subcontractors manufacturing everything from fighter aircraft to GI socks.

Over nine million tons of new shipping was required for 1942, and nearly double that for 1943. Existing shipyards and factories were converted to war production, and dozens more built from scratch. The lingering Depression-era unemployment, which peaked at 25 percent, fell

---

* Warrant Officer Nobuo Fujita dropped 168-pound incendiaries in several places near Brookings, Oregon. The Japanese did not account for the wet weather, so the fires were very small. Nevertheless, the attack sent the West Coast into a near panic, so any attack on the Panama Canal would inevitably accomplish the same. Fujita survived the war and visited Oregon to apologize. On his fourth trip, he was made an honorary citizen of Brookings shortly before his death in 1997. A portion of his ashes were scattered over the very forest he bombed fifty-five years earlier.

to 4.7 percent in 1942, then effectively disappeared until 1946. America was now in the war with a vengeance—but the six months following Pearl Harbor were critical, and any gains made would have to be paid for in blood. For the first six months of 1942 it was imperative to disrupt and blunt enemy momentum until the United States could stand firmly on a war footing. This was especially true in the Pacific, where America stood virtually alone against Japan.

A gesture was needed.

Franklin Roosevelt had been thinking of this since Wake Island and Guam. Some act of defiance against overwhelming odds to demonstrate to the world, and more important to the American people, that the Japanese Empire was not unassailable. That it also could be attacked and wounded.

# 2

# THE DRAGON'S MOUTH

Engines roaring, Captain Ed York muscled the B-25 through a sluggish left turn away from the *Hornet*'s bow. On the ragged edge of a stall, he wanted to drop the nose to gain airspeed, but the tossing wave tops were so close he could see into the troughs. There was no real horizon to watch, and he didn't want to fly on instruments fifty feet over the ocean, so Ski eyeballed the cloud bottoms to stay level.

One heartbeat.

Two heartbeats . . . he felt the props bite into the heavy, wet air and slowly lift the bomber up away from the sea. Easing the yoke back and further left, York brought the Mitchell up to one hundred feet, then rolled out parallel to the carrier heading in the opposite direction. Leaving the flaps down, he accelerated to 170 miles per hour, then retracted the flaps. Tugging the throttles back to hold the airspeed, he stared back through the side window and let the *Hornet*'s fantail drift under the wing. When it passed beneath his tail, York booted the rudder and twisted the yoke left again. Leaning forward against his harness, he stared from the front quarter window and then played the turn to roll out a half mile behind the carrier and about two hundred yards off her starboard side. Fighting the gusts to stay level and stable, Plane 8 charged ahead and passed the carrier as another B-25 lumbered off her bow. Before takeoff, the *Hornet's* navigator had given them all the ship's heading, and down in the nose compartment navigator Nolan Herndon adjusted his compass to match it. Both pilots did the same.

310 degrees.

With the *Hornet's* coordinates, 35°43' N, 153°25' E, and now a baseline heading, Herndon computed Plane 8's inbound course. A heading of 243 degrees for 710 statute miles would bring them to the Boso Peninsula—Cape Inubo, to be precise. The best landmark on eastern Honshu, Inubo was an eight-mile shark tooth jutting out from the mouth of the Tone River between Toriakeura Bay and the Kashima Sea. At 170 miles per hour, no wind, Herndon calculated it would take them four hours and six minutes to make landfall. From the cape it was about the same heading for their target, and if York pushed the airspeed up to at least 240 miles per hour, Plane 8 would cover the sixty miles into Tokyo in another fifteen minutes. Confirming this via intercom, the navigator promised a fuel-consumption update in an hour. Ten feet behind Herndon and five feet above, the two pilots exchanged glances. That, they knew, would be an interesting number. Loosening their lap belts and shoulder harnesses, both men were relieved to be airborne and, not for the first time, wondered how they'd gone from flying bombers over Oregon to this bleak spot in the Pacific heading straight into the mouth of the imperial Japanese dragon.

Sixteen Army bombers flew off an aircraft carrier that morning because on a cold Saturday in January 1942, a weary Navy captain came to a historic decision. Francis Stuart Low, known as Frog to his Annapolis classmates and friends, had just returned from Norfolk, Virginia, with a startling idea. While waiting for takeoff back to Washington, he'd noticed several Army bombers making practice attacks on the runway, which was painted to simulate a carrier deck. The sight of medium-range, land-based bombers and the outline of an aircraft carrier suddenly combined into a shocking notion, and he thought of nothing else on the short trip back to the capital. Upon his return, Low, who served under the Commander, U.S. Fleet (COM-INCH), proceeded immediately to the gunboat USS *Vixen* (PG-53), docked at the Washington Navy Yard on the Anacostia River. He intended to risk a conversation with his notoriously short-tempered chief.*

Sixty-three-year-old Admiral Ernest Joseph King was generally disliked personally but widely admired for his blunt, decisive nature and comprehensive naval experience. He'd been a surface naval officer, attended the New London Submarine School, and then, at age forty-eight, became a naval aviator. A veteran of the Spanish-American War, Veracruz, and the Great War, King had commanded several ships, including the aircraft carrier *Lexington*. Brilliant and acerbic, the admiral was widely feared for his abrasive personality. One of his daughters would later famously remark, "he is the most even-tempered person in the United States Navy. He is always in a rage." Nevertheless, Low came aboard the converted motor yacht, where he was also quartered, then proceeded to the admiral's stateroom, paused, and knocked. Hearing a muffled command to enter, Francis Low turned the knob, then opened the door—and changed the course of events in the Second World War.

Despite Washington's rhetoric and stubborn defense on Wake Island, Japan's explosive expansion was still materially unchecked. The British had surrendered Hong Kong, and imperial forces were moving into Borneo. The day Wake fell the Japanese landed on Luzon in

---

* *Vixen*, a converted motor yacht, had arrived on December 28, 1941, from Newport, Rhode Island. She served as King's flagship and office until relieved by the USS *Dauntless* (PG-61) in June 1942.

the Philippines, and General Douglas MacArthur met this challenge by hosting a Christmas party for his three-year-old son, Arthur. The following day, the general took himself, his family, and personal staff by steamer across Manila Bay to the island fortress of Corregidor, leaving the Philippine capital to its fate. While MacArthur fled to safety, the North Luzon Force's American and Filipino troops withdrew to the Bataan Peninsula and dug in along a series of defensive lines. The First Battle of Bataan, marking the onset of a grueling three-month campaign, began the same day Frog Low knocked on Admiral King's door.

As a submariner, Low expected a rebuke for proposing an aviation operation but was surprised at King's reply. "You may have something there," the admiral grated. "Talk to Duncan about it."

That night Low called Captain Donald Bradley Duncan and asked to meet the following morning at the Navy Department in downtown Washington. At forty-six years old, Duncan was one of the most experienced naval aviators in the service. Nicknamed Wu due to his slightly Asiatic features, he was a 1917 graduate of Annapolis and earned his gold aviator wings in 1920. Between sea duty Duncan obtained a Master of Science from Harvard and served aboard battleships as well as the carriers *Langley*, *Lexington*, and *Saratoga* before assuming command of the Navy's first escort carrier, *Long Island* (CVE-1), in 1941. Ordered back to Washington after December 7, Duncan was Admiral King's chief of air operations and was slated to command the USS *Essex* (CV-9) later in 1942.

"There are two big questions to be answered," Low told Duncan that Sunday morning. "First, can such a plane—a land-based, twin-engine medium bomber—land aboard a carrier?" The Navy pilot wasn't overly shocked by the question. Such inquiries had already emerged whenever carriers ferried bombers to wherever they were needed in the world, and Wu already knew the answer. "A definite negative." Low looked surprised, but the pilot continued. "A carrier deck is too short to land an army medium bomber safely. The newest bombers, the North American B-25 Mitchell and Martin B-26 Marauder have tricycle landing gear. The tails are so high off the deck that there is no way to install a landing hook." He didn't add that bombers also had a very high landing speed, and even if a hook *could* be attached the airframe wasn't designed to take the stress of a sudden, full-stop, arrested landing; it would rip the tail off. There also was no place to stow them below even if they did land since a medium bomber could not fit on the elevator that moved planes down to the hangar deck.

Low exhaled. As a submariner he knew none of this, but plainly Duncan did, though the aviator was surprised by the next question. "Alright. But can such a plane, stripped down to its bare essentials and loaded with bombs and gasoline, *take off* from a carrier deck?"

Duncan blinked. Ferry missions were not uncommon, but the planes were manually loaded and off-loaded—not flown off. And bombs ... Wu blinked again. Obviously, there was more to this than his chief was telling him. "That," he finally answered, "will take some figuring. I'll get to work and let you know."

"All right," Low replied, then added softly, "But the boss said not to tell another soul what you're doing."

Duncan found an empty office and immediately began his preliminary evaluation, slowly becoming more excited as he worked. There had been a lot of speculation about attacking Japan's Home Islands, but always with carrier aircraft. Though he divined the intent of this request immediately, Wu was too much the professional to let on, and if Frog had wished him to know officially then he would have said so. Someone, probably Low himself, had thought of using army bombers from a carrier, and this appealed to Duncan for several tactical reasons. Medium-range bombers, unlike carrier aircraft, could be launched at least one hundred miles beyond the Japanese pickets that guarded the Home Islands, some three hundred miles out to sea.

Japanese military leaders had considered such an option but were focused on a land-based attack from American bombers potentially operating west from China, not a carrier threat from the east. However, with the success of the recent U.S. carrier raids, especially against Marcus Island, this might have changed. Nevertheless, if Army bombers could take off four hundred miles from Japan's coast, then there was a very good chance of arriving over their targets undetected. The point was moot, though, as landing on a carrier was not feasible. But Wu had a startlingly obvious thought: just because a plane took off from a carrier didn't mean it had to land on one—and *that* raised some fascinating possibilities.

Any plan would hinge on the selected bomber's capabilities and limitations, so from operations manuals and through U.S Army Air Force staff officers he knew, Duncan began noting available aircraft.* He eliminated the Douglas B-18 Bolo, which was already obsolete in 1942. Lockheed's Hudson light bombers were almost all slotted for the Royal Air Force, and Consolidated's B-24 Liberator was a heavy bomber; its monstrous 110-foot wingspan made it impractical for use off a carrier. The Douglas A-20 Havoc looked promising: small enough to fit and fast enough for the mission, but most of them were spoken for as well. Besides, if the bomber wasn't going to return to the carrier, that necessitated a landing in friendly territory, which meant Russia or China, and neither was truly an option for the Havoc's 945-mile range. The choice eventually came down to two aircraft: Martin's B-26 and the B-25 from North American. Both were new medium bombers that had first flown in late 1940, and both were regarded as state-of-art, frontline aircraft.

Duncan learned that both aircraft had been designed in response to Air Corps Proposal 39–640, which stated the bombers were to exceed three hundred miles per hour and carry a three-thousand-pound bombload at least two thousand miles. Seven aircraft companies entered bids, and in August 1939, twenty-two days before the German invasion of Poland, Secretary of War Henry Woodring divided the

---

* The U.S. Army Air Corps became the U.S. Army Air Forces on June 20, 1941.

385-aircraft contract between James "Dutch" Kindelberger's North American Aviation and the Glenn L. Martin company.

Martin's Model 179 design would evolve into the B-26 Martian (fortunately, this was later changed to Marauder), but clogged fuel lines, leaking hydraulics, and other issues would plague its production. Though comparable to the B-25 in range, payload, and airspeed, the Marauder was heavier, had a longer wingspan, and carried a crew of seven against five for the Mitchell. After five days of research, Wu Duncan decided Kindelberger's B-25 was the only real choice.

Based in Los Angeles, North American Aviation currently produced the T-6 Texan trainer and would subsequently field the wildly successful P-51 Mustang fighter. A full-scale wooden mockup of its NA-62 medium bomber design was assembled by November 9, 1939, and presented to the Air Corps. After 156,000 engineering hours produced 8,500 drawings, the design was finalized and the aircraft entered production, with the first B-25 #40–2165 completed on August 6, 1940. Thirteen days later, legendary test pilot Vance Breese took the bomber on its maiden flight over the Pacific Ocean, with Captain Frank Cook conducting follow-on military evaluations at Wright Field, Ohio.

Early in the development phase, Lee Atwood, North American's vice president, decided an inspirational name was required for the new bomber, and suggested honoring Brigadier William "Billy" Mitchell. A brilliant airpower visionary decades ahead of his time, Mitchell was also brash, opinionated, and insubordinate, which created numerous enemies for him in the Army hierarchy. "The next war would come in the air," he wrote. "Planes would strike at cities and factories and not simply at armies. The air was now the first line of defense and, without air power to shield them, armies and navies would be helpless."

Earning the ire of Army leadership through his outspoken advocacy of the new weapon, Mitchell was loathed by traditional, hidebound Navy battleship admirals for his conviction that surface warships could be threatened, or even destroyed, by aircraft. Sea power remained the cornerstone of national defense, and Mitchell's loud and persistent claims that aircraft could sink any warship, including the great battleships, were dismissed or ignored. Eventually Congress, always parsimonious in peacetime, warmed enough to the potential budgetary savings and directed a series of tests. Naval aviation sunk a captured U-boat in June 1921, and the following month Mitchell's First Provisional Air Brigade sank a German destroyer and the cruiser *Frankfurt* off the Virginia Capes.

His last target during this test was the *Helgoland*-class dreadnought *Ostfriesland*, a veteran of Jutland and other naval battles that was ceded to the United States for war reparations: she went to the bottom in twenty-five minutes. Mitchell's fliers subsequently sank the obsolete USS *Alabama* (BB-8) in September 1921, followed by the surplus battleships *Virginia* and *New Jersey* in 1923. All three American vessels were smaller and less heavily armed than the *Ostfriesland*—Mitchell had proven his point. Later court-martialed, the general was nonetheless revered by a generation of younger, forward-thinking officers, so Dutch Kindelberger loved the idea of exonerating and honoring him in this manner. Henry Harley "Hap" Arnold, chief of the Army Air Corps since 1938 and a longtime supporter of General Mitchell, enthusiastically approved the name. "Billy," Arnold stated, "was clearly the Prince of the Air." A ceremony was held at North American's Inglewood plant in late 1940, with Mitchell's younger sister attending to christen the bomber. A Vassar graduate who would be captured by the Germans while fighting for Serbian partisans during the next war, Ruth Mitchell chalked "For Fighting Billy. His bomber" on the B-25's bay door.

The Mitchell was now official.

Under contract AC-13258, 184 bombers, worth $11,771,000 to North American, were to be delivered for the rapidly expanding Air Corps.* But before this could happen, several issues revealed from

---

* Valued at $223,295,870 in 2022.

testing at Wright Field had to be corrected. Frank Cook discovered that when the aircraft controls were coupled with the Norden bombsight, any small trim corrections would be overcompensated for by the rudders, and the B-25 would begin an uncoordinated bank. This led to a "Dutch roll," the tail wagging in a side-to-side yaw while the wings banked up and down.

Fortunately, these problems were relatively easy to fix. Lateral stability was largely a function of the dihedral, or the angle formed by the wings joining the fuselage. In the Mitchell's case, only the outboard wing panels had to be adjusted to zero degrees, which was called a "broken dihedral" and gave the bomber a gull-shaped wing. The other alteration was to the vertical tail and rudders, which were too small and subsequently broadened. In early 1941, Major Donald Spence took B-25 #40–2174 flying for an hour and was so satisfied with the results that the basic redesign remained unchanged for the next ten thousand Mitchells off the production line.

In speaking with Army Air Force officers, Wu Duncan learned that the Army and North American Aviation had been quick to incorporate into the Mitchell combat lessons gleaned from the Royal Air Force. Armor was installed to the crew positions, with an extra ⅜-inch plate in the pilot and copilot seats. Newly added, and just patented in January, were self-sealing fuel tanks. Trapped gases, and the fuel itself, are highly flammable, which create a critical weakness during combat. Armored fuel tanks added too much weight, so other methods were fielded. The Royal Air Force and Luftwaffe both utilized different options to plug leaks, especially the larger, jagged holes made by exiting rounds. Firestone, Goodyear, and United States Rubber all had differing versions, but the concept was basically similar. When a tank or cell was penetrated by gunfire, the fuel would come into contact with multiple layers of vulcanized and natural rubber that would swell and seal the puncture. The principal drawback was decreasing capacity to make room for the rubber lining, which, in the Mitchell's case, brought usable fuel down from 912 to 694 gallons, with a corresponding loss of range.

Reclassified as the B-25A, the first of forty bombers were assigned to the 17th Bombardment Group (BG) based at McChord Field in Tacoma, Washington. These pilots accumulated flying time and experience in the new bomber while participating in Army maneuvers around the country. They would need it. During November 1941, the group took its newly modified B-25B Mitchells and operated from Pendleton Field, Oregon, mainly flying combat patrols in preparation for the expected war with Japan. Essentially a more heavily armed B-25A, the new B-model was a bit shorter and carried five .50-caliber machine guns. The added weight dropped the airspeed down to just over three hundred miles per hour, but was regarded as a good tradeoff due to the heavier armament.

Duncan knew the 17th BG had the pilots he needed.

New aircraft, but not too new. They'd been flying the Mitchell for about six months, which was enough time to work out the bugs and gain valuable experience. Since December 7, the group had conducted antisubmarine patrols along the Pacific Northwest coast, and on Christmas Eve 1941 attacked a Japanese fleet submarine near the mouth of the Columbia River.* Not true combat experience, Duncan knew, but at least these men had made the mental jump from peace to war and were operating at a higher level because of it. With the plane and unit decided, he had two other questions to answer: which aircraft carrier to use and, equally crucial, who would lead the mission?

---

* Following the attack on Pearl Harbor, I-25 and eight other submarines took up positions off the West Coast. Intending to shell several cities, she was driven off by American defenses, including the 17th BG Mitchells. On 28 December, 1941, the I-25 did torpedo the tanker SS *Connecticut* near Cape Disappointment, west of Baker Bay, Oregon.

Everything around the bomber was a shade of gray.

Smoky wisps of cloud tendrils waved beneath an overcast sky that stretched off toward the western darkness. The horizon was out there someplace, but Bob Emmens couldn't see it. From two hundred feet up, he could only plainly see the stark outlines of ragged whitecaps blowing across a steel-colored sea. Teeth. They looked like endless rows of teeth. Plane 8 banked up slightly as Ed York eased it a bit further left, then rolled wings level again as the bomber bounced through the rough, wet air. Like all good pilots, Ski could compartmentalize quite well, and up till now that was mainly what he had done. The myriad details of having the crews trained, then getting the bombers to the west coast and aboard the *Hornet*, plus the other matter that he arranged, were behind him. All the planning and details having been completed, the moment when he was actually flying toward Japan was here.

A long, long way from upstate New York.

The second son of Polish parents who immigrated to the United States in 1895, he was born Edward Joseph Cichowski on August 16, 1912, in Batavia, halfway between Buffalo and Rochester, and less than thirty miles from Lake Ontario. The elder Cichowski became a successful building contractor, as did the oldest son. Ed was having none of it. "I knew I wasn't going to stay in Batavia all of my life," he later recalled. "Anyone who wanted to get somewhere left Batavia as quickly as they could."

Enamored of West Point from an early age, a military career "seemed glamorous and something that I would like to do." With a gift for absorbing information, Ed graduated from high school at fifteen and enlisted in the Army. He lacked the pedigree and credentials to seek a nomination to the academy, but after a year in the Army he was selected to attend a preparatory school in San Francisco. Once there, he actually had to apply himself to academics but passed the exams with high enough grades to apply for the final West Point appointment allocated to Senator Hiram Johnson (R-CA).

"I loved every minute at the Academy," he remembered, and graduated in the class of 1938. Deciding Cichowski was too hard to pronounce, Ed legally changed his name to York after leaving West Point, but the Ski moniker stuck with him.* "I wanted to be a cavalry officer," York related, but he was put off by the $2,000 cost of five pairs of riding boots, pants, and blouses, which was a tall order during the Great Depression. Ski was told "anyone going to flying school has to buy one shirt and one pair of slacks," and that did it for him. Heading off to flight school, after the basic course, Ed went through fighter training at Kelly Field in Texas, but then the army abruptly changed the rules and anyone over five foot ten inches could not go into fighters. However, at Kelly he met his future wife, Justine, at a big social, so when he departed for March Field, California, she went with him. Later stationed at McChord Field in Tacoma, Washington, by 1942 Ed York had risen to command the 95th Bomb Squadron of the 17th Bombardment Group, and he was there when the whole outfit was moved to Columbia, South Carolina.

Lurching upward, the bomber's jolt brought Ski back to the present. Out of habit, both pilot's eyes flickered over their instrument panels. As the pilot in command, York's panel on the left side of the cockpit displayed the primary flight instruments. The altimeter and airspeed indicator were just forward of his left knee, but not obscured by the thick steering column and heavy yoke. The big flight indicator, with its bright yellow horizon line, was easy to see midpanel in front of his right knee. From the right seat Bob Emmens could see this as well, in case he needed to fly. Between the pilots the center panel was dominated by two oversize circular gages: the directional gyro with its heading indicator and the bank-and-climb gyro unit. Both were

---

* This was in reference to Sergeant Alvin C. York, the Great War hero awarded the Medal of Honor for single-handedly killing twenty-five Germans and capturing 132 more during the 1918 Meuse-Argonne Offensive.

essential for instrument flying and had to be accessible from either pilot's seat.

Below this was a center console more or less divided into three main quadrants. In clusters of two, the throttle, propeller, and mixture controls were on the top along with a hockey-puck-sized knurled knob that could be twisted to lock the throttles in place. There was also a lock lever for the mixture controls so they wouldn't vibrate out of their setting. About a foot lower, the next quadrant held two pairs of levers for operating the superchargers and oil-cooler shutters, though Bob wasn't worried about anything over-heating today. Like every other aircraft he'd flown, the Mitchell was noisy and either too hot or too cold. Today was cold, and he wrig-gled his fingers inside the leather gloves to keep them nimble. York's hand came off the wheel and pointed down to his left, and the co-pilot nodded. The floor-mounted quadrant held a single lever for the wing flaps, which Ed raised to neutral, and engine cowl flaps that Bob now slid forward to close.

Running his eyes again over the gages, Emmens thought about the first plane he'd ever flown and chuckled to himself. A Taylor Cub—and he'd soloed after less than three hours of flying back in 1935. Seven years ago. That was hard to believe. So was being here, and for certain if he'd gone to medical school like his older brother had and followed his father into medicine, someone else would be the copilot of Plane 8. Born in Medford, Oregon, on July 22, 1914, just eleven days before Germany began the Great War, Bob grew up in a "medical atmosphere" but had no interest in the field. Following his father's sudden death in 1934, Emmens had to drop out of the University of Oregon so his older brother could finish and go on to medical school.

"Flying always fascinated me," he fondly recalled, and he became acquainted with the manager of Medford's airport, who taught him to fly the Cub. One day his mother showed him an ad in the paper that read:

COME TO THE WEST POINT OF THE AIR,
RANDOLPH FIELD, AND LET THE ARMY
TEACH YOU TO FLY AND PAY YOU AT THE
SAME TIME!

After passing the physicals, he was accepted into flight school during February 1937 and left for Texas. "I loved every minute of it . . . and that gave me my start in flying." With three years of college to his credit, he was commissioned a lieutenant and rated a pilot in 1938. Bob left for his first duty station with the 89th Reconnaissance Squadron of the 17th Attack Group, which became the 17th Bombardment Group, at March Field. Here he met Ski York, and though they were in different squadrons, their wives became friendly. When the initial twenty crews were picked for a special mission down in Florida, Ski went as the operations officer while Bob remained in South Carolina. Emmens glanced at the pilot and remembered the phone call that put him in this cockpit today. "We need another airplane right away down here," York told him. One of the other pilots, Lieutenant Jimmy Bates, stalled on takeoff and crashed his Mitchell. Bob never hesitated. "I will see you about 1530 or 1600," he had replied, and left to pack his footlocker. He'd run across the group commander, Lieutenant Colonel William C. "Newt" Mills, who had asked him what he was doing, so Bob told him. Mills, who'd already lost twenty crews to Doolittle's unknown excursion to Florida, made Emmens promise to return. "Oh sir, I will be back!" Bob smiled at the memory because the last thing Mills told him was, "If you don't come back, I am going to have your ass."

Another smile. Mills could certainly have his ass now, if he could get out here to collect it, wherever "here" is. Tugging the lap belt to loosen it a bit, the copilot stared through the forward windscreen but saw nothing but pewter sky. Same thing from his right-hand window—nothing but waves and clouds. No other aircraft were in sight, nor would they be. After launch every plane was on its own, though he'd heard talk of some trying to join up for the ingress to Japan, the target area, and out to the safety, hopefully, of the Chinese coast.

As for Plane 8 . . . Bob Emmens leaned forward and squinted at the big magnetic compass mounted atop the glare shield. Bouncing through the rough air as they were, the jiggling numbers were hard to read.

243 degrees.

It was just over seven hundred miles, and Herndon said holding 170 miles per hour would place them over Cape Inubo in approximately four hours, depending on the wind—so just before 1300 hours, ship's time, or about noon over Honshu. Starting with the center console, Bob's eyes dropped down and then right to the panel in front of his knees. Manifold and oil pressure were in the green; the tachometer was fine; fuel pressure and cylinder head temperature were also just where they should be. Fuel. The gage was big, a vertical rectangle rounded on both ends and impossible to miss. Emmens stared at the little glass window for a minute, but he knew it was too early in the flight for any issues to reveal themselves.

That would come later.

Taking off from a carrier had never really been a large question, at least not in Wu Duncan's mind. Naval aviators were trained to do it, so Army pilots could be likewise trained. Landing on a carrier, however, was a different matter entirely, and thankfully not a consideration in this case. The bomber to use had already been determined, so now the remaining question was, Which aircraft carrier to use? In January 1942, these warships, which had struggled for years to find their place in the modern peacetime American Navy, had suddenly become irreplaceable assets for the war against Japan. Only now, faced with bloody proof of the carrier's efficacy, was the influence of the battleship admirals—the "Gun Club"—

waning in favor of aviation. This was especially true in the context of a Pacific war fought across vast distances over specks of land few cared about before the attack on Pearl Harbor.

Yet in January 1942, America had only eight flattops available; one of those, the USS *Langley* (CV-1), was obsolete and currently in Australia, while the Navy's newest carrier, the USS *Hornet* (CV-8) was on her shakedown cruise in the Caribbean. *Wasp* (CV-7) and *Ranger* (CV-4) were needed in the Atlantic Fleet, which left only *Enterprise* (CV-6), *Lexington* (CV-2), *Saratoga* (CV-4), and *Yorktown* (CV-5) to cover a 63-million-square-mile Pacific battleground. None of these could be spared to return to Hawaii, let alone California, to pick up army bombers. No, he decided, *Hornet* was the only option, and in several ways she was the perfect choice.

Currently at sea conducting her shakedown trials, the carrier was due back to Norfolk by the end of January, so the timing seemed good to Low. Commanded by Captain Marc Andrew Mitscher, *Hornet* was in supremely able hands. His father, Oscar Augustus Mitscher, was a federal agent with the Bureau of Indian Affairs who moved his family to Oklahoma City. Unimpressed with the local educational environment, the elder Mitscher sent his son to Washington, D.C., to complete school. Gaining an appointment to the Naval Academy in 1904, Mitscher proved an indifferent student lacking in deportment and military bearing. Nicknamed Pete, poor grades and excessive demerits forced his resignation in 1906, but his father demanded he reapply, and Mitscher was readmitted as a plebe.* Applying himself in earnest this time, he graduated in 1910 and went to sea in battleships.

Designated Naval Aviator Number 33 in June 1916, three years later Mitscher, now a lieutenant commander, took off in Curtiss flying boat NC-1 from Naval Air Station Rockaway outside Queens,

---

* This was in reference to Peter Cassius Marcellus Cade, Oklahoma's first academy appointment, who washed out in 1903.

New York, bound for Newfoundland's Avalon Peninsula. Two other flying boats, NC-3 and NC-4, were part of the Navy's attempt to cross the Atlantic in a powered aircraft. On May 16, 1919, Mitscher left Trepassey, Newfoundland, for the Azores but was forced down by mechanical issues. He and his crew were rescued while NC-3, piloted by Commander John Towers, also came down, but taxied two hundred miles over the waves into the Azores.* In the end, only Lieutenant Commander Albert Cushing Read and NC-4 made it all the way into Plymouth on May 31, 1919; yet the die was cast, and naval aviation was growing up fast.

Working tirelessly to advance naval aviation, Mitscher commanded the *Saratoga's* initial air group and was the first to land on her flight deck. Promoted to captain in 1938, he was assigned as deputy chief of the Bureau of Aeronautics while awaiting completion of the *Hornet*. Mitscher was present on October 20, 1941, when Annie Reid Knox, wife of Secretary of the Navy Frank Knox, christened his warship and for the next two months he was completely absorbed with the Byzantine issues surrounding a new command. Putting back into Hampton Roads on Christmas Eve 1941, the new carrier stood out three days later with the battleships *Washington* and *North Carolina* for her shakedown cruise in the Caribbean.

Straddled by the York and James Rivers and jutting southwest into the Chesapeake Bay, Virginia's peninsula has always been a hub of naval activity. About five miles south of its tip across the Hampton Roads channel lay Naval Operating Base Norfolk and the headquarters of the 5th Naval District, which included the Norfolk Navy Yard and Naval Air Station. Like a spiny growth, a sprawling line of jutting piers clung to the peninsula's sheltered western edge along the wide James River, and it was here in late September 1939, at Newport News Shipyard and Drydock, that

---

* John Henry "Jack" Towers would command both the *Langley* and *Saratoga*, and all three men survived the Second World War to retire as admirals.

the keel for hull number 385 was laid down three weeks after Germany invaded Poland. Last of the *Yorktown*-class carriers, *Hornet* was designed largely by lessons derived from extensive war-gaming and the Navy's collective experience with the previous *Lexington*-class warships.

*Saratoga* and *Lexington* were built from partially completed battle cruiser hulls, and with an 888-foot length overall they were considerably larger, heavier, and slower than the 824-foot *Hornet*. Her nine Babcock & Wilcox water-tube boilers produced 120,000 horsepower for two pairs of Parsons-geared turbines that could muscle the carrier through open seas at thirty-three knots, if needed. With eight five-inch guns and over two dozen smaller pieces, *Hornet* was better armed than previous carriers, but she carried less armor so her engineering spaces were particularly vulnerable. Mitscher was doubly concerned by this since the fire rooms, which produced the steam, were collocated with the engine rooms that spun the shafts. This meant a single torpedo in the correct spot could put the carrier out of service, or cause mortal damage. However, with an air group comprising up to ninety aircraft and the addition of a search radar, the risk was acceptable, not that Mitscher had a choice.

Saturday, December 14, 1940, was cold and rainy, but that didn't stop Annie Reid Knox from launching America's newest warship. "In the name of the United States I christen thee *Hornet*," she proclaimed, and with flags flying from the towering scaffolding, the big carrier slid stern first down the slipway as onlookers cheered and waved beneath their umbrellas. Free of land and committed to salt water, *Hornet* was moved to a "fitting out" pier and, while Hitler invaded Russia, she received her engineering plant, electronics, some weaponry, and other systems necessary to transform the empty hull into a fighting ship. Those preparing *Hornet* had few illusions that war was indeed coming, particularly Captain Marc Mitscher, who arrived to take command in July 1941.

Sea trials normally took place along the Maine coast, but through the fall of 1940 nearly three hundred merchantmen and freighters totaling over 1.5 million tons now rested on the Atlantic floor. As America stepped up its assistance to Britain, Nazi U-boats became bolder, and wolf packs, small groups of submarines, were attacking in force. Roosevelt responded during April 1941 by extending the Pan American Security Zone, through which convoys were escorted by U.S. warships, to within fifty miles of the Iceland coast. Just before Mitscher took command, the SS *Robin Moor*, a U.S.-flagged cargo steamship, was stopped by U-69 and sunk after the crew was allowed to abandon ship. Based on the rising risk, America's newest carrier largely remained in the Chesapeake Bay until completely armed; then she stood out from the Virginia Capes to complete high-speed testing.

The Navy's caution was well founded.

September 4, 1941, found the old four-stack destroyer *Greer* (DD-145) off Iceland when a British patrol plane radioed the position of a German U-boat. After dropping depth charges, the aircraft returned to its base, and *Greer* began trailing the submarine. Obviously believing the destroyer to be hostile, U-652 fired several torpedoes, and *Greer* began laying the first of nineteen depth charges. Neither ship was damaged, and the U-boat escaped. On October 17, three days before *Hornet's* commissioning, the USS *Kearny* (DD-432), a modern *Gleaves*-class destroyer, sortied from Reykjavik Harbor in defense of Canadian warships escorting a British convoy. Attacking the wolf pack with depth charges, *Kearny* took a torpedo from U-568 and was forced to disengage with the loss of eleven dead Americans. Finally, on Halloween Day 1941, the USS *Reuben James* (DD-245) was escorting HX-156, a fifty-one-ship convoy eastbound from Halifax to Liverpool, when another wolf pack attacked. Immediately laying depth charges, the destroyer was struck by a torpedo from U-552 intended for a merchantman. *Reuben James's* forward magazine exploded, and the ship broke up and sank with 115 of the 159-man crew, including all her officers.*

After commissioning, *Hornet* was moved down the Elizabeth River to the Norfolk Naval Shipyard at Portsmouth until late November. The historical symmetry was pleasing for Marc Mitscher, as it was here that an eighty-three-foot-long wooden ramp, the first flight deck on a ship, was added to the bow of the light cruiser *Birmingham* (CS-2). In November 1910, five months after Mitscher's graduation from Annapolis, Eugene Burton Ely wobbled into the air off the cruiser's bow flying a fragile Curtiss Model D Pusher. Twelve years later, this same shipyard then saw the conversion of the collier *Jupiter* into America's first aircraft carrier, the USS *Langley* (CV-1). Captain Marc Mitscher was proud to bring his carrier, the modern offspring of those historical events, back to where naval aviation arguably began.

On Saturday morning, December 6, 1941, *Hornet* was brought back up the Elizabeth River to Norfolk Naval Base and tied up to the starboard side of Pier 4. She was here, alongside the USS *Yorktown*, when the Japanese attack on Pearl Harbor was announced the next afternoon. Relayed through the naval base to the carriers, an urgent ALNAV signal, which was transmitted to all Navy and Marine units, simply read: "EXECUTE WPL FORTY SIX AGAINST JAPAN."

Such a dispatch triggered an immediate, preplanned response and placed all recipients on a war footing. "WPL," or "War Plan," 46 was part of the 1939 RAINBOW series of plans that replaced the Joint Planning Committee's older, color-coded interwar-period plans, and dealt with a two-ocean war against multiple enemies, with or without

---

* *Reuben James* was not flying the U.S. ensign when she was hit and was actively attacking the wolf pack, so the confusion, though tragic, was understandable. U-552 was commanded by Kapitänleutnant Erich Topp, who, along with his boat, would survive the war. He later served in NATO as a rear admiral for the Bundesmarine, the West German Navy.

allies. The immediate tasks involved safeguarding sea lanes, destroying any enemy raiding forces, and protecting U.S. territory. However, as of December 7, only Japan had attacked the United States, and President Roosevelt would not deliver his famous six-minute speech to the House of Representatives asking for a declaration of war until the following afternoon. "Yesterday, December 7, 1941, a date which will live in infamy," Roosevelt said, his well-modulated, patrician voice mesmerizing politicians and citizens alike, "the United States of America was suddenly and deliberately attacked by the naval and air forces of the Empire of Japan."

Upon hearing the news from Oahu, Winston Churchill gratefully remarked, "No American will think it wrong of me if I proclaim that to have the United States at our side was to me the greatest joy . . . but now, at this very moment, I knew the United States was in the war up to the neck and in to the death."

The Pacific Fleet's immediate mandate included defending the British, destroying Japanese vessels, and to "CAPTURE AND ESTABLISH CONTROL OVER THE CAROLINE AND MARSHALL ISLAND AREA" while defending Guam and the American Samoa. A tall order given the paucity of forces available, even with the forthcoming addition of the USS *Hornet*, but with shots now fired and 2,403 dead Americans at Pearl Harbor, the United States squared off to fight. Three days later, the Axis declaration of war on America, which dismayed Hitler's generals and truly plunged the world into global war, simplified the issue considerably. There was now a clear, unambiguous objective to rid the world of tyranny in any of its forms, providing a moral imperative that the Great War had lacked. On December 10, *Hornet* stood out of Norfolk to Lynnhaven Bay, then into the Chesapeake for degaussing.* On the same day, *Yorktown* cleared Hampton Roads bound for the Panama Canal

---

* This involved passing a charged electrical cable over the ship's steel hull to reduce the effects of Earth's magnetic field.

and then the Pacific; she would never again pass through the Virginia Capes.

She would never see home again.

The following day in Rome, Benito Mussolini strutted from his office onto the balcony of the Sala del Mappamondo overlooking the Palazzo Venezia and postured pompously before a crowd of 100,000 screaming Italians. "The powers of the steel pact," the pudgy, self-styled former journalist arrogantly pronounced, "Fascist Italy and Nationalist Socialist Germany, ever closely linked, participate from today on the side of heroic Japan against the United States of America."

Fifteen minutes later Hitler followed suit, addressing a rapturous Reichstag. "First, he [Roosevelt] incites war, then falsifies the causes, then odiously wraps himself in a cloak of Christian hypocrisy and slowly but surely leads mankind to war." The latter half of his eighty-eight-minute speech was a rant directed at the "the Anglo-Saxon Jewish-capitalist world." As this was occurring, the German chargé d'affaires in Washington, Dr. Hans Thomsen, managed to pass Germany's formal declaration of war to the head of the American Division of European Affairs.

The lineup was complete—and the world was once again at war.

An angry, vengeful wave swept across America, unifying a divided populace and transforming a largely isolationist nation into the largest war machine in history. On January 16, Wu Duncan presented Frog Low with his handwritten, thirty-page study of the proposed mission; then both officers went to see Admiral King. Terse as always, the admiral read the report and told the pair, "don't mention this to another soul." He looked up and stared grimly at each man. "Go see General Arnold about this and if he agrees with you, ask him to get in touch with me."

Despite his nickname, "Hap" Arnold was not particularly happy at the moment. Admitting that the Air Corps was "practically non-existent" in 1940, he found himself in the unenviable position of having been proved correct about the necessity for a modern air force, and now forced to deal with the wartime reality of desperately needing such an air force. Two decades of American isolationism and pacifism had left the Great War military disgracefully emasculated and utterly unprepared for another global conflict. History's premier lesson, that peace must be built on strength rather than false hopes, had been promptly discarded again after November 1918. The enervating years of the Great Depression and its accompanying budgetary realities only exacerbated the American military's malaise, and the harsh reality now was that the United States was unable to do much but defend itself—and could barely do that. Too many years of Washington's complacency, neglect, and indifference had created a frightening reality in early 1942, and Hap Arnold *was* frightened.

Son of a prominent doctor from Gladwyne, Pennsylvania, at seventeen Henry Harley Arnold entered the U.S. Military Academy at West Point. Nicknamed "Pewt" by his classmates, he was a mediocre student but an excellent athlete with a penchant for practical jokes. "I skated along without too much effort in a spot just below the middle of the Class," he wrote of his years at the Point, graduating in 1909 and commissioned a second lieutenant. A skilled polo player, Arnold hoped for the calvary but was assigned to the 29th Regiment in the Philippines and disliked the infantry enough to manage a transfer to the Signal Corps.

En route home in 1909 via the Suez Canal, he rendezvoused with friends in Lucerne, Switzerland, and went on to Paris, there witnessing an event that changed not only his life but the lives of hundreds of thousands of men who would be part of the vision resulting from his first view of manned flight. Louis Blériot's high-winged monoplane was ungainly, barely managing sixty miles per hour, and Hap recalled, "I was not very greatly inspired by its appearance for it seemed to be too fragile looking to have any real value as a means of transportation." Yet Arnold quite clearly saw the military potential of not only operating above the battlefield but also transforming the sky into a battlefield. It was the ultimate high ground in a fight.

Returning to America, he was garrisoned at Governors Island, New York, when he received Special Order 95 transferring him to Huffman Prairie, an eighty-four-acre pasture northeast of Dayton, Ohio. Joined by Thomas DeWitt Milling, the two lieutenants were ordered to undertake instruction from the Wright brothers themselves, and on May 3, 1911, Arnold flew for the first time. Twenty-eight flights later, each no longer than eight minutes, he soloed with three hours and forty-eight minutes of flying experience. Designated Military Aviator No. 2 in 1912, the twenty-six-year-old pilot quickly began pushing limits and setting records. Arnold was the first to fly the U.S. mail and the first pilot to carry a congressman as a passenger. He won the first Mackay Trophy offered by the Aero Club of America in 1912 and flew as a stunt pilot for several silent films.* It was on these movie sets that Arnold acquired the nickname that stuck to him the rest of his life: "Happy," or simply "Hap" due to his amiable demeanor.

Witnessing firsthand the firestorm fanned by Billy Mitchell, Arnold agreed with the man's arguments, if not his methods. Arnold was a major in 1926 when the Air Corps Act granted an expansion to 1,800 serviceable aircraft and 20,018 personnel, including 1,518 officers and 2,500 flying cadets. By 1934 the Air Service had become the Air Corps and Hap was a lieutenant colonel, when the politically motivated airmail scandal erupted. Seeking to strengthen their reelection prospects, Democrats dug into former Republican president Herbert Hoover's administration looking for dirt. A report

---

* The Mackay Trophy is awarded for the "most meritorious flight of the year," which Arnold won for a reconnaissance competition in Virginia. The films were *Military Air-Scout* (1911) and *The Elopement* (1912).

emerged linking lucrative airmail contracts to Herbert Hoover's tenure as commerce secretary. With no hearing or due process of any sort, President Franklin Roosevelt canceled all airmail contracts, and through Executive Order 6591 directed the Army Air Corps to now carry mail.

Army Air Corps Mail Operations (AACMO) divided the country into western, central and eastern zones and did the best it could to carry out the president's orders. Unfortunately, of the 262 military pilots used, all but one were junior lieutenants with comparatively little experience, and what flight time they did have had generally been performed during the day in fair weather. Only a fraction of these men had any flight time at night, and just two officers had more than fifty hours of instrument flying. Seventy-eight days later, after sixty-six accidents with thirteen dead aviators only one zone, the Western Zone, incurred no fatalities; it was commanded by Lieutenant Colonel Hap Arnold.

Fallout from the AACMO fiasco generated public outrage and political embarrassment.

"If we are unfortunate enough to be drawn into another war," fumed Speaker of the House Henry Rainey, "the Air Corps wouldn't amount to much. If it is not equal to carrying the mail, I would like to know what it would do in carrying bombs." A scapegoat was needed, and Major General Benjamin Foulois, chief of the Air Corps and the first Army aviator (airships) was a convenient target. With his term expiring in December 1935, Foulois chose to retire and was succeeded by Major General Oscar Westover. The other immediate consequence was the activation of the General Headquarters Air Force (GHQ), a sort of compromise command structure that inched the Air Corps toward a separation from the army, and the advancement of Hap Arnold to the temporary rank of brigadier general as assistant chief of the Air Corps. On September 21, 1938, the fifty-five-year-old Westover was landing a Northrup A-17 in Burbank, California, when he stalled the aircraft, crashed, and died in the front yard of a little house on Scott Street. Hap was immediately promoted to major general (temporary) and assumed command of the Air Corps.

A resolute man with a curious mind, Arnold could see what was needed and sought solutions to make it so, even if that meant working beyond the established system. He also possessed an uncanny instinct for putting the best men in the positions where he needed them most, and, unlike Billy Mitchell, Hap understood how to work with people to achieve his objectives. Mitchell had once written, "But the advent of air power which can go straight to the vital centers and entirely neutralize or destroy them has put a completely new complexion on the old system of war." Arnold fervently believed that, and intended to make the Army Air Corps into America's sharpest sword. To do that he needed the best men available—not just fine pilots, but men who understood engineering and technology, men who were gifted tacticians, and, most of all, men who were bold enough to take the fight straight to the enemy.

Duncan's analysis was quite good, detailed and thorough, and Hap Arnold was pleased. The type of mission the aviator outlined would strike directly at the heart of Japan and figuratively knock them back on their heels. It would also be done with aircraft, and that would fire the imaginations of the public while loosening Congress's parsimonious budget strings. What a mission. Hundreds of miles of open sea from a carrier straight into Tokyo. Arnold suddenly hated his office and wished he could physically be a part of this, but he knew that bombing the Japanese capital was for someone else.

Someone else.

Arnold needed a man who could turn Duncan's pages into reality: a resourceful officer who could overcome the unforeseen yet inevitable technical challenges that were bound to occur, a pilot whose flying ability and reputation was beyond question and who could inspire others to follow him without hesitation. Above all, he needed an aggressive combat leader who would get this done, no matter the risk or ramifications. As these qualities flitted through his mind, Arnold's thoughts returned again and again to one name and one face.

There really was only one man to put this mission together—and he was sixty feet away down the hall.

Easing the throttles back a few inches, Ski York set 170 miles per hour on the airspeed indicator directly in front of his yoke, then ran an eye over the other vibrating gages.

All good.

Staring through the cockpit windows, Plane 8 appeared suspended in a world layered with shades of gray. Smoky lace swayed from pewter cloud bellies hanging low over white-flecked waves. The horizon, where he could see it, was just a thin charcoal thread running across the blurry, rain-smeared windscreen.

It didn't matter.

They had instruments and a chart. Bob Emmens held his up and tapped the single black line running west from their launch point. York nodded and banked slightly right to steady the heading indicator on 273 degrees. Near as he could calculate, they were now about six hundred miles from their landfall on Cape Inubo, west of Tokyo. That had definitely *not* been the plan. They were supposed to launch four hundred miles east of the cape, but the Japanese had changed that. Glancing at the chart on his knee, York half smiled and then stared out through the front quarter panel to the left of his control panel, then down at the map. There was nothing to see—not this far out. Just a heavy black line from *Hornet's* planned launch point to Cape Inubo. Tucked inside his coat pocket, he had a map of Honshu marked with targets past Cape Inubo, carefully chosen targets divided up among the other raiders based on their entry into the target area and vulnerability to the four bombs each Mitchell carried.

So . . . 170 miles per hour was 196 knots. Doing the math in his head, York calculated Cape Inubo was about three and a half hours of flying from here, depending on the wind, and downtown Tokyo, Doolittle's main target, was fifty miles past the cape, but that didn't matter either.

Plane 8 wasn't going to Tokyo.

# 3

# JIMMY AND BILLY

Australia, through the United Kingdom, had been at war since 1939, yet she was even less prepared initially than the United States, and with none of the latter's astonishing manufacturing potential. The Royal Australian Navy (RAN) possessed six cruisers and five obsolete destroyers in 1939, and had barely three thousand full-time professional soldiers. Raising the 6th Division through volunteers, Melbourne dispatched it to aid the British in North Africa, which left very few troops to defend the homeland and provided a compelling reason for the United States to keep Japan occupied away from Australia's shores. Australian troops were among the very best in any theater of operations: tough, independent, and resourceful—but in early 1942, there simply weren't enough available in the Pacific.

Distance, which compounded Japanese logistical limitations, worked for the Allies, but time did not—time that had to be gained, now, by blunting Japan's momentum wherever possible. To the surprise of the Japanese, American forces in the Philippines did not surrender, but instead fell back defensively to the Bataan Peninsula. Nevertheless, a defensive mind-set did not sit well with the two generals and two admirals appointed to the recently created Combined Chiefs of Staff. Though now competing with the European Theater for men and materiel, the admirals were well aware the Pacific would be primarily a naval and marine war, and they also knew the value of keeping an enemy, particularly a stronger one, off balance. So did the new Commander in Chief, Pacific Fleet (CincPac) Admiral Chester Nimitz.

In the dark weeks following Pearl Harbor this seemed a tall order indeed, and the worst was yet to come. After largely destroying the Far Eastern Air Force in the Philippines on December 8, the Japanese invasion began with Batan, an island off the coast of Luzon. December 22 brought enemy landings along Lingayen Bay, and within twenty-four hours three more divisions landed in Lamon Bay. The day after Christmas 1941, General Douglas MacArthur declared Manila an open city, yet the Japanese bombed it anyway. Withdrawing to the Bataan Peninsula, U.S. and Filipino forces began a successful delaying action that would bog down imperial forces until May 1942.

MacArthur, with a secret $500,000 cash gift from President Manuel Quezon of the Philippines, was more concerned with relocating his headquarters to the island fortress of Corregidor and had little to do with this heroic, desperate action. In fact, the general never spent a single night on Bataan and did whatever he was doing over the next two months from deep inside Corregidor's Malinta Tunnel. When ordered out of the combat zone by Roosevelt, MacArthur, who obeyed no one but himself, leapt on the opportunity. After dark on March 11, 1942, the general slipped aboard PT-41 on Corregidor's South Dock and headed south toward Mindanao, abandoning tens of thousands of Filipino troops, American soldiers, and Marines. Of course, he didn't go alone. His wife, Jean, and son, Arthur, in company with the general's personal physician and family cook, would also be spirited away from danger to the finest suite at Menzies Hotel in Melbourne, Australia.

While the Philippines were invaded and without a declaration of war on the British Empire, on December 10 the Imperial 38th Division pierced the Gin Drinkers' Line north of Hong Kong. Capturing the Shin Mun Redoubt, the Japanese headed south toward Kowloon. Major General Christopher Maltby had fallen back to the island fortress but, with no relief or escape possible, surrendered his remaining forces on Christmas Day 1941. Brutality from the Imperial Army toward the helpless populace and captured military personnel quickly mirrored widespread incidents reported from China. At least ten thousand civilians from Hong Kong were massacred, and various British, Canadian, and Indian military personnel were murdered, including fifty prisoners of war taken following the battle at the Ridge near Repulse Bay. Soldiers of Colonel Rysaburo Tanaka's 229th Regiment killed all the patients in the Salesian Mission, and at least fifty more were bayoneted at St. Stephens College on Stanley Point. Here also, on Christmas Day, twelve British and Chinese nurses were gang-raped.*

During January 1942, Rommel's Afrika Korps captured Benghazi, and the German 9th Army would eventually turn the Soviet Rzhev–Vyazma offensive into an aptly nicknamed "meat grinder," inflicting more than a million Russian casualties. In the Atlantic, Nazi submarines were enjoying what they called the *Zweite glückliche Zeit*, the "Second Happy Time," and within a few months 609 merchant ships totaling 3.1 million tons would lie on the seafloor. In the Philippines, the Japanese were slowly breaching the defensive lines strung across Bataan and inexorably pushing the remnants of the United States Army Forces in the Far East (USAFFE) south toward Corregidor. With three main prongs, the Imperial Southern Expeditionary Force was thrusting southwest through Borneo and Sarawak toward Java,

---

* Many Japanese units behaved decently toward prisoners and civilians. No one at the Kowloon Hospital was harmed, and some Japanese officers often discreetly aided captured personnel. Rape, torture, and murder were largely condoned and encouraged by individual commanders who believed such acts were inalienable prerogatives due a conqueror.

south through the Celebes toward Timor, and southeast into New Guinea. If the offensive was successful, then northern Australia would be vulnerable and hopefully unusable to the Americans.

Chester Nimitz wasn't going to wait for this. During January 1942, in the first of two bold moves that would blunt Japanese objectives, Nimitz turned Vice Admiral William Halsey loose with a pair of task forces to raid the northern Gilberts and southern Marshall Islands. Nicknamed "Bull," Halsey's aggressive spirit matched his countenance.* He was a fighting admiral who declared, "Before we're through with them, the Japanese language will be spoken only in hell," and he meant it. During the first month of the war, two audacious plans were put into action that would buy time for the United States by derailing Tokyo's plans and send a defiant message to the Axis and to the world. The Japanese might have easily climbed Mount Niitaka, but the Americans were now resolute, united, and utterly enraged. Washington intended to strike deep into the Empire's black heart and ensure it climbed no higher.

On January 25, while *Hornet* was finishing her shakedown cruise in the Gulf of Mexico, Task Force How (Halsey), built around the *Enterprise*, and *Yorktown*, leading Task Force Fox (Fletcher), sortied from Pago Pago Harbor in American Samoa and headed two thousand nautical miles northwest toward the Marshall and Gilbert Islands. Imperial submarines were based in the Marshalls, and supposedly long-range Kawanishi flying boats were operating from bases in the Gilberts. Believing the Japanese would strike toward Samoa to cut the United States–Australia supply line, Nimitz wanted to hit them first. Offensive action would hopefully catch the enemy off guard, disrupt his plans, and give vital experience to American carrier aircrews and a much-needed morale boost all around. Skirting How-

---

* Halsey always claimed it originated from a war correspondent who misspelled "Bill." Some of his brother officers claimed it was given in recognition of amorous conquests ashore. Whichever is true does not detract from his willingness to seek out and destroy the Japanese whenever possible.

land Island, Halsey and Fletcher split and approached from the vast empty ocean east of the Marshalls and Gilberts.

At 0443 on February 1, 1942, *Enterprise* began launching her strikes from northeast of the Marshalls, and *Yorktown*, between the island chains, followed suit at 0517. At the end of the day, twelve Japanese vessels had been sunk and thirty-five aircraft destroyed. Taken completely by surprise, enemy shore installations, warehouses, and ammunition dumps were all hit by American aircraft. After-action reports revealed that the startled Japanese had not responded aggressively, and anti-aircraft fire, though heavy, was largely inaccurate. After destroying what they could, both carriers slipped away to the east having lost just five dive-bombers and no fighters. The heavy cruiser *Chester* took a bomb hit that killed eight men but retired in good order, while the *Enterprise* recorded a single near miss from a Japanese air attack.

Nineteen days later, a thousand miles southwest of the Marshalls, the USS *Lexington*, flying the flag of Vice Admiral Wilson Brown, was within striking range of Rabaul. The plan was to launch an attack from 125 miles east of the harbor against ships, or any aircraft, that could be found. However, at 1442 the carrier's radar detected a group of planes inbound from Rabaul preparing to assault the task force. *Lexington's* VF-3 Wildcats shot down five Mitsubishi "Betty" bombers on the way in, and three of the remaining four on their way out. None of the bombs came within a half mile of the carrier, but while this was happening another group of nine Bettys attacked. Lieutenant Edward Henry O'Hare and his wingman, Marion Dufilo, were the only two fighters able to intercept them. O'Hare, a 1937 graduate of Annapolis and son of a prominent Chicago lawyer, slashed into the bombers a mere nine miles from the *Lexington*.*

---

* The lieutenant's father, Edward J. O'Hare, was once Al Capone's lawyer and confidant, but it was O'Hare's tip-off to the Internal Revenue Service that led to the gangster's indictment. It was also O'Hare who revealed the jury had been bribed, which sent Capone to prison. The senior O'Hare was assassinated in 1939.

Dufilo's guns jammed, so "Butch," as O'Hare was known, attacked alone, damaging one bomber and sending three more down in flames. Originally it was believed he destroyed five aircraft, but by single-handedly disrupting the attack, Butch very likely saved the carrier from severe damage and perhaps prevented its total loss. A hero when America desperately needed one, Edward O'Hare became the first World War Two naval aviator to be awarded the Medal of Honor.* Having lost the element of surprise but determined to create as much confusion for the enemy as possible, Admiral Brown continued toward Rabaul until sunset, then reversed course out to sea. The Japanese lost sixteen of eighteen bombers during their two strikes and a pair of four-engined patrol planes. Wilson's task force lost two Wildcats, but one of the pilots was safely recovered.

In the meantime, Nimitz ordered Halsey to sea again, and after a quick turnaround *Enterprise* sortied from Pearl Harbor on Valentine's Day, headed toward Wake Island. February 24, sixty-three days after the Japanese flag broke over Wake, *Enterprise* swung into the wind and launched fifty-one aircraft against any enemy shipping, aircraft, and shore batteries in place on the atoll. Opening fire at 0742, the heavy cruisers *Northampton* and *Salt Lake City*, with a pair of destroyers, pummeled the atoll with 1,868 rounds of high explosive. Again caught by surprise, Japanese defenses responded sporadically, and the task force vanished back out to sea with the loss of a single Dauntless scout bomber.

The following day Nimitz ordered Halsey, fuel permitting, to continue seven hundred nautical miles northwest from Wake and attack Marcus Island. Annexed by the Japanese in 1898, the island was only 1,148 miles from Tokyo, so striking it would be hitting Japanese territory, certainly rattling the Imperial General Staff. On March 4, *Enterprise* once again turned in to the wind and launched

---

* In Butch's honor, the USS *O'Hare* (DD-889) was commissioned in 1945, and in 1949 Chicago's Orchard-Depot Airport was renamed O'Hare International Airport.

a thirty-seven-aircraft strike, but with overcast skies navigation to the 372-acre flyspeck would be problematic. However, the Americans hit on a novel solution. Unlike imperial carriers, U.S. carriers were all equipped with radar, and the *Enterprise*'s CXAM-1 set was used to vector the aircraft to Marcus, where they achieved complete surprise. Fuel storage and hangars were badly mauled, and the carrier air group again vanished out to sea with the loss of a single aircraft.

Six days later, in the first U.S. Navy combined carrier action, *Lexington* and *Yorktown* launched 104 aircraft, led by Commander Bill Ault, over the Papuan Peninsula's rugged Owen Stanley Mountains against Japanese forces landing at Lae and Salamaua. Sliding in from the Coral Sea along the Australian side of New Guinea, the flattops were undetected, and the Japanese again badly surprised. Four transports were sunk, a destroyer badly damaged, and the light cruiser *Yūbari* hit so hard she was sent back to Japan. One Dauntless from the *Lexington* was lost over Lae.

By now the Imperial Japanese Navy General Staff was alarmed, and the carrier raids forced a shift from grand strategy to tactical details. The Americans were in no way defeated, and the raids proved they could, and would, attack anywhere at will as long as their carriers remained operational. The General Staff had been pushing Operation FS, a major southeasterly thrust toward Fiji and American Samoa, and now this became a priority. But shipping, exacerbated by the American raid on Lae, was a problem. Japan had limited logistical capacities, and any loss or damage of crucial transports would inhibit operations in the southwest Pacific. The American carrier raids also demonstrated to some that the Home Islands might be vulnerable, but the Imperial General Staff dismissed such concerns, though they did order the line of early-warning picket ships moved farther out to some seven hundred miles east of Honshu. This was sufficient, Tokyo believed, as the Americans did not possess the means from which to attack the sacred Home Islands. Carrier aviation was range-limited, and the pickets would provide ample warning. As for land-based bombers, there was no evidence of U.S. bases on mainland China or in the Maritime Territory of the Soviet Union.

One vote.

On the heels of the war in Europe and the embargo against Japan that would certainly lead to war, the U.S. House of Representatives extended the military draft by a single vote on August 12, 1941. Men were easy enough to train, but what of modern equipment, specifically aircraft, to fight the imminent war? Years of budget cuts, isolationism, and financial upheavals had left the American military emasculated, and the Air Corps was no exception. More funds were allocated for hay and calvary horses than for aircraft development during the 1930s, and now the piper had to be paid. Nonetheless, in less than twenty years warplanes had evolved from underpowered fabric kites into serious and expensive weapons—particularly in nations now aligned against the United States. Fighters, still known as pursuit aircraft, were undergoing their own metamorphosis due to lessons learned from the 1940 Battle of Britain, but bombers were another matter altogether.

A medium bomber, one that packed a punch, could protect itself, and fly at near fighter speeds for long distances, was deemed an acceptable compromise between cost and capability. In March 1939, the Air Corps issued Proposal 39–640 to top American manufacturers for just such an aircraft. North American Aviation, which would also produce the iconic P-51 Mustang fighter, answered with an innovative design they called NA-62, but would later be designated the B-25 medium bomber.

As Wu Duncan surmised, this was the only aircraft for the mission, but he did not know enough about the technical details to completely vouch for its feasibility. Fortunately, the man sitting sixty feet down the hallway from Hap Arnold did know, and he was promptly called to Arnold's office. Short, balding, and with a certain professorial air, the man hardly fit the image of the stereotypical military pilot. But then he never had.

"I had long curls, which promptly classified me as a sissy," James H. Doolittle later wrote of his childhood in Nome, Alaska. "At about age five, I had my first fight." Apparently, one day an Eskimo boy began punching the little *chechako*, or newcomer, and Jimmy promptly struck back, smashing his opponent's nose: "Blood spurted over his parka . . . I ran home to my mother, certain I had killed an Eskimo."

Doolittle's father, Frank Henry, was a skilled carpenter from Alameda, California, who had gone north with the Klondike gold rush in 1897 after the birth of his only son. Eventually buying passage for his family on the SS *Zealandia*, Jimmy and his mother joined Frank during the summer of 1900. Moving into a comfortable house built by Frank, who was doing well enough as a carpenter he had no need to become a miner, as an only child Jimmy described his upbringing as "spoiled." Nome was a tough place to grow up. One day he and a friend were walking through town and the other boy tripped. Before he could get up, a half dozen ferocious malemute sled dogs tore the child to pieces.

Shorter than the other boys, Doolittle grew up tough; "I had to fight all the time," he recalled, though he had no idea how much this pugnacious attitude would shape most of his life. Always a scrapper and not much interested in school, Jimmy was frequently at odds with his father and later wrote, "I told him when I was big enough, I was going to whip him."

It was a short childhood.

Three things changed the course of his life forever. At seven years of age, he took a six-week trip with his father to Seattle, Los Angeles, and San Francisco and "saw everything in a new perspective." There were trains, automobiles, trolley cars, and modern houses; the world suddenly and irreversibly opened up for him. When his mother moved back to California, Jimmy happily accompanied her, and it was there, in January 1910, that Doolittle discovered aviation at the Los Angeles International Air Meet. Captivated by a sky full of biplanes, monoplanes, and blimps, he decided to build his own glider and promptly began selling newspapers and doing odd jobs to make enough money for the project. From a 1909 *Popular Mechanics* article, Jimmy painstakingly constructed his aircraft from wood, fabric, and piano wire, then towed it to a cliff in a wagon. Demonstrating the absolute fearlessness that would serve him so well later in life, the boy "strapped it on and ran toward the edge."

He plummeted straight down with the glider on top of him. Bruised, bleeding, but undeterred, the boy decided "what was needed was more speed." One friend of his could get to his father's car, so after repairing the glider Doolittle tied it, and himself, to the rear bumper while his buddy drove. The car quickly outpaced the boy and his glider, so in desperation Jimmy jumped into the air hoping to fly rather than be dragged. Though he managed to briefly get airborne, there was no lift, so boy and glider crashed back to the ground and were dragged behind the car. With no money to build another aircraft, Doolittle took up boxing courtesy of Forest Bailey, his English teacher. Once the five-foot-four-inch teenager learned the difference between street brawling and the science of boxing, he began winning flyweight and bantamweight amateur bouts along the West Coast. His mother, unenthused by his battered face and ungentlemanly behavior, bought him a motorcycle in hopes that he would quit boxing. Jimmy simply used it for travel to matches beyond walking distance, but tinkering with the machine awakened a latent interest in machinery that would serve him well in later years. Now fifteen, a final significant event occurred that truly changed the course of his life.

A girl.

Josephine "Jo" Daniels was not just any girl but a beautiful, intelligent southern belle from Louisiana. She was everything Doolittle was not: cultured and well mannered, a straight-A student, and admired by all, especially Jimmy. He knew if he was to have any hope with her, then he would have to change—and change he did. Enrolling in Los Angeles junior college, he transferred to the School of Mines at the University of California, Berkeley. Doolittle's initial plan was a degree in mining engineering, but this was altered with America's entry into the Great War. Enlisting in the Army's Signal Corps, he was sent to aviation ground school back at Berkeley and married Josephine on Christmas Eve, 1917, before his commissioning as a second lieutenant.

Unable to get to Europe to fight before the war ended, Jimmy went on to receive his degree from UC Berkeley, then served as a test pilot before earning a master's of science and a doctorate in aeronautical engineering from the Massachusetts Institute of Technology. Winning the Schneider Cup and the Mackay Trophy, Doolittle resigned his commission and headed to Shell Oil's Aviation Department, where he was largely responsible for the development of hundred-octane fuel. Jimmy went on to win the Bendix and Thompson Trophies, then became president of the Institute of Aeronautical Science. He had come a long, long way from the undersized, unruly boy off the streets of Nome that no one, except Jo, believed would amount to anything. By 1940, with war looming, he was accepted back on active duty as a major and was serving at Army Air Forces Headquarters in Washington when Pearl Harbor was attacked. At age forty-five, he was promoted to lieutenant colonel the week before Frog Low went to see Admiral King about his bomber notion.

Hap Arnold briefed Doolittle on the concept of the raid, Admiral King's interest, and Wu Duncan's preliminary assessment. "Jim . . . I need someone to take this over and—"

"And I know where you can get that someone!" he interrupted excitedly, and Arnold smiled.

"Okay . . . it's your baby. You'll have first priority on anything you need to get the job done. Get in touch with me directly if anybody gets in your way."

And that was it. Jimmy had his "verbal marching orders" from the head of the Army Air Forces, and that was sufficient. Arnold despised paperwork and gave verbal orders whenever possible. In any event, there wasn't time to put together staff packages and feasibility studies. He had to trust the expert knowledge and professionalism of those he selected to do jobs for him. Hap was also under pressure to explore the feasibility of another concept: bombing Japan from China or the Soviet Union. On January 28, he was at a meeting with Secretary of War Henry Stimson, Admiral King, and President Roosevelt, who wanted to know what progress was being made on attacking Japan from the Asian continent. Arnold had some thoughts about that that were tied to the Doolittle Raid, but for now they would have to wait.

Doolittle also loathed paperwork, but organized his thoughts about the raid and its requirements in memorandum form for Arnold. In part, it read:

**Subject: B25B Special Project**
**To: Commanding General Army Air Forces**

The purpose of this special project is to bomb and fire the industrial centers of Japan. It is anticipated that this will not only cause confusion and impeded production but will undoubtedly facilitate operations against Japan in other theatres due to their probable withdrawal of troops for the purpose of defending the home country.

An action of this kind is most desirable now due to the psychological effect on the American public, our allies and our enemies.

The method contemplated is to bring carrier borne bombers to within 400 or 500 miles (all distances mentioned will be in statute miles) of the coast of Japan, preferably to the south-southeast.

They will then take off from the carrier deck and proceed directly to selected objectives. These objectives will be military and industrial targets in the Tokyo-Yokahama [sic], Nagoya and Osaka-Kobi areas.

Simultaneous bombings of these areas is contemplated with the bombers coming in up waterways from the southeast and, after dropping their bombs, returning in the same direction. After clearing the Japanese outside coastline a sufficient distance a general westerly course will be set for one or more of the following airports in China: Chuchow (Lishui), Yushan and or Chien. C ... chow is about seventy miles inland and two hundred twenty miles to the south south-west of Shanghai.

After refueling the airplanes will proceed to the strong Chinese air base at Chungking, about 800 miles distant, and from there to such [ ... ] as may, at that time, be indicated!

The greatest nonstop distance that any airplane will have to fly is 2000 miles.

Eighteen B25B (North American Medium Bomber) airplanes will be employed in this raid. Each will carry about 1100 gallons of gasoline which assures a range of 2400 miles at 5000 feet altitude in still air.

Each bomber will carry two 500# demolition bombs and as near as possible to 1000# of incendiaries. The demolition bombs will be dropped first and then the incendiaries.

The extra gasoline will be carried in a 275-gallon auxiliary leak proof tank in the top of the bomb bay and a 175-gallon flexible rubber tank in the passageway above the bomb bay. It is anticipated that the gasoline from this top tank will be used up and the tank flattened out or rolled up and removed prior to entering the combat zone. This assures that the airplane will be fully operational and minimizes the fire and explosion hazard characteristic of a near empty tank.

In all other respects the airplanes are conventional.

The work of installing the required additional tankage is being done by Mid-Continent Airlines at Minneapolis. All production and installation work is progressing according to schedule and the 24 airplanes (6 spares) should be completely converted by March 15th.

Extensive range and performance tests will be conducted on #1 article while the others are being converted. A short period will be required to assemble and give special training to the crews. The training will include teamwork in bombing, gunnery, navigation, flying, short take off and at least one carrier takeoff for each pilot.

If the crews are selected promptly from men familiar with their jobs and the B-25-B airplane the complete unit should be ready for loading on the carrier by April 1st.

General operational instructions in the use of his particular equipment will be supplied to each crew member for study and practice. Final operational instructions will be issued just before take-off from the carrier.

Due to the greater accuracy of daylight bombing a daylight raid is contemplated. The present concept of the project calls for a night take off from the carrier and arrival over objectives at dawn. Rapid fueling at the landing points will permit arrival at Chungking before dark.

A night raid will be made if due to last minute information received from our intelligence section or other source a daylight raid is definitely inadvisable. The night raid should be made on a clear night, moonlight if Japan is blacked out, moonless if it is not.

All available pertinent information regarding targets and defenses will be obtained from A-2, G-2 and other existent sources.

The Navy has already supervised take off tests made at Norfolk Va. using three B25B bombers carrying loads of 23,000#, 26,000# and 29,000#. These tests indicate that no difficulty need be anticipated in taking off from the carrier deck with a gross load of around 31,000#.

The Navy will be charged with providing a carrier, (probably the Hornet), loading and storing the airplanes and with delivering them to the takeoff position.

The Chemical Warfare Service is designing and preparing special incendiary bomb clusters in order to assure that the maximum amount that limited space permits, up to 1000# per airplane, may be carried. 48 of these clusters will be ready for a shipment from Edgewood Arsenal by March 15th.

About 20,000 U.S. gallons of 100 octane aviation gasoline and 600 gallons of lubricating oil will be laid down at Chuchow and associated fields. All other supplies and necessary emergency repair equipment will be carried on the airplanes.

1st Lt. Harry W. H . . . e, now with the Air Service Command and formerly with the Standard Oil Company of New Jersey, will be charged with making arrangements for the fuel caches in China. He will work through A-2 and A-4 and with Col. Clare Chenault, a former Air Corps officer and now aviation advisor to the Chinese government. Col. Chenault should assign a responsible American or a Chinese who speaks English to physically check and assure that the supplies are in place. This man should also be available to assist the crews in servicing the airs. That the supplies are in place can be indicated by suitable radio code signal. Work on placing supplies must start at once.

Shortly before the airplanes arrive the proper Chinese agencies should be advised that the airplanes are coming soon, but the inference will be that they are flying up from the south in order to stage a raid on Japan from which they plan to return to the same bases. Radio signals from the bombing planes immediately they drop their bombs may be used to indicate arrival at gassing points some six or seven hours later.

Care must be exercised to see that the Chinese are advised just in time as any information given to the Chinese may be expected to fall into Japanese hands and a premature notification would be fatal to the project.

Lt. Col. J. H. Doolittle, Air Corps, will be in charge of the preparations for and will be in personal command of the project. Other flight personnel will, due to the considerable hazard incident to such a mission, be volunteers.

Each airplane will carry its normal compliment [sic] of five crew members; pilot, co-pilot, bombardier-navigator, radio operator and gunner-mechanic.

One crew member will be a competent meteorologist and one an experienced navigator. All navigators will be trained in celestial navigation.

Two ground liaison officers will be assigned. One will remain on the mainland and the other on the carrier.

At least three crew members will speak Chinese, one in each of the target units.

Should the Russians be willing to accept delivery of 18 B-25-B airplanes, on lease lend, at Vladivostok our problems would be greatly simplified and conflict with the Halverson project avoided.

Doolittle was now actively traveling back and forth to Wright Field tasking engineers to draw up plans modifying twenty-four Mitchell bombers with three extra fuel tanks, each a leakproof, 225-gallon rubber cell made by the U.S. Rubber Company that would be installed in the top of the bomb bay. It had to fit above specially designed shackles that would hold each bomber's four-bomb payload. The crawl space at the very top of the bay was to house a 160-gallon rubber cell that could be collapsed when empty and discarded. This would then permit the flight engineer to move freely throughout the aircraft. Finally, the belly turret was to be removed, and a sixty-gallon tank put in its place. This could be refilled in flight by the engineer with the ten five-gallon cans each plane would carry. These modifications would increase the B-25's fuel capacity to 1,141 gallons, of which 1,100 were usable—and they'd need every drop of it. If the tanks could not be properly installed, then the mission was moot.

February 3, 1942, saw an order sent to Lieutenant Colonel William Mills of the 17th Bombardment Group, endorsed by Hap Arnold, directing that twenty-four Mitchells, with all their flight crews and required mechanics, armorers, and ground-support personnel, be sent immediately to Columbia Army Air Field, Columbia, South Carolina. En route, they were directed to land at Mid-Continent Aviation in Minneapolis to have the fuel tanks, labeled "special equipment," installed. The selection of crews was left to Major Jack Hilger, newly appointed as Doolittle's deputy, who delegated this to three squadron commanders from the 17th; Captains Karl Baumeister, Al Rutherford, and Edward "Ski" York.

Doolittle would not command a unit flying aircraft he was unqualified to pilot, so while the details were worked out and with the Mitchells en route, he got himself checked out to fly the B-25B by March 3, 1942. Once the bombers landed in Columbia, Jimmy had already picked Eglin Field in Florida as a forward operating and training base, though the administration for his "B-25 Special Project" would remain in South Carolina. Eglin was perfect: off the beaten track, with auxiliary fields available for short takeoff training, and right on the Gulf of Mexico so the pilots could hone their overwater navigation and flying skills. As their new fuel tanks were installed, the crews left Minnesota and trickled into Eglin by March 3, and training commenced immediately.

The Navy ordered Lieutenant Henry "Hank" Miller, a carrier-qualified instructor, to teach the Army pilots the fine points of taking off from a carrier at sea. The bombers would take up about half the available deck space since they could not be stored below, which would leave about four hundred feet for the first several Mitchells to get airborne. From an earlier experiment flying Mitchells off the

*Hornet* while it was in Norfolk, Miller knew the bomber could get airborne with full flaps at about seventy miles per hour; of course, this assumed the carrier was making twenty knots and there was at least a twenty-five-knot wind over the bow—but it could be done with room to spare.

While the pilots trained, *Hornet* sortied from Norfolk and headed down the East Coast. Doolittle was making regular trips to Wright Field and Washington, as well as the Edgewood Arsenal, to have his bombs built. He did this in his own B-25, both for expedience and to build up his flying hours in the Mitchell. By the middle of March 1942, Jimmy managed to backdoor his way into actually leading the mission, replacing Captain Vernon Stinzi, who fell ill, as pilot in command of B-25 #40-2344. Also during this time, *Hornet* passed through the Panama Canal heading for Alameda, ostensibly on her way to the war in the Pacific. In a manner of speaking, this was true, though only Captain Marc Mitscher was aware of the carrier's true mission.

On the final day of training in Florida, Captain Ski York replaced Lieutenant Jimmy Bates, who stalled and crashed his bomber on takeoff. This was a bit odd, as there were already seven other fully trained spare crews ready to go, but York was a squadron commander and Doolittle's chief of operations, so no one gave it too much thought—at the time. Jimmy, like Hap Arnold, relied on verbal orders and kept no written records. "Typically these men," Hap's grandson Robert confirmed, "were given tasks, huge or narrow, with verbal authority." As March 1942 drew to a close, Doolittle gathered his men and told them the next step of the special project: head to McClellan Field in Sacramento, and then to Alameda Naval Air Station on San Francisco Bay. Those who had postulated they were going to North Africa were left scratching their heads. No one openly discussed the mission—Doolittle's explicit orders—but in privately discussing their destination, none of the pilots had satisfactory answers. Those who did know—Doolittle himself, Jack Hilger, Davey

Jones, and Ross Greening—said absolutely nothing. The last man that knew the overall mission details, and his own recently disclosed mission details, also said nothing. But then Ski York never was much of a talker.

# 4

## PAYBACK

Lurching upward, the B-25 cocked sideways, then corkscrewed sick-eningly as it hit a pocket of warm air. Swearing under his breath, Bob Emmens muscled the bomber back to level flight and stared ahead through the curved rectangular windows at the Japanese coast. For the past hour the horizon had noticeably darkened, stretching from end to end with what had to be the island of Honshu, largest of the Home Islands. Running his eyes over the gages, Bob was satisfied with the engine revolutions per minute, cylinder head temperatures, and oil pressure. What worried him, and York, was the fuel. By their reckoning, Plane 8 was still at least an hour east of Cape Inubo, and they had switched to the specially installed 260-gallon bomb-bay tank forty-five minutes ago. This was supposed to be done at the cape, but the 160-gallon collapsible rubber tank in the passageway atop the bomb bay had already run dry.

"Hey Bob," Ed leaned right and held up his kneeboard. "Take a look at this." Down the center of the paper were two columns of numbers, one for each engine, with lines drawn under both at the bottom. Beside this he'd written 1,141, the total gallons carried, and subtracted the first number from it along with the fuel burned during takeoff. There was a circled total at the bottom. Glancing outside at the horizon, he looked back at the kneeboard, then met York's eyes and nodded.

It was not enough.

Not enough to get to China anyway, but the two pilots already knew that. They also knew exactly why they were short of fuel. This aircraft, #40-2242, was the only B-25 on the mission with factory carburetors installed. Of course, the bomber's carburetors had been previously modified for low-altitude flying, as were those on all the Mitchells—but these were changed back at McClellan Field, and the carburetors on each of Plane 8's Wright-Cyclone engines were now the original unmodified type, which would burn fuel at unacceptable levels. Unacceptable, that is, for the 1,200-mile flight across the East China Sea to Chuchow, China. Though Doolittle knew Plane 8 was going to Russia, the colonel purposely left the details to Emmens and York so he could plausibly claim ignorance of the whole affair. The pilots had no intention of telling him about the adjustment, so Doolittle's very genuine anger at the mechanic added further realism to the cover story. During their remaining day at McClellan it would have been simple enough to undo the adjustments, but the carburetors were never "fixed," and fortunately no one ever asked if the original mission settings had been restored.

York's numbers showed they'd spent over two hundred gallons thus far and were about forty gallons into the bomb-bay tank. That meant Plane 8 was burning something like ninety-eight gallons per hour, over twenty-five gallons more per hour than the modified B-25s, and this was at optimum cruise speed, not the combat speed they'd fly over Japan. From the center of Tokyo to the tip of Kyushu was just over five hundred miles, which at 250 miles per hour would take two hours and burn over 250 gallons of fuel. Chuchow was another thousand miles past Kyushu, and even at a reduced speed the B-25s with modified carburetors would be sucking fumes over the Chinese coast.

Plane 8 could not make half that distance, and the two pilots now had the math to prove it. Replacing his kneeboard, Ed York tapped the yoke and wrapped his hands around it, and Emmens released the controls. Sitting back, Bob wriggled his fingers and stared out the side window at the waves. They seemed a lighter blue now, though that could just be the light. Suddenly, movement above the horizon caught his eye and he leaned forward, heart pounding. There! Again! Opening his mouth to speak, Emmens abruptly stopped. A bird. It was just a bird, though a big enough one for him to see it. Some type of albatross, he reckoned. Waving to get York's attention, he pointed toward the bird. The other pilot craned forward and scanned a moment, then nodded. Relieved it wasn't a Japanese fighter, Emmens knew the bird meant land was reasonably close. After 450 miles of open water, land, even enemy land, was something of a relief. Yet it was Japan; 140,000 square miles brimming with several million Japanese who would joyfully cut his head off and stick it on a pole if they could. That, he knew, was at least one certainty if Plane 8 went down in enemy territory. The thought made his mouth dry, and he forced himself to concentrate on the cockpit instruments rather than whatever lay past Cape Inubo. Death or destiny, he would meet it soon enough.

Jimmy Doolittle was troubled by no such thoughts at the moment. Fifty minutes ahead of Plane 8, he pushed both throttles forward and roared over the Joban beach on Japan's east coast at 250 miles per hour while Emmens was watching his seagull. Passing close to an enemy cruiser and beneath a long-range patrol aircraft on the way in, Jimmy had no idea what type of reception awaited the raiders.

But all was quiet for the moment.

He had also periodically angled into the wind during the ingress, and his navigator, Lieutenant Hank Potter, called over the interphone that the spike of land they'd overflown was *not* Cape Inubo.

As near as he could calculate, they were about forty-five miles north of the intended landfall, which would put them about eighty miles from Tokyo. Doolittle didn't care. In fact, he instantly decided not to correct, but to fly on west a bit, then turn south for the Japanese capital. This way, he figured to avoid the airfields and anti-aircraft guns situated between Tokyo and the east coast. Lieutenant Travis Hoover, flying #40-2292, had caught up with Doolittle thirty minutes after takeoff and flown loose formation with the colonel all the way into the Japanese coast. Passing the beach, as it became obvious Doolittle was heading west, Hoover waggled his wings and "promptly turned off toward his target area."

Racing over Honshu at treetop level, Jimmy passed Kasumigaura Bay and zigzagged past Mount Yamizo. Popping out onto the central plain, he kept the bomber low and fast, angling southwest now toward the Tone River. Far away to the south he could make out a solitary fuzzy peak silhouetted against the clear sky. Fuji. It had to be. Crossing the river twenty miles north of the Japanese capital, he rather absently noted the beautiful landscape turn into innumerable clusters of small buildings, seemingly built at random, with no straight roads visible anywhere. Potter called out course corrections, and with light touches to the yoke and rudder, Doolittle lined up on a target that he still couldn't see. People on the ground were waving, he was surprised to see, and "there were many planes in the air," he later recalled, "mostly bi-planes."

Trav Hoover, who had turned over Joban, was actually first into Tokyo. Crossing the Edo River at fifty feet, he paralleled the Naka then pulled up to nine hundred feet just northeast of the Awakawa River. His primary target was the Senju Steam Power Plant, a large complex in the triangle formed as the Sumida and Awakawa Rivers converged. Such a low-altitude run-in allowed no time for fine-tuning anything, and visual references were nonexistent. So when Hoover spotted smokestacks off his nose, next to a river, he twitched the yoke and lined up on them. It was a huge rectangle with buildings and smokestacks built up to the edge of the southern river, and this is what Lieutenant Dick Miller, his bombardier, tried to hit.* In fact, it was the Kinukawa Steam Electrical Plant collated with the Asahai Electro-Chemical Industries Ogu factory a mile west of Senju on the other side of the Sumida River. His first bomb missed long of the target by some two hundred yards, impacting in an intersection in front of the chemical factory forty yards from the riverbank. Hoover's remaining bombs hit two hundred fifty yards farther southwest in the Ogumachi residential area, causing fires and panic.

About ten miles out from Tokyo, Doolittle shoved the throttles forward to their stops and eased back on the yoke. Surging upward now, feeling exposed and vulnerable, he was looking for the Tokyo Arsenal, which, from the scanty maps provided, was a military complex just west of a wooded park. There! Jimmy saw it and bunted over to hold twelve hundred feet. Light in the seat as the dust floated upward, he was thinking no one had spotted them when several black puffs appeared off the nose, like burnt popcorn against the blue sky. Still, none of the enemy aircraft seemed to notice the American bomber zipping over their sprawling capital city.

That, he knew, would change in less than a minute.

At 1130 *Hornet* time, 1230 local time, some sixty-five miles east of downtown Tokyo, Plane 8 thundered clear of the haze one hundred feet over the surf about the time the colonel's incendiaries were detonating. York and Emmens knew the next *planned* leg perfectly: 262 degrees from Cape Inubo for sixty-two miles, just over fifteen minutes, basically straight ahead to the center of the imperial capital. But as the coast appeared, York pushed both throttles up, pulled back on the yoke to climb up a few hundred feet, then booted the right rudder and banked Plane 8 hard to the northwest—away from Tokyo. Bracing his forearm against the side window, Bob Emmens

---

* The chemical factory area is now the headquarters to the ADECA Corporation, and the site of the Kinukawa Power Plant is now a sewage treatment facility. The block where his last bombs impacted is now a kindergarten.

stared down the wing line at Japan. He could see the mouth of a big river, eight football fields wide, oozing into the ocean. A sandy beach flashed past, and he suddenly saw a fenced-in area filled with people, maybe two hundred of them.

A fifty-foot watchtower stood in one corner, and as the bomber raced overhead, he saw waving arms and men jumping up and down—then they were gone. "At that speed it was just a glimpse," he recalled, "but I'd swear those faces were the faces of white men, not Orientals." A prisoner of war camp, perhaps? They'd seemed excited to see the bomber, and if they were Caucasian prisoners, they had also seen the American star painted on the wings. Maybe, he thought, a ray of hope illuminated their black existence for that brief moment.*

He hoped so.

Ed cranked the yoke back to the left and rolled out heading northwest. Keeping the airspeed high and the bomber low, Plane 8 raced over the Japanese countryside just above the trees. They were so low Emmens could make out peasant men with broad-brimmed hats and women with tight bands across their chests. So low he could make out the woman's tight black bun knotted behind her head. People waved, including a group of schoolchildren being bunched into a ramshackle building. The air felt different after hours over the sea; it was rougher, and the briny smell had been replaced by a heavier, earthy odor. After five minutes of paralleling a river, the terrain steepened, and York threaded his way up into the hills between two lakes.† Cresting a ridgeline, Bob caught a glimpse of the Atlantic less than ten miles off the right wing, then it disappeared

---

* There is no evidence of such a camp at Cape Inubo, though the Hiraoka Sub-Camp 3 lay some four miles inland near the confluence of the Hirachitone and Tone Rivers. Another possibility, though unlikely based on York's timing, is that Plane 8 came ashore farther north near Joban. Two camps, Shimomago and Hitachi, were in that area by 1944, but their status in 1942 is unconfirmed.

† Lake Kitaura and Kasumigaura Bay.

as Ed dove down into a narrow valley. Up ahead was a line of north-south mountains, and York headed for a visible saddle that would hopefully shield them from the formations of Japanese planes the gunner, Sergeant Dave Pohl, kept calling out.

As far as the crew was concerned, this dash across Japan was a last-minute decision based on fuel. Nolan Herndon added his course corrections, which York largely ignored in order to hug the terrain. The pilot had his own map, made weeks earlier, that showed a straight black line from Cape Inubo over central Honshu to the west coast near Nagaoka. From there, the line continued past Sado Island and across the Sea of Japan to a circle drawn around a harbor on the far eastern edge of a Russian peninsula.

As Plane 8 headed for the saddle in the Yamizo Mountains, Jimmy Doolittle cleared western Tokyo at rooftop level in the haze. Rippling his incendiaries together, he initially banked hard to the west, dropped to roof level, then pushed the throttles up to hold three hundred miles per hour. Turning south, the colonel dipped through the foothills, passing east of a spur running off Mount Tanzawa, confident that he'd hit his target. Later analysis would show that Jimmy's bombardier, Staff Sergeant Fred Braemer, also missed his primary target—not that it mattered at the time. There was indeed a park, but the adjacent complex he aimed for was the Toyama Military Academy, and Braemer's incendiaries impacted four hundred yards south of the academy's firing range in the Nishi Okubo neighborhood. Fires quickly spread, and a piece of debris killed a student seven hundred yards northeast at the Waseda Middle School.

Cresting a slope, Doolittle could now clearly see the wide blue sheen of Sagami Bay maybe ten miles away to his east. Following a river, Doolittle was threading the bomber through the foothills when they suddenly dropped away into a wide, flat valley. To his right, about the three o'clock position, a solitary triangular peak rose dramatically from the mist. It was striking: dark, almost black, from its base up to a gleaming snowcapped summit wreathed in faint clouds.

Mount Fuji.

No other landmark was as prominent in all Japan. Keeping the Mitchell at fifty feet above the flat valley, he figured the terrain would hide them from spotters and certainly from any radar—if the Japs even had any. This had been a concern in planning, but Army intelligence had no concrete technical information. Any radar, they had concluded, would be around Tokyo and once clear of it the chances of being found were small. That sounded fine from a warm office 6,700 miles away in Washington, but now, deep inside enemy territory and having just bombed their capital, it was not much of a comfort.

Hugging the foothills, Doolittle weaved south down the valley toward some higher terrain looming from the haze ahead. Abruptly, the ground again flattened, and as the haze rolled back, he picked up buildings from a small city and more blue water off the nose bordered to the east by a long peninsula. Suruga Bay, his map indicated, protected by the Izu Peninsula, so the town was likely Numazu. Roaring across the city, suddenly they were past the beach and over the bay. Edging the bomber a bit southwest, Jimmy could see a faint coastline off to his west curving back toward them. Four minutes later he spotted Cape Omaezaki, a hook-shaped spit of land that, according to his map, marked the southernmost edge of the bay. Truly out to sea now, he eased back on the yoke, climbed slightly, and smoothly banked up to the right.

Exhaling slowly, Doolittle rolled out heading 230 degrees, then walked the throttles back to lean out the mixture and save fuel. From this point, staying fifteen to forty miles offshore, there were some five hundred miles to cover before passing Cape Sata and the island of Yakushima. He would turn west from there, fly south of the Satsuma Peninsula, then west for another thousand miles across the East China Sea, and over occupied China to Chuchow. It seemed insurmountable now, at wavetop level just off the enemy coast. He took a deep breath. One leg at a time, mentally and physically. Glancing at the map again, Jimmy did the math in his head; about two hours and fifteen minutes to Yakushima, and then at least they'd be clear of mainland Japan.

Right now he'd settle for that.

Eighty-odd miles northeast of Doolittle, Bob Emmens could see a rugged, mountainous skyline, and as the lake disappeared aft, he felt the bomber lurch sideways as Ed York lined up on a gap to the right of a big peak.* Dropping back to fifty feet, Plane 8 roared northwest across the same flats Doolittle had crossed just thirty-five minutes earlier. Glancing down at York's map, he figured they were about thirty miles from the "initial point," or IP, which was a prominent landmark used to initiate a bombing run into a target. From this point, a time, distance, and heading were meticulously calculated to put a bomber in an optimum position for dropping its payload. Though officially assigned Target Number 331 in Tokyo, he and Ed York knew they were really dropping on a factory in the city of Utsunomiya, which lay nearly halfway across Honshu on the direct route to the Soviet Union's far eastern Maritime Territory.

Nine minutes.

York had both hands on the yoke now and was leaning forward as he threaded Plane 8 through the mountains. On the upper pedestal between them both, throttles were forward of the halfway mark and the twin black PROP levers were full forward. Occasionally, York would drop his right hand to the red MIXTURE knobs and nudge them forward. After watching the instrument panel for a minute, Bob Emmens reached over and tapped the big round CYL HEAD TEMPERATURE gage. Both engines were in the high yellow arc, and the CARB TEMP gage was also climbing toward red. York nodded,

* Mount Tsukuba.

and pointed down toward his copilot's left thigh. There was no chance of icing at fifty feet over Japan in April, so Emmens reached down and slid both CARBURETOR AIR knobs aft, which opened the ducts to the outside air. Farther down on the floor between them, were the levers for the ENGINE COWL FLAPS, which he also opened. This would let relatively cool outside air flow over and through the engines, hopefully cooling them a bit.

Off both wings, the dark green hills seemed to compress as the valley narrowed. Left, then right, the Mitchell banked as York flew toward a saddle at the north end. Pulling up suddenly, he crested a cluster of small hills and both men floated up against their lap belts as he bunted forward to stay low. Grabbing the edge of the glare shield for support, Bob looked right, then left, then down at the map spread across his knees. The solid black route line was left of them as York purposely hugged the ground along the mountain slopes.

Suddenly a light gray ribbon appeared off the nose and both pilots pointed. Nodding again, York reached over and tapped the map. Emmens looked left and saw the road vanish into the foothills as Ed pulled back to climb a bit, then cranked the yoke over hard left. Arcing around the diminishing terrain, Plane 8 shot out onto a mesa about two miles square where tails from four mountain ranges formed a sort of crossroads. The road angled off to the northwest, and York banked left again to follow it, which Emmens knew would lead them to their IP: a bridge over the Kinugawa River. He couldn't see the aircraft clock on the right-hand panel in front of Ed, but he flipped his left arm over and glanced down at a battered Bulova A-11–type watch that, like most pilots, he wore reversed with the black face on the inside of his wrist. Though the glass face was scratched from long use, he could plainly see the white minute tick marks outside of the white numbers on the face. Glancing at a scrawled number on his kneeboard, he did the math in his head: three and half minutes to the bridge.

About five feet below, and ten feet in front of the pilots, No-lan Herndon crouched in the Mitchell's nose and stared at his own map. He'd rapidly plotted the new course suddenly passed from the cockpit, and had been catching up on the details since they'd made landfall. As the navigator/bombardier, Herndon would normally have been part of the planning for any low-level penetration into hostile territory, especially the IP-to-target segment. He'd done all that, in painstaking detail, for this mission—to target number 331 in Tokyo. Yet, not thirty minutes ago, York informed the crew they would not be bombing the aircraft plant but, because of low fuel, head northwest across Honshu for a bay on the east coast of the Soviet Union. Sergeant Ted Laban, the engineer, had said nothing about a leak or any problems transferring fuel, so this was unwelcome news to the navigator.

The Soviet Union. Russia. A far cry from his home in Texas.

The twenty-three-year-old navigator had enlisted on July 27, 1940, in Dallas, hoping to eventually become a pilot. By that time, general officers like Hap Arnold were well aware that war with Japan was increasingly likely, so after the fall of France the U.S. Army Air Corps expanded rapidly. After eleven months as an enlisted man and with two years at Texas A&M University behind him, Herndon was commissioned a second lieutenant on June 25, 1941. Stationed at McChord Field, he was there with the 89th Reconnaissance Squadron when the word went out for volunteers for the secret B-25 project—and now here he was, bouncing through the foothills somewhere north of Tokyo. Staring down through the glass, he could see rice paddies and dikes, also some houses that looked to be made from straw and mud. The navigator squinted at the penciled lines he'd drawn on his map after York named a Russian city as their destination. Like the Jap rising-sun emblem, headings radiated in all directions from Tokyo, because Herndon assumed they would proceed to Russia *after* bombing the capital— but the pilot had turned northwest as soon as they'd reached Cape

Inubo. Frowning, he realized that meant Emmens and York already knew the course away from the cape to Vladivostok. It also meant Plane 8 had never been headed to Tokyo.

What in the hell was this really all about?

Making landfall on the Chiba Peninsula east of Tokyo, Lieutenant Robert Manning Gray of the 95th Bombardment Squadron was the third B-25 over the imperial capital. A square-jawed Texan from Killeen who wore cowboy boots, Gray had a degree in aeronautical engineering from the Agricultural and Mechanical College of Texas (renamed Texas A&M in 1963) and named his B-25 *Whiskey Pete* after a favorite horse. Vowing never to become a prisoner of the Japanese, if forced down over the city Gray intended to get his crew out if possible, then "pick out the biggest building in Tokyo and stick *Whiskey Pete* right in the middle of it." By now, scattered anti-aircraft batteries had realized the planes overhead were definitely not part of the citywide air-defense drill conducted that very morning, but were the enemy. They were Americans.

Gray cut across Chiba, recognized where he was, and crossed northern Tokyo Bay to the mouth of the Edo River. Following it northwest, he popped up to 1,450 feet; his first bomb hit the Kamakura residential area in the vicinity of an electrical substation. About twenty seconds later, 1.5 miles to the north, his second five-hundred-pounder impacted very close to the Kanamachi railway station in an industrial area containing a paper mill, chemical factory, and other targets clustered between the Naka and Edo Rivers. During the run-in, Gray later reported seeing "a burning oil tank . . . just west of the Ara Waterway," which had to be Travis Hoover's bombs near Arakawa. Continuing another mile north, Gray racked the bomber up on its left wing, came left to west, and sped across an open area of rice paddies between the rivers. The bombardier, Sergeant Aden Jones from Pasadena,

California, saw an orderly quadrangle of white buildings that he took for an army barracks and fired his nose-mounted Browning .30-caliber as the Mitchell thundered past.*

Racing six miles across Tokyo, Gray saw the Nihon Diesel Kogyo Plant nestled just west of a bend in the Shinshiba River, then banked up hard to the southwest looking for the Tokyo Armory. Mistaking an enormous complex off his nose for the armory, he lined up on a huge collection of buildings that was, in fact, the Imperial Army Powder Magazine. But Jones released early, and the M-54 incendiaries struck six hundred yards northeast in the Iwabuchi residential neighborhood. Dropping back down to the rooftops, Bob Gray dashed over western Tokyo, then headed southwest toward the coast.

Sixty miles due north of *Whisky Pete*, Ed York walked the throttles back a bit to hold 250 miles per hour. Lighter now with so much fuel burned, the Mitchell wanted to fly faster, but gas was tight as it was, and four miles per minute was quick enough for what they had to do.

Japan flashed past, under, and around the cockpit, but neither pilot was interested in the details. Easing left around a rocky spur, the bomber again popped out over a fertile plain dotted with farms. York leaned forward, then pointed straight ahead. Craning his neck, Bob saw the road wind off across the flats and disappear toward a rising line of mountains. But to the right off the nose, maybe ten miles distant, he saw what attracted the other pilot's attention. Pillars of thick gray smoke that were big enough to be seen at low altitude from this distance rose up against the hills.

During a quiet trip to Washington in March, York had planned the route across Honshu and collected the very sparse information available on military targets. Once he let Emmens in on the mission, they studied targets in Kashiwazaki and Jōetsu on the northwest

---

* It was not a military installation but rather the Mizumoto Primary School, and the quick burst accidentally killed a fourteen-year-old student named Minosuke Ishide.

coast, where they planned to exit Honshu, but that meant lugging two thousand pounds of bombs thirty more minutes to the coast. Another hundred miles, which would burn at least fifty gallons of fuel that Plane 8 did not have to burn. Once the two pilots decided on the route then the targeting choice was plain: Utsunomiya, the 400,000-person capital city of the Tochigi Prefecture, was really the only option. Old Army Map Service city plans showed a mine, salt warehouses, substations, a factory of some sort on the Ta River, and an extensive rail yard. West of the city there were military installations that included the 14th Division headquarters, with home garrisons for the 59th Infantry and 18th Cavalry Regiments. No one was certain if the target was a power plant or a factory, but it was of military significance and therefore fair game. If the bombs landed short they'd hit the rail yard, and if they went long there were official-looking buildings along the river. York didn't really care at this point—he just wanted to drop his bombs, hit the enemy hard, and get out of Japan.

Reaching over with his right hand, the pilot pushed both red MIXTURE knobs all the way forward, left the PROP levers where they were, and then wrapped his right hand around the throttles. Winding left and right beneath the nose, the road suddenly straightened and he banked up to follow it.

There!

A river and a bridge. He frowned . . . there were actually two rivers coming together.* Glancing at the map he couldn't tell, but the maps were so bad it didn't mean anything. His Initial Point (IP), the last landmark prior to the target, was supposed to be a bridge over the Kinugawa River. Then a flat plain would appear, with a town about eight miles northwest.

"334 degrees to the target," Herndon called.

Banking left as the foothills flattened and spread out, York had the

* These were the Naka and Hoki Rivers, not the Kinukawa. Plane 8 exited the Yamizo Mountains twenty miles north of the intended target area. York and Emmens never realized this, and always assumed they struck Utsunomiya as planned.

impression that the terrain on the map didn't quite match what his eyes were seeing. Neither did the heading. Not quite. Leaning forward, both pilots stared at the flat area ahead, and Emmens pointed left to the eleven o'clock position. Ski saw it—a dark smudge that had to be the town. Flicking the yoke, he corrected left to 314 degrees and wrapped his fingers back around the throttles.

It didn't matter.

Eyes flickering inside, the pilot glanced at the OIL and MANIFOLD PRESSURE gages left of the console, then the airspeed indicator in front of his yoke: 250 . . . just below the 275-knot red line. A village flashed past, then a tree line, and as the bridge slid under the Mitchell's nose Ed pulled back, kicked the rudder pedal, and twisted the yoke to the right. The bomber's left wing lifted, and Plane 8 thundered over the river. Almost as soon as he banked, the pilot kicked the opposite rudder and brought the yoke back left to level out.

"Seven and a half miles to target," Herndon's voice came over the interphone. "One minute and forty-eight seconds."

York and Emmens already knew that.

"Bandits . . . four o'clock high," Pohl's voice suddenly broke in. "Opposite direction."

Twisting in his seat, Bob stared from the side window back and right above the wing, but couldn't see anything. Even if the Japs saw them, they wouldn't be able to stop the bombs from falling. Facing forward again, he saw another road slide beneath the nose, then ahead the green fields abruptly ended in the sprawling gray outskirts of a town. It was smaller than he thought, but Ski held up two fingers, then pointed at several lines of rising smoke.

Two miles. Thirty seconds.

"Two miles," Herndon's voice sounded nervous.

York's eyes darted over his panel again, and he frowned. "Open your bomb bay doors Herndon."

"Jesus." He glanced at the other pilot. "That would be a fine thing at a time like this . . . to forget to open your bomb bay doors!"

Seconds later the Mitchell shuddered as the hydraulically actuated doors dropped open into the slipstream. Like scales on an immense emerald hide, an irregular patchwork of small farms fell away under the wings, and a darker green river snaked away north of the town. Pushing the throttles all the way forward, Ed pulled back on the yoke and Plane 8 soared upward. As the ground fell away, Bob felt horribly exposed. Naked. Surely every anti-aircraft gun was lining up on them to blow the bomber from the sky.

But no tracers arced into the clear air, and no ugly puffs wracked the Mitchell. Next to him, York's face was deadly serious, but calm, as he craned forward and kept Plane 8's nose on the smoke plumes.

"PDI!" Herndon called over the intercom, and Ed glanced down at the big instrument on his left forward panel. The pilot director indicator, or PDI, was a single needle that, when aligned with the navigator's course, lined up on a large 'o' at the top of the gage. Normally, Herndon would use the aircraft's AFCE (automatic flight control equipment, or autopilot) to make minor adjustments that kept the bomber on its final heading to the target. But that was only possible with the complex and generally accurate Norden bombsight, which had been removed for this mission.

During the twenty-odd years following the Great War, bombing had progressed from nails hammered into wing spars to "iron sights" that relied on the pilot's eyes to a line of technical improvements that steadily compensated for aircraft parameters, temperatures, and, most crucially, winds. Gimbals, gyroscopes, and mechanical computers all combined to give a bombardier or pilot the best aim point possible from which to release bombs. As anti-aircraft fire and enemy fighter planes advanced, so did the necessity of a bomber's reactive capability to maneuver and not be tied to long, predictable run-in headings. Also, the capability to fly above anti-aircraft fire, beyond the reach of fighters, and to deliver accurately from high altitudes was an ongoing quest for bomber development. After all, what was the point of risking life, limb, and aircraft only to arrive over an essential target and then miss? While Naval aviation was tactical and focused primarily on dive-bombing, the Army had both strategic and tactical missions.

Enter the Norden.

Designed by a Dutch émigré, its basic concept solved the fundamental problem with aerial bombing accuracy: the release point. Looking like a muscular microscope, the forty-five-pound apparatus was mounted in the aircraft's nose, and with a small internal telescope and movable mirrors, the bombardier could maintain a stable image of the target while it was far ahead of the aircraft, and fine aiming adjustments were made using horizontal and vertical tuning knobs. It was supposed to make high-altitude bombing deadly accurate, which would enable bombers to surgically remove essential targets, cripple the enemy, and shorten the war. Nolan Herndon, like many professionals, had his doubts. In any event, the Norden was not effective for a level drop at fifteen hundred feet, and the weight saved could be carried in extra fuel, so Doolittle had them all removed. There was also the unspoken knowledge that if a bomber went down during the raid, this precaution would prevent the latest American bombing technology from falling into Japanese hands.

Leaning forward, Herndon squinted down at the ten-thousand-dollar Norden's replacement, the twenty-cent "Mark Twain" designed by Captain Charles Ross Greening, pilot of the *Hari Kari-er*. Appointed as the raiders' gunnery and bombing officer, Greening had given the basic problem some thought and applied the simplest solution possible. A thin, seven-inch quadrangle topped by a ninety-degree arc marked with ten-degree increments was installed on the existing Norden mount. With a handle attached, the bombardier could swivel the sight right or left, which correspondingly deflected the PDI in the cockpit and accounted for any horizontal corrections.

The vertical solution, or the release point, was similarly basic. A sighting bar, which rotated vertically on the quadrangle's right face, could be aligned with the desired release angle, and when the target appeared at the end of the bar, the bombs were dropped. Herndon had already set the angle since the bombing parameters for all the planned targets were essentially the same: a fifteen-hundred-foot release, when the target hit the thirty-degree down angle on his Mark Twain sight. Leaning right, he checked the angle and tightened the thumb screw to hold it, then stared through the plain V notch cut into the near end of the bar—just like a rifle sight. It was a very Great War solution and would be useless at altitude. But from a low altitude level delivery, his bombs would fall in ten seconds and avoid running the gauntlet of changing wind speeds or directions encountered from medium or high altitudes.

Kneeling over the mount, Herndon stared through the glass nose panels as small roads widened, buildings became larger and closely packed, and railroad tracks converged. Eyes flickering between the sighting bar and the looming pillars of smoke ahead, he fine-tuned the PDI, although no bombardier could miss such an obvious target from this distance. With the bomb toggle switch between his left thumb and forefinger, Herndon aimed at the base of the smoke trails and watched them slide up. As they appeared to touch the sighting bar, he released the bombs.

"Bombs away!" The Mitchell jolted upward, and Herndon called again, "bomb bay doors closed."

York immediately banked left thirty degrees and pushed the yoke down. Time to disappear again. Pulling back at one hundred feet, he let the bomber settle slightly and left the throttles wide open. Eyes darting between the gages and the ground, Ski checked the bomb bay's door-open light and confirmed it was out. A muddy gray river flashed past, he felt the tail lift, and Plane 8 rocked sideways as he rolled out heading northwest.* From the tail cone, Sergeant Dave Pohl described the impact where the smoke was rising. Glancing at his watch, which was set on *Hornet* time, he saw 1215—so 1315 in

---

* The Hoki River.

Tokyo. Three hours and twenty-nine minutes since they'd skidded down the carrier's wet deck.

Ignoring the navigator's course corrections, York kept the Mitchell headed straight for the foothills rising off the nose to the west. There was a flat valley and a road to follow, but he angled slightly to the right, directly for the higher terrain. Roads meant people, and people meant a sighting that could be passed on to Jap fighters. He and Bob Emmens had planned the egress and knew the fastest way out of Japan was a 330-degree heading just south of a big peak rising in the distance.* It was ninety-seven miles from Utsunomiya, which York believed they'd just hit, to the Sea of Japan, then another 450 miles or so to the Russian coast. Both pilots had the same thought and looked at each other. Whatever lay ahead was certainly better than being caught in the firestorm behind them. Nothing York or Emmens knew about Imperial Japan gave hope for fair or respectful treatment if they went down over Honshu, especially after having the audacity to bomb the sacred Home Islands.

Now, at all costs, they had to get out of Japan.

While Plane 8 dashed over Honshu toward the dubious shelter of the Echigo Mountains, the assault on Tokyo continued. Lieutenant Everett Holstrom, nicknamed "Brick" due to his red hair, was fourth off the *Hornet*. Pilots are notoriously superstitious, and Holstrom had already dealt with a leaking left-wing tank, a failed top gun turret, and a miscalibrated compass that put them over land fifty miles south of Tokyo against a fully alerted enemy. Making landfall at 1330 Tokyo time, he decided to approach the capital from the south, reasoning that there would less opposition from that direction. Mistaking Sagami Bay for Tokyo Bay, Holstrom, also of the 95th Bomb Squadron, was now heading the opposite direction from the first three Mitchells. Under attack from four fighters, which looked alarmingly like Nazi Bf-109s, Brick dumped

* Mount Nantai.

his bombs in Sagami Bay six miles southwest of Eno Island, then turned back down the coast.*

The next three Mitchells, led by Captain David "Davey" Jones, were slated against targets in central Tokyo. Eventually rejoining after takeoff, they stayed together until entering Tokyo Bay from the Chiba Peninsula. Stating in his official report that his first bomb fell on "an oil tank south of the palace," Jones, with Lieutenant Ted Lawson's *Ruptured Duck* off his left wing, mistook the Kawasaki industrial district for the Omori and Nihombashi dock areas north of the Tama River. Kawasaki, like much of the Tokyo Bay area, is fringed with artificial islands that are heavily utilized for commercial and military development, so any of the built-up harbor areas would look alike as he popped up from fifty to twelve hundred feet.

Roaring in over the Nichiman Wharf fully twelve miles southwest of the Imperial Palace, Davey's first bomb landed in the Nippon Pipe Manufacturing compound north of a canal separating the artificial island of Ogimachi from the mainland. Banking up hard right away from Lawson, he raced back toward the bay over shipyards and a partially reclaimed island rising from the mud. Coming in from the east this time, he dropped an incendiary and a five-hundred-pounder on another Nippon Pipe facility south of the canal, and his remaining bomb hit the Yokoyama Manufacturing Company eleven hundred yards to the northwest. The incendiary did little to the concrete and metal structures, but both bombs caused extensive damage.

Flying the seventh bomber off the *Hornet*, Lawson stayed in loose formation with Jones over Kawasaki and released his first two bombs at roughly the same time. His first fell into the canal,

---

* These were Kawasaki Ki-61s, a newly fielded Imperial Army Air Service fighter. Japanese designs favored air-cooled radial engines, but the "Tony," as it became known, used a liquid-cooled inline engine. With its rounded wingtips and pointed nose, the Tony resembled the German fighter, and its sudden appearance gave cause to much speculation.

but the second impacted very close to Jones's weapon within the Nippon Pipe area and similarly did little damage. Also banking to the right away from the city, the *Ruptured Duck* wheeled around Kawasaki, dropped another bomb on the Japan Steel Pipe Manufacturing plant, then pitched back in from the east. Blitzing straight down the patchwork of reclaimed islands, Lawson's incendiary hit the Tsurumi Dockyard a mile and half west of his first bomb. Dropping back down to the rooftops, *Ruptured Duck* turned toward Yokohama, then scooted southwest out over Sagami Bay.

Like many others, Lieutenant Chase Nielson, navigator for the *Green Hornet*, had a dodgy compass and no chance over water to update his navigation. Arriving over Japan, he quickly determined the sixth bomber's position for the pilot, Lieutenant Dean "Jungle Jim" Hallmark. A former collegiate football player, the six-foot-tall, two-hundred-pound pilot split off from Jones and Lawson, then initially headed deeper into Tokyo Bay, perhaps realizing he wasn't far enough north. With fighters overhead, anti-aircraft bursts pockmarking the blue sky, and barrage balloons strung over the waterfront, it is certainly possible that Hallmark decided his original targets were too risky. Or maybe he, like Jones, mistook Kawasaki for his primary target area. In any event, he suddenly turned west and flew up the mouth of the Tama River separating Tokyo from Kawasaki. Spotting a big orderly compound past a bridge, Hallmark evidently decided it wouldn't get much better than this and attacked.* Aiming for the Fuji Steel Mill on the south bank of the river, bombardier Sergeant William Dieter's first bomb hit the street instead.

Banking sharply left, Hallmark muscled the *Green Hornet* around to the east, rolled out, and dropped on another factory at the bend in the river.† Wheeling right over the Chidori Canal,

---

* The Daishi Bridge connecting Tokyo to Kawasaki.
† Nippon Kako Company, currently the Nippon Yakin Kogyo Company.

the Texan leveled off, pushed the throttles to the stops, and tore across Kawasaki heading southwest toward Yokohama. Largely destroyed by the 1923 Great Kantō Earthquake, it had been rebuilt into the Keihin Industrial Area and boasted a formidable array of shipyards and drydocks. Approaching the piers and warehouses along the north end, Dieter aimed, but missed again, and *Green Hornet's* third bomb went into the water short of the piers. Zooming overhead, Hallmark flew straight southwest across the thirteen-mile neck of the Miura Peninsula toward Sagami Bay. A mile past the dockyard, Dieter, probably mistaking buildings along the Nakamura River for military or government structures, opened fire with the .30-caliber nose gun. Unfortunately, the buildings were schools, and his bursts went into the Uchikoshi residential area, killing an infant. Letting go of the Browning, Dieter quickly hunched over the Mark Twain, sighted down the bar at a factory complex at the confluence of the Horiwari and Nakamura Rivers, and dropped his incendiary. Assuming he was aiming at the factories, again he missed and hit the Horinouchi neighborhood south of Maita Park.

At the same time, roughly one hundred miles northwest, Ed York reached the Echigo Mountains and, two thousand pounds lighter now, was dipping and banking toward the coast. The bombs were gone and the Japanese were outraged, humiliated, and vengeful—roughly the same emotions that had pervaded the United States since December 7, 1941, yet now the tables were turned. The objectives of the main mission, Arnold's special bomber project, had been fulfilled, and for fifteen other B-25s and their crews the only remaining mission was to get as many home alive as possible.

But not Plane 8.

Throttling back to hold 250 miles per hour, York tapped Emmens on the shoulder and nodded at the yoke. Moving his feet to the rudders and wrapping both hands around the controls, Bob flew the Mitchell through a distinct saddle between two peaks and held a 305-degree course over Honshu's backbone.* Off to the south, just visible on the horizon, both pilots could plainly see the solitary snowcapped peak that could only be Mount Fuji. Ten minutes later they "crossed the peak of the backbone" and the terrain fell away drastically. "Ahead stretched a magnificent view of some 50 miles of flat, green land," Emmens recalled.

Sliding down the foothills, York took back the controls and picked a distant peak for a reference as Plane 8 crossed a pewter-colored river threading its way through a wide valley patched with fields and dotted with tiny hamlets.† They were so low that the Mitchell's shadow looked like another bomber flying formation with them, and that made Bob feel less exposed somehow. Rolling hills appeared, and for the next two minutes there was little to see but trees. York periodically banked left or right permitting Laban and Pohl a better view of the high six o'clock position above the tail, which is certainly where any Japanese fighters would likely appear.

But none did.

As they darted across another river valley and up over a ridge-line, a silver sheen blended with the darker blue horizon, and Bob Emmens tore open another pack of cigarettes. The Sea of Japan . . . they were so close. His heart beat quicker at the thought of actually pulling this off and getting out of enemy territory. "I'll bet we're the first B-25 crew to cross Japan at noon on a Saturday," he said into the interphone to break the tension. York managed a grim smile but did not reply as another valley suddenly opened up off the nose. People in the fields looked up and some even waved, then thirty seconds later Plane 8 roared over another river, then dropped back into the foothills. Rocks and trees filled the windscreen as this hillside was much steeper than the others. Grunting, York pulled harder

---

* Mount Nantai and Mount Nyoho.
† Mount Echigo.

and Bob felt the added g-forces push him back into the seat as Plane 8 soared over the ridge.

There!

Hills instantly melted away into clear air, and a flat coastal plain yawned from wingtip to wingtip. The sea . . . less than ten miles ahead! Pushing the bomber down, Bob strained against the lap belt and braced himself against the glare shield with his right hand as the Mitchell bottomed out one hundred feet over the countryside. Two rivers appeared and came together just beyond the nose as York pushed the throttles up and accelerated to 250 miles per hour for the final dash to the shore. "We passed low over a well-constructed railroad bridge . . . double track,"* Emmens wrote, then, after paralleling the rail line, a minute later they were over a "low sprawling city outlined against the sea beyond."

The bomber's shadow mirrored every twitch of the yoke as York continued checking their six o'clock. Both pilots were slightly incredulous that they'd made it this far without being intercepted. *These damn Japs must have an aircraft warning system,* Emmens thought as he leaned forward and stared ahead. The railroad tracks curved off to the left, intersecting another set coming in from the north, and the copilot could plainly see that "tall stacks reached up from the center of town . . . the chimneys might have indicated the blast furnaces of a steel mill."† Thundering overhead, a thin ribbon of sand spread sideways like a brown mustache, and they were sud-

---

* Very likely at the confluence of the Nagatori and Sabaishi Rivers, approximately five miles east of Kashiwazaki on Honshu's northwestern coast.

† Kashiwazaki lies on the southern edge of the Nugata oil fields and the Nippon oil refinery in this city was the largest in this section of Japan. This complex, later identified as target number 1,649 by the U.S. Army Air Force, was nearly seven hundred yards long and two hundred yards wide with at least six chimney stacks. The Niigata Iron Works, which constructed small naval craft and had a pair of smokestacks, lay three hundred yards west, next to the U River. Somewhat ironically, both complexes were separated by a candy factory.

denly over water again. "Our shadow," Bob recalled, "big and smooth now, [was] chasing alongside of us."

Both pilots exhaled, and Ed banked up to 320 degrees as the coastline faded behind the wings. Now all they had to do was cross 450 miles over the Sea of Japan, which was the Imperial Navy's backyard, then use outdated maps to find an airfield they'd never seen, and land unannounced and uninvited in a country at war. Assuming that was all possible, what facilities existed to service Plane 8 and send it on its way? Were there runways or just airfields? Were there gas, oil, and weapons—and what sort of cooperation would Americans receive? Lots of unknowns. But, of course, those very unknowns were the object of Plane 8's right turn over Cape Inubo and disappearance into central Honshu.

Rolling out, York climbed up to a more comfortable two hundred feet and stared ahead. Off to the right, about two o'clock, a humped outline showed above the haze. Sado Island. Their maps showed that at least, and for the first time since Cape Inubo, Emmens knew exactly where they were. He hadn't been completely certain over Utsunomiya, not that it mattered, and relief at one less variable made him relax slightly. York pointed at the instrument panel, and Bob understood. New cruise tables had been prepared, and the other crews had trained to maximize every gallon of gas. Despite not training for this, Ed York had helped develop the procedures and had more B-25 flying time than anyone on the raid except Jack Hilger. The idea was to keep manifold pressure high and control gas consumption by lowering the revolutions per minute through fine-tuning the propellor pitch and adding more air, or "leaning out" the fuel-air mixture entering the engines. Emmens fiddled with the MIXTURE knobs, which were on his side of the pedestal, while York adjusted the PROP controls and eased the throttles back slightly.

As Plane 8 was the only bomber with unmodified carburetors, the best they could manage was 170 mph, 1,400 rpm, and about 28 inches of manifold pressure. Without the two thousand pounds of extra weight from the bombs, this burned approximately ninety gallons per hour, and there was about 475 gallons remaining.* Bob craned forward and looked out of his window as they passed a point of land that hooked around to form a bay on the west side of Sado Island. Up ahead, the horizon was darker and blurry for the first time today. What, he wondered, was the worst enemy now? Weather, lack of fuel . . . or the Soviet Union.

Probably all three.

---

\* By comparison, the other fifteen modified bombers could use 1,300 rpm, twenty-five inches of manifold pressure, and reduce their fuel burn to sixty-three gallons per hour.

# PART II

Only a foolish optimist can deny the dark realities of the moment.

—Franklin Delano Roosevelt

# 5

## THE DARKENING

The events placing Plane 8 over the Japanese coast on April 18, 1942, are a veritable Gordian knot of deception, intrigue, political failures, and rampant nationalism. Nonetheless, as with all knots, there is a beginning buried somewhere within the tangle. To some degree, that Ed York, Bob Emmens, and their crew found themselves south of Sado Island westbound for the Soviet Union was indirectly the fault of another American—Commodore James Biddle of the United States Navy.

In 1845, Biddle anchored the USS *Vincennes* and USS *Columbus* in the Uraga Channel at the mouth of Edo Bay, and was promptly surrounded by several dozen oared Japanese gunboats.* Snubbed by the Tokugawa shogun, Biddle was not permitted to land and was actually knocked down by a Japanese guard after being invited aboard one of the gunboats. Seven years later, Commodore Matthew Calbraith Perry entered the same channel, steamed through the startled Japanese toward their capital city, and trained his eight-inch Paixhans

---

* Edo Bay became Tokyo Bay in 1868. Incidentally, Ted Lawson, Davey Jones, and Dean Hallmark overflew this exact spot in 1942 while inbound to their targets.

guns on the town of Uraga. Pugnacious, with the face of a bulldog and a temperament to match, Perry had no intention of suffering Biddle's fate. Thunder filled the bay as he fired blanks from his seventy-three cannons; then he sent a letter ashore with a white flag informing the astonished Japanese that if they chose to fight they may keep the flag and use it for their surrender. Not only did Perry refuse all commands to leave, but he blatantly conducted surveys of the bay and its fortifications. Deeply disconcerted by their invincible warrior caste's inability to intimidate or prevent Perry's actions, the Japanese agreed to negotiate.

For insular Japan, which had resisted western influences and trade, this opened the door to the modern world. With this fracturing came the Boshin War and the restoration of the emperor over the shogunate in 1869. Prince Mutsuhito, ascending to the Chrysanthemum Throne as Emperor Meiji, realized that without western technology Japan was doomed. Promptly embarking on a series of reforms to ensure his country's survival, he was most keen to create a modern navy. Somewhat ironically, Japan's first new vessel was the USS *Stonewall*, a former Confederate ironclad, and over the next two decades Meiji ordered more warships than any other nation except the United Kingdom. This race to catch up and take its position as a major power would lead to Japan's conflict with Imperial Russia and Tokyo's participation on the Allied side during the Great War. Imperial Japanese ambitions would lead to its expansion into China and the Pacific, and eventually be manifest in the conflict that put five Americans in Plane 8 over the Honshu coastline.

Franklin Roosevelt and his military commanders had been aware that war was likely unavoidable since Poland fell in 1939, and the outlook was quite bleak. The United States military was rapidly emasculated after the Great War, and two decades of neglect from Congress coupled with indifference from the American people had turned a formidable war machine into a "muleback army hardly large enough for an Indian campaign." Its weapons were generally obsolete, and there were too few of them. Hap Arnold, chief of the Army Air Corps, reported that his force was "practically nonexistent." Fortunately, with abundant natural resources and the geographic shields of the Atlantic and Pacific Oceans, America had some time to prepare—but not much.

While industry shook off its cobwebs and began converting its awesome potential to war, Roosevelt reasoned that the best immediate defense of America was to keep her allies fighting, yet there were several complex problems with this. Many Americans had not supported involvement in the Great War, and isolationism had become a political lightning rod. As Italian fascism, German national socialism, and Japanese imperialism took root, an overwhelming majority of Americans felt no compunction to spend more treasure or blood solving the world's problems, and beginning in 1935, four Neutrality Acts were passed that legally prevented armed U.S. involvement in overseas conflicts. Roosevelt was now in a political corner as he faced overwhelming public opinion against engagement, while realizing that eventually America would become involved in the looming global struggle. His challenge was to survive politically until an event occurred that changed public opinion and permitted overt participation.

The first Neutrality Act, invoked in response to Italy's invasion of Ethiopia, prohibited trading in materiel or arms to any parties at war. Roosevelt imposed a separate "moral embargo" that applied to any other commerce not covered by the act that provided support to belligerents. In this way, it was hoped, no sides would be taken and America would not be involved in overseas military actions. In 1936 this act was extended and went further by forbidding loans or credits by U.S. banks to belligerents. However, provisions in the act did not cover *civil* wars, and companies like General Motors, Ford, and Standard Oil, amassed at least $100,000,000 selling goods to Franco's Spanish Nationalists during the Spanish Civil War.

The 1937 act corrected this oversight by extending coverage to include civil wars, and U.S ships were now also prohibited from carrying passengers and war materiel to belligerents. American citizens were banned from traveling on vessels belonging to belligerent nations, but there were loopholes. A civil war or an outright war was only such a conflict if "the President shall proclaim such as a fact." If he did not so proclaim, then the conflict was something else that may or may not allow commerce. This worked with aid for China following Japan's 1937 invasion since Tokyo never formally declared war. Another significant loophole was a "cash and carry" provision permitting the sale of arms to those who could immediately pay, with cash, for such materiel, and if they arranged their own transport on non-U.S.-flagged vessels. This was a clever way of circumventing opposition and aiding Britain and France, since their navies controlled the seas over which such materiel would travel.

By October 1937, the Imperial Japanese Army had taken Beijing and was engaged in a vicious battle for Shanghai. In Chicago, Roosevelt freed a metaphoric trial balloon against isolationism by giving a speech designed to weaken domestic opposition for American involvement in the worsening situations overseas. Superficially, this was about China, but the president was attempting to lay the groundwork for intervention in Europe.

"Without a declaration of war and without warning or justification of any kind, civilians, including vast numbers of women and children, are being ruthlessly murdered with bombs from the air," Roosevelt said. His intent was to appeal to inherent American sympathy for an underdog and, perhaps, to focus on halting Imperial Japan's aggression in Asia. "If those things come to pass in other parts of the world," he continued, "let no one imagine that America will escape, that America may expect mercy, that this Western Hemisphere will not be attacked and that it will continue tranquilly and peacefully to carry on the ethics and the arts of civilization." Plainly a warning, the president sought to weaken the isolationist's position by revealing war would come to the United States regardless of efforts to remain neutral.

"I am compelled and you are compelled, nevertheless, to look ahead. The peace, the freedom, and the security of ninety percent of the population of the world is being jeopardized by the remaining ten percent who are threatening a breakdown of all international order and law. Surely the ninety percent who want to live in peace under law and in accordance with moral standards that have received almost universal acceptance through the centuries, can and must find some way to make their will prevail," he asserted. Couching the speech in moral terms, Roosevelt hoped to convey that the shadow slowly darkening the world must be fought to preserve civilization, the rule of law, and basic human decency. This was not an overseas adventure bent on expansionism or economic colonialism but a righteous struggle of good against evil, as he put it:

> It seems to be unfortunately true that the epidemic of world lawlessness is spreading. When an epidemic of physical disease starts to spread, the community approves and joins in a quarantine of the patients in order to protect the health of the community against the spread of the disease. War is a contagion, whether it be declared or undeclared. It can engulf states and peoples remote from the original scene of hostilities. We are determined to keep out of war, yet we cannot insure ourselves against the disastrous effects of war and the dangers of involvement.

> Most important of all, the will for peace on the part of
> peace-loving nations must express itself to the end that na-
> tions that may be tempted to violate their agreements and
> the rights of others will desist from such a course.

Unfortunately, as a catalyst for a more robust foreign policy, the speech backfired. Leading newspapers mocked the content, and opinion polls suggested even more Americans now identified with isolationism. Washington's reluctance was noted in Tokyo, and the Chinese capital of Nanjing fell just two months after Roosevelt's speech. Emboldened by America's apparent indifference and Brit-ain's appeasement, Hitler continued unchecked in his quest for a "Greater Germany," and smoldering events in Europe rapidly fanned the flame of war.

On March 12, 1938, the German 8th Army crossed the border into Austria, followed by a triumphant Adolf Hitler, ostensibly to liber-ate ethnic Germans who were being "oppressed." Austrian himself by birth, the forty-nine-year-old chancellor and führer of Germany entered the country through Braunau am Inn, his birthplace, and three days later announced the *Anschluss*, or "Union," from the Hel-denplatz in Vienna. Long coveting the Sudeten regions of northern Czechoslovakia, for some time Hitler had been sowing internal dis-content, hoping to create a pretext for annexation. However, with a modern army of forty-seven divisions and alliances with France, the Soviet Union, and Great Britain, the Czechs were in no mood to be bullied.

Ultimately, neither London nor Paris was inclined to actually fight for a region that was predominately German and inhabited by many who considered themselves German and wished to join Nazi Germany. Hitler approved the final version of Case Green, his invasion of Czechoslovakia, but was persuaded to join Mussolini,

French premier Édouard Daladier of France, and Britain's Neville Chamberlain for a last-ditch effort at peace. Meeting in Munich on September 29, 1938, it was agreed that the Wehrmacht would occupy the Sudetenland and that Prague could either acquiesce or fight Germany alone. With little choice, Czech president Edvard Beneš agreed. Six months later, Hitler violated the accord and annexed the rest of Czechoslovakia.

At 0445 on the morning of September 1, 1939, the Dirschau Bridge over the Vistula River vanished in a roaring explosion as pieces of its Polish defenders cartwheeled through the gray dawn. Flushed with success and emboldened by the perceived weakness of his adversaries, Hitler initiated Case White—the invasion of Poland and the total destruction of its army. From newly acquired Slovakia, East Prussia, and Pomerania, four German army groups thrust eastward into Poland, and by September 3, both Britain and France declared war on Germany—for the second time in two decades Europe was again at war. Roosevelt, shrewd politician and opportunist that he was, used the worsening situation to revoke the 1935 and 1937 Neutrality Acts. Victorious over the isolationists on November 4, he signed the 1939 Neutrality Act, which permitted the open sale of arms to belligerent nations, meaning France and Great Britain, but again on a cash-and-carry basis. Selling arms without a government-issued license also now became a federal offense.

Within days of Hitler's Polish invasion, France declared itself fully mobilized and, in a little-heralded campaign, invaded Germany. Eleven divisions left the Maginot Line, and advanced north into the Warndt Forest toward the Westwall, the 390-mile fortified line stretching between the Netherlands and the Swiss border. Believing the Wehrmacht too heavily engaged in Poland to threaten them, the French insisted on Great War tactics and crawled forward relatively slowly under heavy artillery cover. Managing to occupy the Warndt Forest but advancing only five miles into Germany after six days, the French panicked as Poland collapsed and, on September 21, retreated back to the Maginot Line.

A period somewhat inaccurately dubbed "the Phony War" now ensued in Europe—inaccurate because, while war did not officially exist for the western powers, it was real enough in the east and north. The Soviet Union took advantage of the confusion and signed a nonaggression pact with Germany in order to bully Finland. Always wary of its huge and deceitful southern neighbor, the Finns had refused claims against several of their offshore islands, as well as the extension of Soviet territory westward though the Karelian Isthmus. Helsinki also rebuffed Moscow's attempts to gain a thirty-year lease for a naval base at Hanko.

On November 26, 1939, in a typically clumsy "false flag" operation, the Red Army shelled the Russian border village of Mainila northwest of Leningrad, then claimed an attack by Finland.* On the last day of November 1939, with no declaration of war, four Soviet armies crossed into Finland. In violation of the 1920 Treaty of Tartu, the 1932 Soviet-Finnish Non-Aggression Pact and the 1934 Covenant of the League of Nations, a half million Russian soldiers surged over the border along an eight-hundred-mile front stretching from Murmansk to Lake Ladoga.

Overestimating their own capabilities, the Soviets planned for a two-week war, and even commissioned Dmitri Shostakovich to compose his *Suite on Finnish Themes* to be played as the Red Army marched triumphantly through Helsinki.† Redoubtable winter fighters that they were, the Finns stopped them cold. To Stalin's

---

* A "false flag" operation is designed to disguise an act by shifting responsibility to another party. In this case, the Finns had already moved their artillery away from the border, and Mainila was quite out of range. Helsinki requested a neutral investigation, which Moscow refused. Declassified post-Soviet documents, namely the papers of Andrei Zhdanov, reveal the incident was orchestrated by the People's Commissariat for Internal Affairs (NKVD).

† Shostakovich later disowned the work, and it was not played in its entirety until 2001.

fury, his army lost five times the men, eight times the aircraft, and one hundred times the tanks as did the Finns, and for its duplicity and aggression, the Soviet Union was expelled from the League of Nations in December 1939. Humiliated, the Russians made little progress until February 1940, when they were finally able to bring heavy artillery to bear and breach the Finnish Mannerheim Line. With no aid from France or Britain, the Finns agreed to cease hostilities and signed the Treaty of Moscow in March 1940.

Hitler used this time to redeploy the Wehrmacht and Luftwaffe back to the west in time to execute Case Green, the assault on Scandinavia, during April 1940. Denmark surrendered in a single day, but Norway held out until June 9, 1940. Sweden's prime minister, Per Albin Hansson, declared neutrality the day Poland was invaded and continued supplying all sides, even signing a trade agreement with Berlin in December. With a 55–67 percent iron content, Swedish ore was the purest in Europe, and ten million tons were imported to the Third Reich in 1940 alone. This composed over half of Germany's stock, and was so prevalent that industrial giants such as Thyssen and Krupp had adapted their machinery to accommodate the high-grade Swedish ore. Thyssen later stated that "without the ore from Sweden it is possible to calculate the date upon which Germany must capitulate."

Sweden's other ace in the hole, at least as far as insurance against invasion went, came from Philadelphia, Pennsylvania. Founded thirty-two years earlier in Gothenburg, Svenska Kullagerfabriken (SKF) was the largest global manufacturer of ball bearings, the finely engineered metallic balls used to reduce loads and minimize friction between moving parts in engines, machine guns, tanks, and especially aircraft. The Luftwaffe alone required a continuous supply of over two million bearings per month, and between its Gothenburg and Schweinfurt plants, SKF supplied 80 percent of all European demands. Even after the United States entered the war, SKF Philadelphia made up production shortfalls and shipped over six hundred thousand bearings per year to Axis countries via South American ports. Germany could not survive without Sweden, so as Allied soldiers fought and died for freedom, Stockholm remained free to conduct business as usual in return for its iron ore and ball bearings.*

A month following Denmark's surrender, the Phony War erupted into real war for the West as Hitler launched Case Yellow—the invasion of France. Chamberlain's appeasement at Munich and Allied failure to halt his conquests of Czechoslovakia, Poland, and Scandinavia, convinced Hitler that with France gone, Britain would have no alternative but to sue for peace. Then, with his western front secure, he could turn back east again and fulfill his lifelong dream of eradicating communism by facing his real enemy—the Soviet Union. But first, France had to be destroyed and, if possible, the entire British Expeditionary Force, which represented the bulk of England's regular army.

On May 10, 1940, the German panzer spearhead commanded by General Heinz Guderian crossed the Luxembourg border, then turned in to the Ardennes, following trails, paths, and especially rail lines. Plowing through the forest, which French Marshal Philippe Pétain declared "impenetrable," Guderian's immediate aim was to capture Sedan. Strategically situated on the Meuse, Sedan was the key link between the top of the Maginot Line and fortifications along the Belgian border. If taken, the French line would be shattered, and a wedge driven between the Allied armies. Two days later the 10th, 2nd, and 1st Panzer Divisions appeared out of the Ardennes north of Sedan, and by nightfall Guderian's tanks were rumbling through the city.

---

* In 1943 the U.S. Eighth Air Force raided Schweinfurt, Germany, to destroy the SKF ball bearing manufacturing facilities and other targets. Over 130 bombers were lost, and some 200 were heavily damaged, at the cost of over 1,100 Americans dead, wounded, or missing. It is considered likely that SKF warned its German subsidiary of the raid in order to protect its financial interests, and again SKF Philadelphia made up the loss in production.

Poor communications, complacency, and, most damning, a defensive mind-set that obviated any meaningful tactical response doomed the French. German forces had taken the bridge across the Ardennes Canal west of Sedan, and now, with three bridgeheads over the Meuse, the panzers were a sword clearly aimed at the heart of France. General Alphonse Georges, commander of the entire North East Front facing the German onslaught, "flung himself into a chair and burst into tears." Shattered, demoralized, and obviously lacking effective leadership, the French military began collapsing. To the north the Dutch surrendered on May 15, and the Belgians were buckling. Caught in the middle, with its flanks now exposed, the British Expeditionary Force (BEF) had no choice but to fall back west toward the English Channel.

At great cost, fighter pilots of the Royal Air Force covered the withdrawal, and London ordered the BEF commander to attack south into the German advance to aid the French. Fortunately, John Vereker, Viscount Gort, a Victoria Cross holder from the Great War, was too able a tactician to comply. He knew it was futile. The French were surrendering faster than he could intervene, so on May 25, Gort initiated his breakout to the only remaining port from which an evacuation had any chance at all—Dunkirk. Three days later, Belgium surrendered, and Britain's new prime minster, Winston Churchill, initiated Operation Dynamo to save as many fighting men as possible from France. In this he was aided by Hitler himself, who, overly concerned about tank losses and perhaps hoping to make peace with Britain, ordered his panzers to halt ten miles outside Dunkirk on the east side of the Gravelines–Saint Omer Canal. Guderian, Rommel, and the other generals watched furiously, but impotently, as Hitler's pause gave the British the opportunity to evacuate a total of 338,226 soldiers by June 4, 1940.

The cost was enormous.

A quarter of the RAF fighters sent to cover the evacuation never returned, and hundreds of highly trained, irreplaceable pilots were lost. Nearly 2,500 artillery pieces were left behind, along with 63,000 vehicles and a half million rounds of ammunition. Though now alone, England was still in the war. Equipment could be replaced, but it took eighteen years to grow a soldier, and those saved from the beach would now fight another day. Cold, often wounded, and hungry, they represented one desperate sliver of hope as the United Kingdom now stood against the Axis. The other hope lay with the United States, 3,700 miles west across the Atlantic Ocean, and deeply divided about participating in, as many viewed it, just another European war. Beyond strategic concerns, beyond common ties with Britain, and even beyond humanity, in the summer of 1940 it appeared nothing could stir America into action. Nothing short of some horrific event would rouse the anger and might of the United States.

Timing was also quite bad for Franklin Roosevelt. In office now for eight years, Roosevelt believed he was the only man with the knowledge and experience to see America through the next war, which meant breaking tradition to run for a third term.* He had two overarching domestic issues to face: isolationism and criticism for New Deal entitlements, which his political opponents labeled socialism. Navigating difficult politics was nothing new to FDR, but his real concern was fickle public opinion regarding another conflict in Europe. As many Americans viewed the Great War, 53,402 U.S. soldiers died and another 204,002 were wounded on the Western Front simply to prop up British and French colonial empires, or to profit American industrialists. Entering into this latest conflict had nothing to do with the security of the United States, and approximately $11 billion of debt by those same erstwhile allies remained unpaid.† Popular sentiment retorted that if they had not learned

---

* The Twenty-Second Amendment, which limits a president to two terms, would not become law until March 1947.

† These were combat deaths. Another 63,114 men died from other causes, mostly influenza, bringing the total to 116,516 dead Americans.

their lesson from the Great War, then this next conflagration was their own fault. Europe could solve it, or perish, on its own.

Yet there were significant differences between the 1914–18 Great War and the current situation. Adolf Hitler was not Kaiser Wilhelm; Hitler intended to rule a global reich controlled by Nazi Germany, and to "purify" the world from, as he saw them, impure subhumans—nothing less than worldwide genocide for those who did not fit his vision. Roosevelt knew if the Axis took Europe and most of the Far East, then it would eventually come for America, and with the rest of the world subdued, the United States would have to fight alone. However, that very likely scenario was dismissed by prominent isolationists such as Senator Gerald Ney (R-ND) and Smedley Butler, a retired Marine major general, two-time Medal of Honor recipient, and combat veteran of multiple conflicts up to and through the Great War, whose views were particularly hard to refute given his background.

"War is a racket," Butler wrote in a pamphlet of the same name. "It always has been. It is possibly the oldest, easily the most profitable, surely the most vicious. It is the only one international in scope. It is the only one in which the profits are reckoned in dollars and the losses in lives."

Yet it was Charles Lindbergh, worldwide flying sensation and U.S. national hero, who irritated Franklin Roosevelt the most. Easily the most famous member of the America First Committee (AFC) and also its public face, Lindbergh was an outspoken critic of any policy or sentiment that would lead the United States into war. This was so strong in 1940 that less than half of Americans would vote for aid if Germany invaded neighboring Mexico. Lindbergh was certainly not alone in his views, but he had badly crossed Roosevelt during the 1934 Army Air Corps mail scandal, and for that the president would never forgive him.

So with public opinion firmly against war in the fall of 1940, the president had to tread carefully, and nowhere was this more critical or contentious than the issue of foreign aid. With his November defeat of Republican challenger Wendell Willkie, Roosevelt could now face the threat posed by Hitler's legions staring across the Channel at their single remaining foe. By December 1940, all of western Europe had fallen except the United Kingdom, which was literally hanging on by coupling newly developed radar with the skill and courage of a thousand fighter pilots. Britain was alone now, and approaching her credit limit with the United States. At the close of a letter, Churchill writes, "Last of all, I come to the question of Finance. The more rapid and abundant the flow of munitions and ships which you are able to send us, the sooner will our dollar credits be exhausted. They are already, as you know, very heavily drawn upon by the payments we have made to date . . . the moment approaches when we shall no longer be able to pay cash for shipping and other supplies."

Essentially, Churchill was asking for free war materiel and, with the Royal Navy stretched to its breaking point, he wanted the United States to deliver the goods to Britain. This would mean a repeal of the Neutrality Act and a public firestorm from those Americans who did not support war. Supplying Britain with arms could also lead to a declaration of war from the Axis, though such an act from Berlin or Rome was not expected—yet.

Tokyo was another problem altogether. Responding to Tokyo's actions in China during July 1940, Roosevelt cut off the export of hundred-octane aviation fuel, aircraft parts, and machine tools to Japan, though he continued to permit shipments of scrap metal and oil. As some 90 percent of the Empire's supply of scrap metal came from the United States, the president's actions were intended as a warning and to incentivize mediation over China. In fact, the United States supplied over 50 percent of *all* materiel Japan required to wage war, and the Imperial General Staff was deeply concerned by this dependency. A dependency that included 82 percent of ferroalloys for steelmaking: over 90 percent of copper imports, heavy machinery, and combustion engines, and about 80 percent of the Empire's oil.

Roosevelt's embargo had the opposite effect that he intended.

With the fall of France in June, its colonial holdings, including Indochina, passed to the collaborationist Vichy government, which was itself controlled by a Germany now allied to Japan. Tokyo demanded naval and air bases, transit rights for imperial troops, and the closure of all routes into China. Vichy cried for help from Berlin, and was ignored. While the diplomats attempted to satisfy Tokyo, on September 22 units of the Imperial 22nd Army crossed the Indochinese border into what is now northern Vietnam and secured Haiphong Harbor four days later. This cut the Allied supply line into southern China, where the Imperial Army was heavily engaged, and put another Japanese-controlled territory within bomber range of American bases in the Philippines. The action also opened a route into British Malaya.

Though lukewarm to an alliance with Hitler, the strategic situation with Washington contributed to Japan's entry into the Tripartite Alliance on September 27, 1940, following the conquest of French Indochina. Roosevelt responded by now placing a total embargo on all shipments of scrap metal from the United States to Japan, which further motivated Tokyo to decrease its dependance and procure, by force if necessary, other sources for its war machine. Consequently, Tokyo increasingly looked south toward Malaya and the Dutch East Indies, but two factors gave them pause: the Soviet Union's Far Eastern Army, and the United States Pacific Fleet.

Four days after Christmas 1940, Roosevelt, seeking to crack the domestic isolationist wall, gave a fireside radio chat, stating:

Some of our people like to believe that wars in Europe and in Asia are of no concern to us. But it is a matter of most vital concern to us that European and Asiatic war-makers should not gain control of the oceans which lead to this hemisphere.

If Great Britain goes down, the Axis powers will control the continents of Europe, Asia, Africa, Australia, and the high seas—and they will be in a position to bring enormous military and naval resources against this hemisphere. It is no exaggeration to say that all of us, in all the Americas, would be living at the point of a gun.

There are those who say that the Axis powers would never have any desire to attack the Western Hemisphere. That [this] is the same dangerous form of wishful thinking which has destroyed the powers of resistance of so many conquered peoples. The plain facts are that the Nazis have proclaimed, time and again, that all other races are their inferiors and therefore subject to their orders. And most important of all, the vast resources and wealth of this American Hemisphere constitute the most tempting loot in all of the round world.

The experience of the past two years has proven beyond doubt that no nation can appease the Nazis. No man can tame a tiger into a kitten by stroking it. There can be no appeasement with ruthlessness.

We must be the great arsenal of democracy.

Roosevelt and more prescient members of Congress, along with the majority of military professionals, could see the war clouds thickening. They did not agree on the timing or even where the sword would fall, but it was coming—and 1941 appeared to be the year of catching up on decades of slashed defense budgets and also, of addressing the atrophying of military technology and capabilities and, most frightening, the decay of the industrial base such that it could no longer build sufficient amounts of war materiel. Not a single operational-level tank had been produced in 1940, and just 1,771 combat aircraft, of which only 46 were heavy bombers. The Army Air Corps had gone from a 1918 complement of 195,023 men to less than 10,000 a few years later, which would remain fairly constant throughout the Roaring Twenties. During the Depression years, manning would creep slowly upward to a 1940 peak of 51,165 officers and men. Now, with war looming and the panic on, an additional 100,000 men would join in 1941.*

Across the country, over 780 new factories were being constructed and existing civilian production slowly switched over to military uses. Not just automobile and aircraft manufacturers, but jewelers were making fuses; washing machine companies made machine guns; appliance makers switched to antitank mines; pipe and valve makers now made hand grenades; and those who made razors a year earlier now produced percussion caps. But the real challenge was constructing the machine tools that physically produced the designs. These precision tools drill, cut, press, and bore; they are the beating heart of the process, and without them there is nothing for assembly lines to assemble. For example, eighty-seven tools were required to build a single propeller shaft, and in 1940 virtually all such tools came from just two hundred companies, most in New England with fewer than one hundred employees. Vermont's Black River Valley was home to the three largest firms, and by the late 1930s Stalin's Soviet Union and Imperial Japan were their best foreign customers.† Retooling for war took up the first half of 1941, but by the end of the year firms ramped up production—like Cincinnati Milling Machine, which was fabricating a new tool every seventeen minutes.

---

* This would increase fivefold in 1942 to 764,415, and by 1944 the Army Air Force's strength reached 2,372,292.
† Over two dozen Kawasaki and Mitsubishi fighters, bombers, and trainers were produced using American-made machine tools.

Looking further ahead, Gibbs & Cox, the nation's top naval archi-
tecture firm, had been tasked with building a new type of merchant
ship to transport the materiel wherever it was needed in the world.
Their answer was the Liberty ship: an ugly little 441-foot-long,
10,856-ton workhorse constructed along straight lines whenever
possible in welded, prefabricated sections to save time. Instead of
coal, the engines were oil-fired so the ship could be refueled at sea,
and all the parts were interchangeable. Steel decks replaced wood,
and there was no electricity or running water for the crew. Oil lamps
were used for interior illumination, and hatch covers were designed
to double as flotation devices if the ship was sunk. Once production ramped up, yards turned out three such ships every forty-eight
hours. Still, by the summer of 1941, only 10 percent of America's
factories were now defense industries—there was a long way yet to
go, and time was running out.

One hour past midnight on June 22, 1941, a full 299 days before
Plane 8 crossed Japan, flashes ripped apart the darkness along the
1,800-mile Soviet border from the Baltic Sea to the Black Sea. Forty-
two thousand artillery pieces on the European-side border opened
fire, heralding Operation Barbarossa, the largest land offensive in
human history and Hitler's invasion of the Soviet Union. Nearly 4
million Germans in ninety infantry divisions with seventeen panzer
divisions lunged east as 3,200 combat aircraft struck airfields, bridges,
communication lines, and other carefully analyzed critical targets.
Having perfected the blitzkrieg in Poland, France, and Scandinavia,
the lightning war paralyzed the Red Army, the Red Air Force, and a
former seminary student and self-proclaimed marshal of the Soviet
Union—known to the world as Joseph Stalin.

Shocked, reeling, and without guidance from Stalin's ineffective
and overcentralized command structure, Soviet forces fell back all

along the front. By the end of the second day, the Red Air Force was missing 3,922 aircraft at a cost of 78 to the Luftwaffe, and by the first week in July the Germans penetrated over three hundred miles through the Red Army toward Moscow. At the end of the month, fifty Soviet divisions, comprising five complete armies, had been annihilated and six hundred thousand Russian soldiers were taken prisoner by the advancing Germans. By July 3, Lenin's body was removed from Moscow and taken a thousand miles east to Tumen. Without Hitler's interference, Army Group Center, commanded by Fedor von Bock, would likely have bypassed major Russian cities and driven straight into Moscow. Hitler did meddle, however, insisting that surrounded enemy armies be destroyed rather than cut off and left to wither. After Smolensk fell on July 15, Berlin ordered Bock to split his forces and reinforce those on his flanks that were subduing Ukraine and thrusting toward Leningrad. By the end of August, Army Group North reached the Volkhov River and was dangerously close to cutting off Leningrad. Eight hundred miles to the south, Field Marshal Gerd von Rundstedt swept through Ukraine to the shores of the Black Sea and penetrated as far east as the Dnipro River. Another seven hundred thousand Soviet soldiers were killed, wounded, or taken prisoner, but Army Group Center was still over two hundred miles from the Kremlin.

Hitler's delay was disastrous, and the drive to Moscow was not resumed in earnest until September 30, 1941. A week later, the snow was falling, and as Russian roads turned to mud, German logistical issues worsened considerably. Most infantry units were half-strength, while motorized and panzer units barely had one third of their original complement. Anticipating a short summer campaign, the Germans lacked winter boots, coats, ammunition, and food, yet Operation Typhoon, the advance to Moscow, still encircled and destroyed four additional Soviet armies at Vyazma and Bryansk. By October 13, the 3rd Panzer Group was within

ninety miles of the Kremlin, with Moscow's defenses were reduced to ninety thousand men and one hundred and fifty tanks.
Two days later, Stalin ordered the *government* to evacuate, not
the people, and pro-Nazi riots accompanied by extensive looting
erupted throughout the capital. In Tokyo during the same week, a
former Kempeitai officer and militant nationalist general named
Hideki Tojo became Japan's prime minister.* On October 27, the
Soviet Union's Marshal Zhukov withdrew east of the Nara River,
and as the Germans attempted a pincer movement to encircle
the Russian capital, reinforcements from the Soviet Far Eastern
Army began appearing, largely due to information provided by a
Soviet spy in Tokyo.

Richard Sorge, born in Azerbaijan to a German father and Russian mother, spent seventeen months in combat during the Great
War as an imperial German infantryman. Badly wounded in 1916,
he was medically discharged and spent the rest of the war attending various universities, eventually earning a doctorate in political
science. Disillusioned by what he had endured, Sorge gravitated
toward Marxism and became a devout communist, which led to
his recruitment into the RU. Also known as the Fourth Director-
ate, this was the Red Army's military intelligence service. Sorge,
under cover as a journalist, traveled to the United Kingdom,
China, and the Soviet Union before accepting an assignment to
Tokyo. A charming sophisticate who spoke fluent Russian, Japanese, German, and English, Sorge set up an effective intelligence
network in the heart of Imperial Japan that provided crucial intelligence to the Soviet Union. Through him, Moscow was informed

---

* Translated as "Military Police Corps" the Kempeitai functioned similarly to the
Soviet NKVD and Nazi Schutzstaffel (SS), carrying out surveillance of all types
and brutal interrogations of anyone it chose, including suspected spies, dissidents,
and prisoners of war.

in May 1941 that a German invasion "will commence in the latter part of June," yet Stalin dismissed the warning.

Though Moscow and Tokyo had signed the Japanese-Soviet Non-Aggression Pact in April 1941, neither side trusted the other and both acknowledged that the erstwhile diplomacy was a delaying tactic that permitted each nation to deal with other issues. For the Japanese, who desperately needed the raw materials provided by its puppet state of Manchukuo, this meant the capability to wage war in China, or against the United States if the prospect of Soviet action in the Far East was somewhat lessened. Stalin, despite Germany's military buildup on his western border, believed his most imminent threat came from the east and the Japanese Empire. If the Soviet Far East was off Japan's menu, even temporarily, he could continue his domestic butcheries and further his territorial ambitions into Eastern Europe unabated.

Even Operation Barbarossa's three-pronged lunge into Russia did not wholly lessen the fear of the Manchukuo-based Japanese Kwantung Army, and it was not until Sorge's October message (which, in part, stated that "the Soviet Far East can be considered safe from Japanese attack") that Stalin began deploying troops from Mongolia to meet the German onslaught. After Zhukov's withdrawal, the exhausted Germans halted on the last day of October to reorganize, resupply what they could, and wait for the ground to freeze. During this halt, Stalin managed to move another thousand tanks into the cauldron around Moscow and reconstitute eleven armies from thirty divisions newly arrived from the Far East.

These fresh troops altered the balance for the Battle of Moscow. Had the Germans suffered less logistically and been better equipped, the additional Soviet forces would likely not have saved the Soviet capital, but added to the Wehrmacht's other woes, these reinforcements were a strategic game changer. Certainly, any deployments from the Far East would not have been possible without intelligence that the Japanese were more concerned with their upcoming "Southern Operation" in the Pacific than they were with a Russian threat from Manchuria.

The situation could be, and has been, interpreted as evidence that Moscow, through Sorge, was made aware of Japanese plans to invade British, French, and Dutch colonial territories in Asia and the Pacific and also to attack the United States. It also meant the Soviets would not do *anything* in the near term to give cause for a Japanese revocation of the nonaggression pact or provoke a Japanese invasion in the Far East, which would force Stalin into a two-front war that he could not successfully fight in 1942.

Against the advice of his generals and with the Germans quite literally at the gates, the Soviet general secretary insisted on holding the November 7 Revolution Day parade in Moscow. Newly arrived reinforcements marched through the streets, then straight out to the front lines, but it had the effect Stalin wished. With morale boosted and the enemy temporarily halted, the Soviets had a few days of metaphoric sunlight while the world, and particularly the Japanese, watched. The respite dissolved on November 15 when the Germans lunged forward again, with the Third Panzer Army capturing Klin, fifty miles northwest of Moscow, eight days later. Taking the last bridge over the Moscow-Volga canal on November 27, Baron Hans von Funck's 7th Panzer "Ghost Division" was now a scant twenty-two miles from the Russian capital.

Unknown to the half-frozen Germans staring through frosted field glasses at the red Kremlin walls, and certainly unknown to the muddy, desperate Soviet soldiers facing them, another event was occurring that would ultimately dictate the course of the war. Obscured by ice, fog, and predawn blackness, 4,300 miles east of Moscow, thirty-two imperial Japanese warships commanded by Vice Admiral Chūichi Nagumo sortied from Hitokappu Bay on Etorofu Island in the Kurile Archipelago. Clearing the sleet- and snow-covered volcanic shoreline the *kidō butai,* or "mobile force," came about to the east and vanished in the mist. Its objective: the Hawaiian Islands and the home port of the U.S. Pacific Fleet at Pearl Harbor.*

During the 1930s the Imperial Navy meticulously plotted sea lanes frequented by foreign ships around the Home Islands, and Nagumo's carriers were following a route carefully chosen to avoid detection. Nonetheless, for over eighty years controversy has existed surrounding the supposed sighting of the Japanese fleet by a Soviet merchantman or freighter. Hiroyuki Agawa, author of *The Reluctant Admiral,* related that "on December 6 the Nagumo force did catch sight of one passing vessel of a third nation," and a conspiracy that Moscow knew of the impending attack on Pearl Harbor, but never warned Washington, was born. Obviously, it benefited the Soviet Union to have the United States in the war since supplies would now openly flow from West Coast ports to the Russian Maritime Territory; the Japanese would be ostensibly too occupied fighting the Americans to threaten Mongolia; and eventually the Germans would have to deal with a true second front in Europe. Sound reasons all, but hardly definitive.

Agawa never identified the vessel's flag, and the likelihood that it was Soviet is virtually nonexistent. On December 6, Nagumo's task force was approximately one thousand miles northwest of Oahu, which was at least fifteen hundred miles south of the standard route used by Russian ships outbound from Los Angeles or San Francisco. This track proceeded north of the Aleutians into the Bering Sea and past the southern tip of the Kamchatka Peninsula, thus skirting Japan via the Sea of Okhotsk to Vladivostok. Japanese agents in port cities along the American West Coast were well aware of "emergency" aid, especially gasoline, supplied to the Soviet

---

* Etorofu was renamed Iturup following the 1945 Soviet occupation.

Union by the United States in circumvention of the Lend-Lease program, which would not be formally extended to Moscow until October.

There were thirty-two Soviet tankers and freighters operating in the North Pacific, but only four departed California ports after November 7 that could conceivably have steamed far enough to encounter Nagumo's fleet. In fact, *Clara Zetkin* and *Uritskii* laid over in Portland and did not depart again until December 6 and therefore could not have encountered the Japanese warships. The other pair, *Uzbekistan* and *Azerbaidzhan*, cleared San Francisco on November 12 and 14, respectively, heading for Vladivostok. Based on a twelve-knot average speed following the prescribed northern route, *Uzbekistan* would have the closest point of approach—four hundred miles north of Nagumo by November 26, on the *other* side of the Kurile Islands, heading the opposite direction. A visual sighting would be impossible and, in the event, Agawa claims the "third nation vessel" was spotted on December 6, a thousand miles north of Hawaii.

Even if a Soviet ship had deviated so far south as to encounter the Japanese fleet, there was no way to relay the information had such a sighting been understood. There was also no way to confirm the report, as Richard Sorge was arrested in Tokyo by the Kempeitai on October 18 and was sitting in a cell in Sugamo Prison as Nagumo approached Hawaii.* More plausible, if such a ship was truly encountered, was that the vessel belonged to a neutral country and had no interest in a fleet of warships, which would be difficult to positively identify so close to the largest U.S. naval base in the Pacific.

In the end, even if Nagumo's ships were sighted, Tokyo was com-

---

* On three occasions, Tokyo offered Moscow an exchange for Sorge but was denied each time. The Soviets refused to acknowledge he was their agent, and he would eventually be hung on November 7, 1944. Hanako Ishii, Sorge's lover, eventually retrieved his gold bridgework from his corpse and had it made into a ring that she wore the rest of her life.

mitted to war with America, and Moscow was equally committed to avoiding war with the Empire. By the time Secretary of the Navy Frank Knox acknowledged that "we are very close to war ... war may begin in the Pacific at any moment," the die had already been cast. During his speech on a cold Thursday evening in Chicago, Knox also stated, "no matter what happens, the United States Navy is ready! Whatever happens, the Navy is not going to be caught napping."

Knox uttered these fateful words on December 4, 1941.

At the same time Knox was speaking, Nagumo's Carrier Strike Force was approximately sixteen hundred miles north of the Hawaiian Islands and turning southeast toward Pearl Harbor. Dawn on Sunday, December 7, 1941, saw the six imperial carriers swing into the wind, and Lieutenant Commander Shigeru Itaya gunned his Zero fighter down Akagi's wooden deck two hundred miles north of Oahu. Within hours 2,403 Americans were killed, and the United States would shortly be at war once again. Stalin, and also Winston Churchill, rejoiced at the news. Oddly enough, so did Hitler. "We can't lose the war at all," he proudly proclaimed, already envisioning full Japanese participation with the Axis in keeping with its 1940 Tripartite Act obligations.

In point of fact, the Tripartite Act stipulated military action only "if one of the Contracting Powers [Germany, Italy, and Japan] is attacked by a Power at present not involved in the European War, or the Japanese-Chinese conflict." Under these terms, Japan avoided intervention in Russia since it was Germany who attacked the Soviet Union, just as Hitler was under no obligation to now go to war with the United States, as Japan was the aggressor. Nonetheless, four days later Hitler did exactly that, to the dismay of his generals and admirals. Cloaked in a euphoric haze at Berlin's Kroll Opera House, at the end of a rambling, ninety-minute harangue to the Reichstag, the führer declared: "Faithful to the provisions of the Tripartite Pact of September 27, 1940, Germany and Italy accordingly now regard themselves as finally forced to join together on the side of Japan in the struggle for the defense and preservation of the freedom and independence of our nations and realms against the United States of America and Britain."

His declaration, Hitler believed, would result in a similar declaration of war on the Soviet Union by Japan, which would certainly lead to an imperial offensive in Mongolia that siphoned men and materiel away from Moscow. The Japanese, he believed, would so fully occupy Washington that aid to Britain and Russia would suffer since the United States could not possibly fight a multifront, global war *and* supply its allies effectively at the same time.

In fact, it could.

"Yesterday, December 7, 1941—a date which will live in infamy—the United States of America was suddenly and deliberately attacked by naval and air forces of the Empire of Japan," the president said. He and his son, Marine Major James Roosevelt, had traveled together to Capitol Hill for the president's short speech to the Seventy-Seventh U.S. Congress. "Hostilities exist. There is no blinking at the fact that our people, our territory, and our interests are in grave danger. With confidence in our armed forces, with the unbounding determination of our people, we will gain the inevitable triumph . . . so help us God."

Within an hour of his speech, a declaration of war unanimously passed in the Senate and subsequently passed the House by a vote of 388:1; the dissenting vote was cast by Jeannette Rankin, a Republican pacifist from Montana.* "If you're against war, you're against war regardless of what happens," she later stated. "It's a wrong method of trying to settle a dispute." She was correct, though like many pacifists, dangerously naive. Such sentiments, admirable in

---

* Deluged by angry reporters, Rankin had to flee to a cloakroom until the Capitol Police could escort her out. She did not run for reelection in 1942.

other circumstances, played directly into the hands of those who continue to take by force, indifferent to the misery inflicted, until they are stopped. Force, when used, must be met by force as the time for diplomacy and compromise has plainly passed. Rankin never understood this, but Charles Lindbergh certainly did.

"Now it has come and we must meet it as united Americans regardless of our attitude in the past," Lindbergh publicly stated the day following Pearl Harbor. "I can see nothing to do under these circumstances except to fight."

America had neither desired nor chosen to be the guardian of freedom, yet no other nation could now do it, and if good was to triumph over evil, then the United States had no choice but to wholeheartedly enter the conflict. Japan, without intending to do so, had sounded the death knell for the Axis. But this was not obvious to anyone at the time; in fact, the global situation appeared to dictate the opposite. Admiral Isoroku Yamamoto's Operation Z had succeeded, temporarily, with its primary objective, which was to prevent the U.S. Pacific Fleet from intervening against the Japanese invasion of the oil-rich Dutch East Indies. On the same morning Oahu was attacked, across the International Date Line the Japanese 14th Army commenced its assault on American bases in the Philippines. Six hundred Marines on Guam were overwhelmed on December 10 by nearly six thousand men of the South Seas Detachment and elements of the 2nd Maizuru Special Naval Landing Force. During the next ten dark days, Hong Kong, Borneo, and Wake Island were invaded. The Japanese caught the Royal Navy battle cruiser *Repulse* and the battleship *Prince of Wales* off Malaysia, sinking them both, and on Christmas Day, the British surrendered Hong Kong. Then Japanese forces invaded the Dutch East Indies and captured Singapore. On February 19 the Imperial Navy bombed mainland Australia and then, four days later and 7,500 miles to the west, the submarine I-17 attacked the Barnsdall–Rio Grande Oil Field near Santa

Barbara, California.* Yamamoto's prediction that he would "run wild" in the Pacific for six months seemed to be accurate. British, Dutch, and colonial troops collapsed under the assault as American and Filipino troops fell back to the Bataan Peninsula. Under the spell of what Yamamoto and others called "Victory Disease," imperial forces became somewhat complacent and arrogant from their "easy" conquests, and in so doing left themselves vulnerable to thoroughly enraged Americans, who viewed the attack on Pearl Harbor as unforgivable duplicity. Roosevelt requested a $56 billion defense budget increase from Congress and got it, while fighting-age men flocking to recruiting stations would swell military ranks to the 2 million mark within a year. Patriotism became a faith, and those disinclined to join the war effort were scorned and vilified. Congress, in its continuous quest to look after itself, discreetly passed Public Law 77–411, providing themselves with lucrative pensions above their current list of benefits. Public indignation and outrage forced a hasty repeal.

New songs rolled out over the airways like "Taps for Japs" and "We Did It Before We Can Do It Again." Barbershops offered "Free Shaves for Japs—Not Responsible for Accidents!" Anything remotely connected with Japan, such as performances of *Madame Butterfly* and *The Mikado*, were summarily canceled, and the fleet carriers *Yorktown* and *Enterprise* surprised the Japanese by raiding the Marshall and Gilbert Islands. While Lieutenant General Jonathan Wainwright stubbornly delayed the Japanese on Bataan, Frog Low stepped through Admiral King's door to articulate his plan to raid Japan with land-based bombers flown from an aircraft carrier.

Low did not know, as King and Arnold did, that the president yearned to strike at Japan, to send a message to Tokyo, to our allies, and to the American people, who were dazed by the sudden-

---

* The area today is covered by the Sandpiper Golf Course.

ness and effectiveness of the Japanese offensives. Now that America had been attacked, Roosevelt meant to pit the entire might of the United States against the Axis.

"We must raise our sights all along the production line," the president said in strong, measured tones during his January 6, 1942, State of the Union address. "Let no man say it cannot be done. It must be done—and we have undertaken to do it."

He increased his 1942 production demands to sixty thousand planes, forty-five thousand tanks, twenty thousand anti-aircraft guns, and fully six million tons of shipping. But this would take time, and Roosevelt wanted to strike now; Frog Low's bomber idea neatly dovetailed with the president's wishes and with the conundrum facing Hap Arnold: how to hit Japan from bases in the Soviet Union.

"As our power and our resources are fully mobilized, we shall carry the attack against the enemy," Roosevelt intoned, adding:

> We shall hit him and hit him again wherever and whenever we can reach him. We are fighting, as our fathers have fought, to uphold the doctrine that all men are equal in the sight of God. Those on the other side are striving to destroy this deep belief and to create a world in their own image—a world of tyranny and cruelty and serfdom. That is the conflict that day and night now pervades our lives. No compromise can end that conflict. There never has been—there never can be—successful compromise between good and evil.
>
> Only total victory can reward the champions of tolerance, and decency, and freedom, and faith.

Roosevelt was calm, decisive, and adamant: "We cannot wage this war in a defensive spirit."

With America now in the war, would the Soviets join the Allies? If so, would they abrogate their nonaggression pact with the Empire?

No one knew the answer, but Washington was certain that Moscow would act solely in its best interests. Allied distrust of the Soviet Union was well founded, and pragmatists were well aware that any alliance with Moscow was an alliance of convenience that would end as soon as the fighting was over.

Japan had never acted in concert with its Axis partners, so perhaps Moscow would not participate in the Allied war against the Empire. But even with no active role, the Russians *could* permit the Americans to establish bases in their Maritime Territory, bases from which the Home Islands could be attacked now, in 1942. Moscow could also permit a Siberian resupply line through Russia into China as well, creating a true second front that would clamp Japan in a Russia-China-American vise.

The Americans were pressing for exactly that. The Tenth Air Force had been created in anticipation of opening such a front against the Japanese with bombers, primarily B-17s, operating from bases in China's eastern Zhejiang province. Aircraft from the 19th and 7th Bombardment Groups were transferred to Australia following the disasters in the Philippines and Java, with the Tenth headquartered in New Delhi, India. Another big part of this planned buildup was the addition of Doolittle's B-25s, which would join the Tenth after bombing Tokyo. The Japanese, who had never been able to subdue China, were very aware of their vulnerability to American air attacks against the Home Islands from bases across the East China Sea in the Soviet Union. The Imperial Army feared and distrusted the Russians, so much so that of the fifty-one divisions available in 1941, thirty-eight of them—some 750,000 men—would remain in China for most of the war due to the unpredictability of the Soviet Union and wariness of an Allied second front.

As for Stalin, he *could* do all that Tokyo feared—but would he? The Americans were hampered by a lack of knowledge concerning Soviet intentions, very probably because Moscow did not know itself what it would do and was not cooperating with Washington. The U.S. Army Air Corps, renamed the U.S. Army Air Force two days before Hitler invaded Russia, was particularly in the dark regarding Soviet infrastructure, attitudes, and capabilities. Before Washington made any type of real demands in return for the extensive Lend-Lease aid Stalin desired, American leaders had to know what sort of hand the Russians were holding in the Far East.

There was no time to build ports, railways, and bases—not if operations were to commence early enough in 1942 to blunt Japanese advances in the Pacific. Therefore, it was imperative to know what the Russians possessed along the Muravyov-Amursky Peninsula, and the only way to do it was to somehow get to the area and conduct a professional on-scene assessment. Even if this could be done through official channels, the Russians would simply stage-manage the entire affair and reveal only what they wished. The key to the Maritime Territory, both for logistics and combat operations, were the coastal ports and any bases close to them. If experienced combat-trained pilots could make a survey, then Washington would have more information than it presently did, which meant valuable leverage in dealing with Stalin.

However, until a possibility was suggested by Hap Arnold during that critical and dangerous winter of 1942, no one, not even Arnold's close friend William Donovan, chief of the Office of Strategic Services (OSS), had figured out how to make this happen. This possibility existed only because sixteen American B-25s would be less than seven hundred miles from Vladivostok while they bombed Japan. What, Arnold, mused, if one bomber was to avoid Tokyo, slip across Honshu, and fly to the east coast of the Soviet Union instead of China? It could conduct an aerial survey followed by one on the ground that would include an assessment of Russian air defenses, and one particularly attractive port and airfield on the far eastern coast closest to Japan.

Roosevelt's desire to hit Japan and Arnold's idea about gaining information supporting that desire were precisely how Ed York, Bob Emmens, and the crew of Plane 8 found themselves a few miles south of Sado Island heading for Russia during the early afternoon of April 18, 1942.

# 6

## GARDEN HOSES

"Well . . . another hour ought to do it," said Nolan Herndon. He had crawled up from his compartment in the nose and was crouched behind the two pilots. Instinctively, Bob Emmens's eyes flickered again to the oblong fuel gage on the instrument panel in front of his yoke. After nearly eight hours of checking, rechecking, and trying not to check it, he felt like the gage's image was permanently burned into his brain.

It was now 1600, *Hornet* time, and with the 275 gallons of fuel remaining they would at least make the Russian coast, but Plane 8 would never have made it 1,100 miles across Japan to China. Emmens figured that after reaching the coast in another hour they would fly maybe another hour after that to find the airfield circled on Ed York's map, and by his calculations this would leave them with about one hundred gallons. In the event the fuel tanks were ever inspected, then the remaining fuel level would lend credence to the necessity of diverting to the Soviet Union, which had been the whole point of having the carburetors switched back at McClellan Field.

The dark haze on the horizon had vanished, and except for a

single freighter they had seen nothing for the past 313 miles over the Sea of Japan. Nothing like danger and adrenaline to take the edge off hunger, but now, with nominally allied territory within reach, all three men realized they'd been ignoring their stomachs. For his part, Bob Emmens was tired of open water. True, it had been extremely welcome after crossing Honshu, but he would later recall thinking "how good dry friendly land would look." After splitting a candy bar between the three of them, York spoke after Herndon returned to the nose. "I hope they have 100-octane gas—if we can find an aerodrome."

The type of fuel available was a big question mark. In fact, everything after reaching Russia was a question mark, but that was part of their purpose. Would they find paved runways capable of supporting medium and heavy bombers, or simply a grass airfield. What about lighting, bomb dumps, roads or railroads from the coastal ports to support the logistics required for a bombing operation against Japan? Lots of questions, and not much time to gather answers.

"We could get away early in the morning," Emmens replied thoughtfully, "and probably beat the rest of the guys to Chungking."

Briefed that Stalin would not allow Soviet territory to be used for combat against Japan, York hoped to gather as much on-scene information as possible, then be allowed to fly on to China—but no one knew how the Russians would react. That was the problem. There was also the possibility of Moscow handing over Plane 8's crew to Tokyo to avoid confrontation, and this was definitely a concern. In Japanese hands, the pilots figured they would be as good as dead for attacking the Home Islands. Well, it was much too late to worry about all that, and besides, there was now no other choice.

Forty-five minutes later "land came slowly into view on the horizon—tall mountains looming dark out of the sea," Bob Emmens recalled. "Lord . . . what a welcome sight!" Relief washed over him. The Sea of Japan had been greatly preferable to the islands of Japan and yet, for Army pilots at least, the water was still alien territory and full of unseen menace. At this point, nearly eight hours after leaving the carrier, even Russian land looked good. But both men knew there was no way to fix a landmark, especially on these maps, at fifty feet above the water. York pushed the throttles up a few inches, then eased back on the yoke. As Plane 8 rose higher over the waves, her shadow, their constant companion for the past three hours, slid aft till it vanished behind the wings.

Leveling off at a thousand feet, York walked the throttles back and began comparing the coastline to his map. Emmens did the same, and they both pointed toward a spit of land jutting out from the coast. There was a peninsula pointing off to the south, but which one? It could be Muravyov-Amursky. It could also be Cape Sysoyeva or Cape Povorotnyy; the maps were so bad it could also be the coast of Korea. Holding 160 miles per hour, they flew to three miles off the coast, then York banked up to the right. "I turned and followed the coastline," he reported to the army assistant chief of air staff, intelligence, in 1943. "This was very inaccurate on your [Military Intelligence] maps."

Rolling out heading northeast, Emmens took the controls so York could better compare the map with the coast. The shoreline looked like bites out of a pizza; a sawtooth of inlets and small bays backed by ridgelines stepping up in height away from the coast. After ten minutes, both men were sure it was not Korea, which had to be at least another hour's flying to the southwest. No, this was the Soviet Union: but where in the Soviet Union? York shook the yoke, and Bob released the controls. Banking left, Ed turned toward land and rolled out heading 180 degrees, back the way they'd come. This time, less than a mile offshore, they picked out more details. It "was rugged, with very little beach," Emmens stated. "One little bay cut inland and a small group of houses could be seen."

Both pilots agreed that flying around the peninsula's tip directly into the harbor would likely be a bad idea. The Soviets flew twin-engine bombers, but any air defenses would no doubt be notified of local flights and would therefore know nothing about a strange aircraft suddenly appearing over their port. Of course, the real fighting was some two thousand miles to the west, but the entire Soviet military was no doubt operating on a war footing, so why take extra chances? Especially after already taking so many today. "We cut inland," Emmens recorded. "As we turned, we could see, off to the left, the fingerlike projection of land extending seaward."*

Clearing the ridgeline at one thousand feet, Ski suddenly flinched. "Jesus . . . look!" He pointed over the glare shield and banked up slightly left so his copilot could see a huge aerodrome just off the nose. Built in an inlet on the east shore of the bay, the pilots could see at least "thirty to forty" orange-winged aircraft. Trainers—they had to be.[†]

"Those must be navy," Emmens said, craning his neck to see as York brought the bomber farther left.

"Well, whatever they are, let's get the hell out of here!"

Emmens nodded. The Soviets might decide to shoot the bomber down, then ask questions. Skimming the hills south of the base, they dropped in over the bay and Emmens glanced sideways at the map, then to the right off the nose. The opposite shore was clearly visible, but Emmens quickly saw what he was looking for and pointed north, right of the nose, past a cone-shaped hill.

A river.

Moments later, both pilots clearly saw that the "river flowed seaward through a wide, flat valley bounded by the hills we had just crossed and another, higher ridge ahead of us."[‡]

York nodded. It seemed close enough to the location circled on his map, so he pulled the throttles back a bit and brought the bomber around to the north in a descending turn up the river. Lev-

---

* Cape Povorotnyy.
† Very likely Po-2 trainers. Thousands were built by Polikarpov from 1927 all through the war.
‡ Partizanskaya River.

eling off at eight hundred feet, both pilots leaned forward, staring at the clusters of little houses and dirt roads dotting the valley floor. Three minutes later they saw it: a "large, square field" with dirty white buildings on the northwest side. Men seemed to be scurrying about, and Ski banked a bit to the right so he could see better. They were arranging a T from long white strips of cloth, and he noted the long stem was pointing down the river the way they'd flown in, meaning the wind was from the north.

Throttling back to 150 miles per hour, the Mitchell roared over the field, and both pilots watched the men on the ground but saw no weapons, or any signs of alarm. As the T disappeared under the tail, Ed banked left and brought the bomber around directly at the river. Bob was easing the MIXTURE to full RICH and the PROP controls forward when a sudden movement off the right wing caught his eye and he flinched. Glancing right, he was startled to see a small fighter was hanging there, maybe fifty yards away. It was a biplane, single-seat, and he could see the pilot's helmeted head staring at them from the cockpit.* Without looking away, Emmens reached over and thumped Ski's arm, then pointed.

"For Christ's sake," he shouted, "let's get our wheels down to let him know we're going to land and he won't have to shoot us down!"

York leaned forward and stared past Emmens at the fighter. Nodding, he dropped his right hand to the pedestal between the seats and moved the FLAP lever aft a notch. The bomber immediately slowed as the wing flaps slid out fifteen degrees, and Ski smoothly eased the throttles forward to hold 160 miles per hour. Rolling out perpendicular to the landing strip, he eyeballed the field, then angled gently away to increase their distance. Planning to cross north of the field and then set up on a left downwind, York glanced right

---

* A Polikarpov I-15 "Seagull," widely used by both the Soviet Air Force and Soviet Naval Aviation.

and jerked his chin toward the floor as the fighter pulled away slightly.

"Gear."

Emmens automatically checked the airspeed indicator, leaned left, and wrapped his fingers around the L-shaped handle. Pulling it back and down, as it clicked he flipped up a wire hook that held the handle to the pedestal.

Whirring filled the cockpit as the hydraulically operated gear lowered and thumped into place. From their respective seats, both pilots could check the main gear on their sides, and Bob also tried to check the nose gear by its reflection in the propeller hub. This worked in peacetime with nice, shiny, and clean aircraft, but Plane 8 was streaked with salt spray and he couldn't see anything. Straightening up, Emmens looked past his yoke to the last round gage on the far right and saw three gear lights on the selsyn indicator. Good enough.

"Down and locked."

Passing north of the field, York was already banking the bomber to the left. With the Russian fighter hanging off the right wingtip, he rolled out paralleling the field heading south. The serpentine river twisted under the American bomber as both pilots stared left at the open landing area. There was a spot on the south side of the grassy field where other planes had obviously landed, and York used it as a reference point like he would use numbers painted on an actual runway. As the spot passed under and beneath the left wing, he slowed to 150 miles per hour and dropped the bomber's nose.

Emmens mentally ran through the GUMP check, and verified the gas, undercarriage and pressures, mixture and prop settings while Ski eased the bomber around toward the grass strip. Halfway through the turn the fighter was still off the right wing as Ski went to full flaps. Plane 8 rapidly slowed to 130 miles per hour, and Bob saw the fighter's belly as it peeled away right and up away from the bomber. Hills bordering the valley slowly swung around as Ed rolled out on final. There was almost no wind, and the late afternoon air was perfectly clear. Playing the yoke, rudders, and throttles, Ski lined up on the patch and held a gentle descent as his copilot scanned the field for signs of trouble.

There were no anti-aircraft guns that he could see, and the group of men were simply standing and watching. Ski noticed his legs were stiff, but his hands and eyes worked together almost unconsciously to bring the Mitchell down. Every landing was different, each one unique in small ways, and this one, on a grass strip on the other side of the world, was no exception. The last time he'd landed Plane 8 was three weeks earlier, at the end of March, at Alameda Naval Air Station, but his experience took over and the bomber dropped in beautifully to a point just short of the bare spot. As the pilot smoothly pulled the yoke back and flared, the nose lifted and the airspeed bled off. Tapping the rudders, Ski leveled the wings, and the B-25 sank to the grass. Then the main mounts touched the Russian earth, but earth nonetheless, and for the first time in nearly nine hours they weren't flying, but rolling. "Good old ground," Emmens recalled. "At last dry, good ground. It was a wonderful feeling."

A line of hills rose up on the right, and as the ramshackle white buildings slid past the left wingtip Ski eased the nosewheel down to the grass and gradually let the aircraft slow. A roar filled the cockpit, and a shadow flitted through the clear overhead panel that suddenly became a plane. Both pilots looked up in time to see the Russian fighter flash past rocking its wings. Ski raised the flaps partway and pointed. "I'm going to taxi over here on the right . . . leave fifteen degrees of flaps down and let's take a look at these jokers to see if they've got slant eyes. If they have, we'll take off straight ahead."

Bouncing slightly on the uneven ground, the Mitchell coasted to a stop and both pilots stared from the side windows at the gathered men. They had round eyes. Round eyes, black overcoats with tight black belts, and blue shoulder tabs. Each man had on a "flat black cap with ribbons in the back and blue lettering on the bands." Bob knew sailors usually wore caps like that, but what would sailors be doing at an inland airfield? Shrugging, he exhaled with relief and glanced over at Ski. Nolan Herndon appeared between the seats and leaned toward the side windows. "Those guys look friendly enough, don't they?"

York didn't know about that, but they weren't openly hostile. Both pilots nodded, and began shutting the aircraft down. The bomb bay doors were opened, the parking brake set, and Bob opened the cowl flaps then turned off all the boost pumps. Ski set 1,200 rpm on each engine, then pulled the red MIXTURE knobs back to IDLE CUT-OFF. As the revolutions per minute dropped, he opened both throttles to full, and they watched the propellers change from spinning discs to individual blades, then lurch to a stop. Bob Emmens puffed out his cheeks and exhaled again. Over 1,400 miles, including 150 miles crossing the most hostile country in the world at the moment. Leaving the *Hornet* at 0835, York shut down the engines at 1745; nine hours and ten minutes later.

"The silence was deafening," Bob remembered. For a long moment neither pilot moved, but just savored the quiet as the hot engines ticked. Unstrapping slowly, he dropped the lap belt ends on either side of the seat and arched his back. Sweat had soaked through his shirt, and Bob realized how hungry he was. Pulling off their caps and headphones, both pilots scratched their scalps then fingercombed their damp hair. Wriggling a bit to get some feeling back in his butt, Emmens saw the black-coated men were openly grinning now, and his arms went weak with relief. Whatever else was going to happen, they had survived a carrier takeoff and bombing Japan. For the moment, at least, they were down safely and Plane 8 was in Russia.

The next part of their mission had begun.

In April 1942, as Ski York and his crew crossed Japan, the Axis powers of Nazi Germany, Fascist Italy, and Imperial Japan controlled upward of one-third of the Earth's surface. Japan alone dictated the lives of some 400 million subject peoples spread over 3,300,000

Crew of Plane 8 (*from left*): Lt. Nolan A. Herndon, Capt. Edward J. York,
Sgt. Theodore H. Laban, Lt. Robert G. Emmens, and Cpl. David W. Pohl.
(*Courtesy of Children of the Doolittle Raiders, Inc.*)

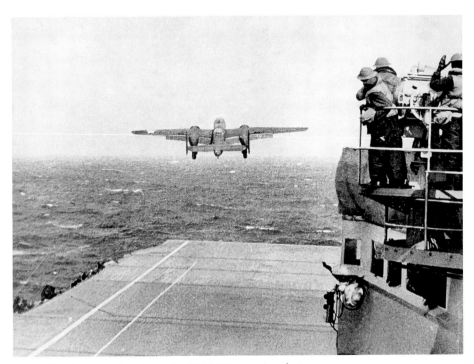

A Raider launches from the USS *Hornet*, April 18, 1942.
(*Courtesy of The United States National Archives and Record Administration*)

Doolittle Raid
duty roster, part I.
*(Courtesy of Children of
the Doolittle Raiders, Inc.)*

Doolittle Raid duty
roster, part II. Note that
Plane 8 was originally in
the seventh position.

*(Courtesy of Children of
the Doolittle Raiders, Inc.)*

Plane 8 stowed aboard the *Hornet*, 1942.
*(Courtesy of Children of the Doolittle Raiders, Inc.)*

Edward J. York. Born Edward
Cichowski in Batavia, New York,
in 1912. *(Public Domain)*

Aviation Cadet Bob Emmens, 1938.
*(Courtesy of Michael Emmens)*

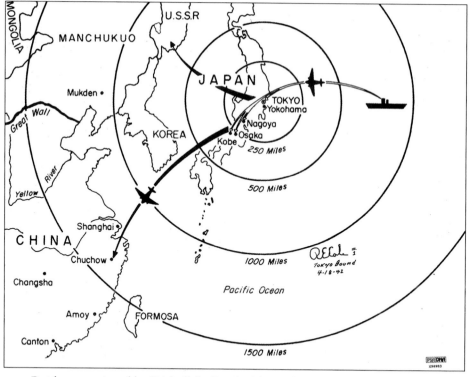

Raider map signed by Dick Cole, Doolittle's copilot.
*(Courtesy of Children of the Doolittle Raiders, Inc.)*

Plane 8 flight path, Japanese sketch.

*(Courtesy of National Institute of Defense Studies, Japan; arranged through Makoto Morimoto)*

Ten-cent bombsight designed by Captain Ross
Greening for the Doolittle mission.
*(Courtesy of Children of the Doolittle Raiders, Inc.)*

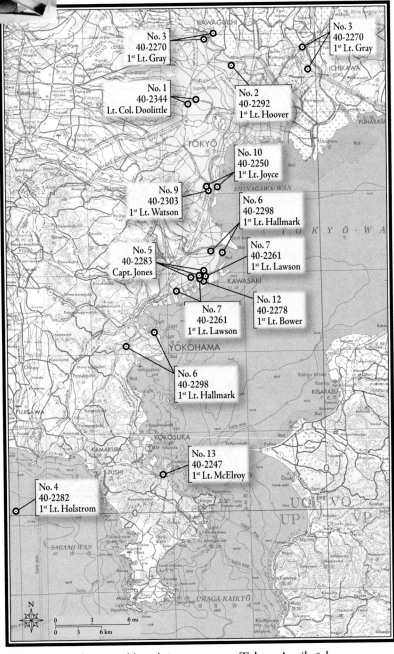

No. 3
40-2270
1st Lt. Gray

No. 3
40-2270
1st Lt. Gray

No. 1
40-2344
Lt. Col. Doolittle

No. 2
40-2292
1st Lt. Hoover

No. 10
40-2250
1st Lt. Joyce

No. 9
40-2303
1st Lt. Watson

No. 6
40-2298
1st Lt. Hallmark

No. 7
40-2261
1st Lt. Lawson

No. 5
40-2283
Capt. Jones

No. 12
40-2278
1st Lt. Bower

No. 7
40-2261
1st Lt. Lawson

No. 6
40-2298
1st Lt. Hallmark

No. 13
40-2247
1st Lt. McElroy

No. 4
40-2282
1st Lt. Holstrom

Doolittle Raider actual bomb impacts near Tokyo, April 18th, 1942.
*(Courtesy of Makoto Morimoto)*

Japanese Army trainers spotted by Bob Emmens from IJAAF Kuoiso, four miles north of Nishi Nasuno.

*(Courtesy of National Institute of Defense Studies, Japan; arranged through Makoto Morimoto)*

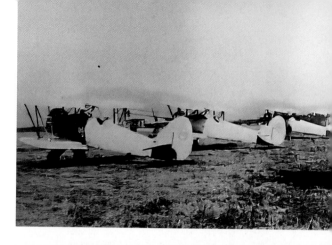

Nishi Nasuno, April 18, 1942. *(Courtesy of Makoto Morimoto)*

Nishi Nasuno, single 500-pound bomb burst filmed from Plane 8.

*(Courtesy of The United States National Archives and Record Administration)*

Imperial Japanese Army retribution against Chinese civilians for
supporting the Doolittle Raiders.
*(Courtesy of The United States National Archives and Record Administration)*

Plane 8 on Unashi Air Field, Soviet Union, April 18, 1942.
*(Courtesy of Ilya Grinberg)*

General of the Army
Iosif Apanasenko, who
arranged the internment
of York's crew.
*(Public Domain)*

Plane 8's crew safe at last in Persia, 1943.
*(Courtesy of Children of the Doolittle Raiders, Inc.)*

square miles. The Rising Sun flew from Manchuria, down the east coast of China, through Burma, French Indochina, Malaysia, and southeast through New Guinea to the Solomons. Germany and Italy controlled continental Europe from the English Channel to the outskirts of Moscow, and Africa from Morocco and French West Africa eastward to within a day's march of Cairo, Egypt. The world was on fire, and metaphoric water was in very short supply.

There were lights of hope, however. The United Kingdom still hung on by a thread following Hitler's failures at Dunkirk and the Battle of Britain. Similarly, though attacked by the Japanese, Australia was another sanctuary and potential staging ground for the Allies if it could also withstand the Empire. Nine thousand miles northwest of Melbourne, Moscow had survived the Nazi onslaught from Operation Barbarossa, and though the Soviet Union's western frontier was occupied by the Germans, to date Hitler's legions had been unable to force a surrender. If Britain and Russia could be supplied with war materiel and, when possible, counteroffensives initiated against the Axis to relieve pressure, then the war was not lost. In early 1942, this hinged on the last hope for continuing the war: North America.

During the 828 days between the invasion of Poland and Pearl Harbor, North America remained more or less untouched and secure behind her oceans. Canada, as a Dominion, had come to Britain's aid during the Great War, and though not obligated it willingly joined the fight in 1939—its Permanent Active Militia had just 4,169 officers and enlisted men. Canada eventually contributed 10 percent of her population to the war, as well as tremendous amounts of agricultural products and fully half of all aluminum used by the Allies, yet Canada's production capacity was dwarfed by her powerful southern neighbor.*

---

* Canada's Eldorado Gold Mines, Ltd., in Port Hope, Ontario, would provide much of the uranium used to construct the Little Boy atomic bomb dropped on Hiroshima in August 1945.

It was the industrial might of the United States that would turn the tide, and American industry was expanding exponentially as the German army stood on the French coast, staring at the faint white Dover cliffs—frustrated by twenty-two miles of water and the Royal Air Force. Still, many American political and military leaders, Chief of Staff General George C. Marshall among them, believed Britain could not survive and would certainly be Hitler's next victim. America would then stand alone against the full weight of the Axis and would desperately need every tank, aircraft, and ship sent abroad. Worse still was the real possibility that captured U.S. equipment would be used against American forces.

Roosevelt was even more committed to aiding Churchill after receiving his eloquent, fifteen-page letter on December 7, 1940, but also painfully aware of London's cash shortage. Britain still possessed some $2 billion in assets, but even if these were liquidated Churchill's existing materiel orders would greatly exceed his available resources. The president also recognized the value of British technology provided by Churchill through the British Technical and Scientific Mission earlier that fall.* The English provided a technological treasure trove, including Frank Whittle's jet engine, self-sealing fuel tanks, gyroscopic gunsights, proximity fuses, and the prize: a technical breakthrough called a cavity magnetron that permitted clear, sharp radar pictures. A key component to winning the Battle of Britain, this development revolutionized radar and even permitted its installation on aircraft.

Recognizing that Britain's survival was crucial to the defense of the United States, Roosevelt stated, "In the present world situation of course there is absolutely no doubt in the mind of a very overwhelming number of Americans that the best immediate defense of the United States is the success of Great Britain in defending itself."

---

* Also commonly referred to as the Tizard Mission, after Sir Henry Thomas Tizard, chairman of the Aeronautical Research Committee that first developed a workable radar system.

Single-minded in his desire to keep Churchill in the war, the president had to conjure a method by which tanks, ships, aircraft, and all the other materiel needed to fight a war could be sent to England without provoking impeachment, or a second American Revolution. The problem was money. Britain still owed over $4 billion to the United States from the Great War, and even American interventionists balked at permitting London to run up its tab.* Sometime during the two weeks before Christmas 1940, Roosevelt arrived at an audacious, yet brilliantly simple political solution, and during a December 17 press conference the money issue vanished like smoke in the wind under the spell of his unique oratory illusion: "Now, what I am trying to do is to eliminate the dollar sign. That is something brand new in the thoughts of practically everybody in this room, I think—get rid of the silly, foolish old dollar sign."

Reporters watched the president raptly, while his aides, somewhat anxiously, eyed the reporters. In their minds the issue was far from settled, and no one knew whether the proposal would be greeted with smiles, derision, disbelief, or angry explosions.

"Orders from Great Britain are therefore a tremendous asset to American national defense; because they automatically create additional facilities. I am talking selfishly, from the American point of view—nothing else. Therefore, from the selfish point of view, that production must be encouraged by us," he said.

Having thoroughly thought the matter through, Roosevelt systematically neutralized all possible objections by agreeing to them—then, in his grandfatherly, patrician tone, he explained that he, like all reasonable Americans, would not support more loans or gifts to foreign governments.

"I am not at all sure," he gravely intoned, "that Great Britain would care to have a gift from the taxpayers of the United States. I doubt it very much."

---

* Approximately $88 billion in 2023.

Leading up to his conclusion, Roosevelt then turned the entire debate into something beneficial to the United States, and to a nation still struggling with the Great Depression this was a point working-class Americans could embrace: "It is possible—I will put it that way—for the United States to take over British orders, and, because they are essentially the same kind of munitions that we use ourselves, turn them into American orders."

Reporters smiled, and his aides breathed easier. Listening to the man, how could one not conclude that such a proposal would boost American industry, strengthen the economy, and provide support against tyranny without risking American lives?

It was genius—and only Franklin Roosevelt could have pulled it off. Yet the dollar sign issue had not yet been explained and financial details were a bit fuzzy to the average citizen, but surely the president had a plan for that.

In fact, he did.

Saving the best, and most risky aspect of his plan, for last, Roosevelt ended his homily with a parable to which everyone could relate: "Well, let me give you an illustration: Suppose my neighbor's home catches fire, and I have a length of garden hose four or five hundred feet away. If he can take my garden hose and connect it up with his hydrant, I may help him to put out his fire."

Smiles widened as the more prescient reporters saw where this was heading.

"Now, what do I do? I don't say to him before that operation, 'Neighbor, my garden hose cost me $15; you have to pay me $15 for it.' What is the transaction that goes on? I don't want $15—I want my garden hose back after the fire is over. All right. If it goes through the fire all right, intact, without any damage to it, he gives it back to me and thanks me very much for the use of it. But suppose it gets smashed up—holes in it—during the fire; we don't have to have too much formality about it, but I say to him, 'I was glad to lend you that hose; I see I can't use it any more, it's all smashed up.' He says, 'How many feet of it were there?' I tell him, 'There were 150 feet of it.' He says, 'All right, I will replace it.' Now, if I get a nice garden hose back, I am in pretty good shape."

However, it wasn't all smooth sailing. The president fielded a few very pointed questions following the press conference.

"Mr. President, before you loan your hose to your neighbor you have to have the hose. I was wondering, have you any plans to build up supplies? There has been a good deal of discussion about lack of authority to tell a manufacturer he should run two or three shifts a day. There is no one now that has that authority."

To which Roosevelt answered dryly, "Isn't there?"

No one doubted that the president's power increased dramatically through initiatives such as this, but his defenders believed it necessary to prepare the nation for what was coming. His detractors, mainly in Congress, saw it as an unnecessary expansion of the federal government and an unwarranted usurpation of their own powers. Not all were swayed by emotion and rhetoric, and several influential Republicans were against the proposal, claiming that it ceded congressional privileges to the president and would lead the United States into war. Among them was Hamilton Stuyvesant Fish (R-NY), who, like Roosevelt, was a scion of a prominent East Coast political family. A product of Swiss and American boarding schools and Harvard, the six-foot-four Fish was no dilettante politician. Serving as an officer with the 369th Infantry Regiment, Fish spent 191 days in combat on the Western Front, ending the war as major with the Silver Star.* Despite this, or very likely because of it, Fish was a hard-liner against interventionism and a formidable opponent of President Roosevelt. Senator Robert Taft (R-OH) bluntly stated, "Lending war equipment is a good deal like lending chewing gum. You don't want it back."

---

* Among other legislation, Fish introduced Resolution 67 to the 66th Congress that established the Tomb of the Unknown Soldier at Arlington Cemetery.

Early in January 1941, Roosevelt addressed Congress: "We cannot, and we will not, tell [Britain] that they must surrender, merely because of present inability to pay for the weapons which we know they must have."

In a determined effort to kill Lend-Lease, Senator Fish called his star witness, a national hero and inspirational icon to the world and most Americans: Colonel Charles Augustus Lindbergh, and asked him testify before Congress. "THIS IS THE MOST IMPORTANT AND FAR-REACHING ADMINISTRATION BILL EVER PRESENTED TO CONGRESS," Fish cabled Lindbergh, pulling out all the stops to get his biggest gun to Capitol Hill. Nearly fourteen years earlier, on May 20, 1927, "Lindy," as he was known, wobbled into the air above Roosevelt Field, Long Island, bound for Paris in a single-seat, single-engine, Ryan monoplane dubbed *The Spirit of St. Louis*. If he made it, Lindbergh would be the first to cross the Atlantic nonstop, from either direction, in a powered, fixed-wing aircraft. Immortality, fame, and wealth were the prizes, just as oblivion and a lonely death in cold, windswept seawater were the consequences if he did not make it.

He did make it.

On May 21, 1927, at 10:22 p.m. Paris time, 33 hours, 30 minutes, and 29.8 seconds after vanishing into the Long Island mist, Lindy rolled to a stop on Le Bourget Field in the middle of one hundred thousand hysterical, screaming Parisians. He, one man, had changed the course of the world by proving the worth of the airplane and its value in bringing the world together. Unquestionably brave and patriotic, Lindy was truly a walking mass of contradictions, not the least of which was his opposition to Lend-Lease in the face of Axis tyranny. He favored America rebuilding its own military, but keeping the equipment that would otherwise be sent overseas for defense of the United States. When asked during his congressional testimony about intervention in the European war, Lindy replied that America's entry "would be the greatest disaster this country has ever passed through." Ten months later, on December 8, 1941, Lindbergh wrote,

"Have we sent so many of our planes and so much of our navy to the Atlantic that Japs feel they are able to get away with an attack on Pearl Harbor?" Yet, like nearly all who opposed the war, once America was attacked, he felt it his duty to enter combat on behalf of his country. "I can see nothing to do under these circumstances except to fight," his diary records. "If I had been in Congress, I certainly would have voted for a declaration of war."

Despite the opposition, House Rule 1776, officially the Act to Promote the Defense of the United States, passed overwhelmingly in the House in February and then, after clearing the Senate, the president signed it into law on March 11, 1941.

"Powerful enemies must be out-fought and out-produced," Roosevelt stated to Congress. "It is not enough to turn out just a few more planes, a few more tanks, a few more guns, a few more ships than can be turned out by our enemies," he said. "We must out-produce them overwhelmingly, so that there can be no question of our ability to provide a crushing superiority of equipment in any theatre of the world war." Brave words, to be sure, but on the same day Roosevelt introduced Lend-Lease to Congress, the Soviet Union signed yet another treaty with Nazi Germany. The Soviet-German Border Agreement of January 1941 settled outstanding territorial issues, mainly Lithuania, which ended up in Russian hands, and this came on the heels of two previous treaties the Soviets signed with Nazi Germany.

Seventeen months earlier, while planning the invasion of Poland, Hitler anticipated a British blockade that would deprive him of war-critical resources like rubber, oil, grain, and industrial metals. The German-Soviet Commercial Agreement, signed in August 1939, gave Stalin ships, machine tools, and factory equipment in return for these resources, and a seven-year, low-interest loan of 200 million reichsmarks. Unsurprisingly, four days later, Moscow approved the Molotov-Ribbentrop Pact, which permitted the Nazi invasion of Poland with no interference from Moscow. The Soviet Union, as always, was prepared to deal with *any* power in the name of its own best interests.

The early months of 1941 also saw Erwin Rommel take command of the Afrika Korps and begin his offensive lunge across North Africa toward Cairo. Bulgaria joined the Axis, and the Germans invaded Yugoslavia and Greece, then took Crete entirely with airborne troops. Faced with these threats and Japanese belligerence in the Far East, opposition to Roosevelt's plans was lessening, with defense spending ballooning to just over $17 billion in late 1940. Plans for a 1.4-million-man army by the end of 1941, plus a two-ocean navy and fifty-four combat air groups were generally a paper tiger until Pearl Harbor. Incentivized by low-cost loans, subsidies, and tax write-offs, companies all over the United States were converting to military manufacturing. Lionel Trains made compasses, Mattatuck Manufacturing switched from upholstery nails to clips for Springfield rifles, Frigidaire and Saginaw Steering Gear made machine guns, Underwood Typewriters manufactured M1 carbines, and many other companies manufactured many more items for war. Nearly eight hundred new factories were being built, and contracts were authorized for 948 naval vessels, including twelve *Essex*-class aircraft carriers. Automobile manufacturers, the largest repository of skilled labor and engineering expertise, switched to tanks and aircraft production.* Now, in the grim aftermath of 1940 and 1941, the American industrial base was flexing new muscles like the awakened giant it was. In 1941, just 3,964 tanks were produced in all combined U.S. factories, but a year later 24,744 rolled off the assembly lines; small-arms production exploded from a prewar high of 617,000 to 2.3 million in 1942, while aircraft production increased eightfold to 47,836.†

---

* With the exception of Ford Motors. Henry Ford, an ardent admirer of Adolf Hitler, refused to fill orders for delivery to Britain until the United States entered the war in December 1941.

† By the end of 1942 alone, American wartime production exceeded the combined efforts of Germany, Japan, and Italy.

Nevertheless, such an effort would only make a difference if the materiel could get to where it was needed, and in 1941 this was still a very real problem. Throughout the Atlantic, the Nazi Kreigsmarine operated twenty-six submarine Wolfpacks, composed of three to twenty-one U-boats each, in an effort to strangle Great Britain. German captains dubbed this *die glückliche Zeit* ("the Happy Time"), as the United States was still officially neutral and the Royal Navy was stretched too thin to protect the growing number of convoys inbound to Britain. Along the western approaches from North America 282 ships totaling 1,489,795 tons of Allied shipping were sunk, and the total climbed to 594 merchantmen destroyed by May 1941. The sinkings were outpacing the combined capacity, for the moment, of British and U.S. shipyards, and if the U-boats weren't stopped, then Lend-Lease was figuratively and literally dead in the water.

Another danger were German raiders. The fast battle cruisers *Scharnhorst* and *Gneisenau* sortied from Kiel on January 22, 1941, broke out into the Atlantic, and in two months sent twenty-two ships totaling 115,000 tons to the bottom. Also departing Kiel, the battleship *Bismarck* passed through the Kattegat and out into the Atlantic in late May to wreak havoc on Allied shipping. Nearly eight hundred feet long with eight fifteen-inch guns, she was more than a match for British surface warships and could annihilate any convoy that happened across her way. Fortunately, *Bismarck*'s career was short-lived. British warships intercepted her and the heavy cruiser *Prinz Eugen* in the Denmark straights, and though she sank HMS *Hood* and killed Vice Admiral Lancelot Holland, *Bismarck*'s fuel tanks were damaged. This forced her to abort the raid and attempt to make the port of Brest in occupied France. Out for blood, the Royal Navy converged forty-two warships on the battleship, including two aircraft carriers. Hit by Fairey Swordfish torpedo bombers from HMS *Victorious* and *Ark Royal*, *Bismarck* herself went to the bottom on May 27, 1941.

Germany's June invasion of the Soviet triggered an immediate response from Churchill, a vehement anticommunist: "No one has been a more consistent opponent of Communism for the last twenty-five years," he said in measured tones. "I will unsay no word I have spoken about it. But all this fades away before the spectacle which is now unfolding."

Roosevelt knew as well that whatever the future ideological risk posed by communism might be, it paled against the very real threat of Hitler and Mussolini. In fairness, both he and Churchill truly believed the larger evil was from the Axis, and both may be forgiven for not viewing the USSR as the long-term, committed danger that it truly was. Two days after the invasion, Roosevelt authorized emergency assistance for the Soviet Union and, with clairvoyance, stated that the German invasion meant the "liberation of Europe from Nazi domination."

Ardently believing the role of a government was to assist its people, Roosevelt was no communist, though his New Deal initiatives and programs like Social Security had been oft labeled "undisguised state socialism." Many people did not, and do not, understand that social-ism permits private property ownership but that the "state" controls industry, which is the true source of national wealth and power. So-cialism, in some forms, also insists on "democratically" elected leader-ship, though the definition of that process varies greatly. Communism is best described as revolutionary socialism, and its basic premise is that violent revolution is inevitable to effect change.

A true communist state is rigidly centralized and controls all property, industry, and resources. A communist society theoreti-cally takes from individuals based on their abilities and allocates resources back to the people based on their needs, while socialism gives back to individuals according to one's contribution. Despite its doctrinal abhorrence of any sort of class system, communism is inherently hypocritical since there always has been, and always will be, a small circle at the top that professes to work for the "state" but exists solely to solidify its own power and influence by controlling the nation in the name of the "state." This reality was personified in the person of Joseph Stalin.

With hindsight, Russia's road to communism seemed unavoidable based on its recent three hundred years of history. By the turn of the twentieth century, it was a vast, underdeveloped, and largely impoverished land. Weakly ruled by Tsar Nicholas II, last of the Romanov dynasty, real power lay in the hands of noble families that controlled the land, the resources, and the peasants. Practicing serfdom, where those born to a piece of land belonged to the landlord, Russian society was still decidedly medieval. Nicholas's father, Alexander, emancipated the serfs yet provided no real opportunities for the massive influx of agrarian peasants now flocking to large cities in search of work. The Industrial Revolution that transformed Europe and the United States had come quite late to Russia and was largely resisted by nobles who would not relinquish control over their agrarian world and by xenophobic peasants whose distrust of foreigners was as ingrained as the dirt beneath their fingernails.

When industrialization did finally creep into Russia, it caused massive overcrowding in major cities and a corresponding shortage of food and jobs. Reforms were desperately needed, but, manipulated by the aristocracy and his own very Russian absolutism, Nicholas resisted changes that might have improved conditions and mollified the masses. He then shocked the world by losing the 1904–05 Russo-Japanese War, marking the first occasion a modern European power was defeated by an Asian nation. Presided over by President Theodore Roosevelt, the Treaty of Portsmouth ceded Russia's Manchurian interests, and Port Arthur, to Imperial Japan. Though victorious, the Japanese people blamed the United States for "cheating" them out of war reparations and control of Sakhalin Island, and anti-American riots erupted in Tokyo. The seeds of Japanese resentment that indirectly led to conflict three decades later were now truly sown.

Russia, always striving mightily to be considered a world power, was embarrassed and humiliated by the loss of its perceived international prestige, and the Russian Revolution of 1905 was sparked largely by disaffected soldiers returning to low-paying jobs and large groups of minorities resentful of national discrimination. Though suppressed, the revolt forced Nicholas to attempt half-hearted reforms that ultimately failed. Russification, which forced a government-imposed cultural standard on the multiethnic, multireligious kaleidoscope that defined Russia, was deeply unpopular. In time-honored Russian fashion, Nicholas sought to focus internal dissent on external threats while regaining some national dignity. Entering the Great War against Germany and Austro-Hungary in August 1914, Russia suffered a string of abysmal military defeats. Fatefully, Nicholas assumed personal control of the Imperial Army a year later and left his German-born empress, Tsarina Alexandra, in power during his absence.

Whatever government competence remained quickly vanished as Alexandra fell under the influence of an uneducated Siberian peasant and self-proclaimed holy man named Grigory Yefimovich Rasputin. Alexandra, though the granddaughter of Britain's Queen Victoria, was distrusted by the Russians because of her German birth and because Kaiser Wilhelm was her first cousin. Her absolute belief in the divine right of monarchs, coupled with Rasputin's meddling, only added fuel to the smoldering fires of rebellion.*

These fires rapidly burst into flame in March 1917, when the Petrograd garrison joined striking workers calling out the tsar's government for corruption and lack of reform.† "Be Peter the Great, or Ivan the Terrible," Alexandra advised her wavering husband, "crush

---

* Convinced Rasputin was a danger to Russia, several nobles murdered him in late December 1916. After poisoned wine and tea cakes had no effect, he was shot three times, including once in the forehead at point-blank range. His body was dumped over Petrograd's (St. Petersburg) Petrovsky Bridge into the Malaya Nevka River.
† Known as the "February Revolution" since Russia used the Julian calendar rather than the more common Gregorian calendar.

them all." In the face of Russia's perennial food shortages, harsh reprisals, and high battlefield casualties, this was the worst advice possible. Nicholas formally abdicated, and the imperial family was eventually sent to the Ipatiev House in Yekaterinburg, where the tsar, his wife, and all the children were later shot and bayonetted at the order of the newly formed Central Executive Committee—and an obscure revolutionary named Vladimir Lenin.

Lenin and his Bolsheviks advocated the Marxist-based violent overthrow of capitalism as the only true method of ridding a society of social classes.* However, like all of his ilk, Lenin then set about creating a new social class structure, with himself at the pinnacle. During the Russian Revolution of 1917, the provisional government was rapidly dissolved and a new government instituted. This was based, theoretically, on the power of councils, or *soviets*, comprised of workers and soldiers. In fact, the true power lay with Lenin, as chairman of the Council of People's Commissars—as much an absolute ruler as any tsar ever was.

Indifferent to the fate of the Allies bleeding in the Great War, Lenin made a separate peace with Germany in March 1918 and pulled his new Russian Soviet Federative Socialist Republic out of the war. This permitted a million German soldiers fighting in the east to be redeployed to the Western Front for an offensive that promised to overwhelm the exhausted British and French and end the war with a victory for the kaiser. Through the Treaty of Brest-Litovsk, Russia agreed to default on all its commitments to the Allies while ceding the Baltic States, Ukraine, and most of Belarus to the Germans. The Russian Caucasian province of Kars went to Germany's Ottoman ally Turkey, and Lenin also agreed to pay six million marks in reparations. The treaty was nullified by the Allied victory in November 1918, but it was a disaster for Lenin and glaringly revealed a fundamental misunderstanding about the West, and this Russian capacity

---

* Bolshevik loosely means "one of the majority."

for duplicity would echo again and again throughout the next century.

From 1919 through 1922, there was a brief hope that widespread resistance to bolshevism would restore normalcy in Russia and provide for a fresh start. Many military officers, if not the rank and file, opposed all for which Lenin stood, as did the bourgeoisie, the remaining nobles, and large property owners. Civil war erupted throughout Russia, as these "White" Russians, backed by western governments betrayed by the Treaty of Brest-Litovsk, fought back against Lenin's "Red" Russians. Troops from the United States, Britain, and Imperial Japan landed in Vladivostok during November 1918 to bolster White Russian forces. Though the western soldiers were soon withdrawn, the Japanese seriously considered adding the entire Russian Maritime Territory to their empire before they, too, eventually pulled out.

Reorganizing what was left of the tsar's Imperial Russian Army, the Bolsheviks utilized the embryonic Red Army to eventually defeat the White Russians. The Red Army also forcibly established soviets in the newly acquired states of Lithuania, Latvia, Estonia, and Ukraine. Drunk with power and consumed with a burning desire to foment a European revolution that would deliver him the continent, Lenin invaded Poland, which had established a parliamentary democracy in the wake of the Great War. Overconfident and dismissive of the Poles, the Red Army came within eight miles of Warsaw but was badly outflanked and lost three field armies in addition to a calvary corps. The Peace of Riga ended the conflict in March 1921 and set the borders that would remain until the Second World War.

Lenin, revolutionary that he was, recognized the threat posed by his fellow revolutionaries and pursued a ruthless campaign of socialist militarism after taking power. Dubbed the "Red Terror," the goal of this democide was the elimination of the entire bourgeois class, as well as counter-revolutionaries, liberals, and organized religion. Marxist-Leninism had no tolerance for competition from the church: the state was God, and Lenin was the state. Violence and bloodshed were to become hallmarks of communist Russia, and it began with the hundred thousand Russians and twenty thousand priests executed during the Terror and culminated in thirteen million killed during the civil war.

Lenin's steadily deteriorating health did not prevent him from binding the soviets of Belarus, Transcaucasia, and Ukraine to a union with Russia through a formal treaty signed on December 30, 1922.* The new entity, a highly centralized, single-party state with Moscow as its capital, was known as the Union of Soviet Socialist Republics: the USSR. This union was, for Lenin, a living Marxist template for the future he, as the man of destiny he believed himself to be, envisioned: a global revolution that would wipe away the past and unify mankind under the banner of Russian communism. A system of control that Lenin maintained was more democratic than the western-style pretensions that were, according to him, "democracies for the rich." However, Lenin's single-minded, revolutionary light burned out on January 21, 1924, following his third stroke. As ideologically deluded and reprehensibly amoral as Lenin was, what came next for Russia and the world was infinitely worse: Joseph Stalin.

Born Ioseb Besarionis dze Jughashvili in eastern Georgia a week before Christmas 1878 and later adopting the name Joseph Stalin, the man who transformed Lenin's ideology into the modern Soviet Union was nothing like his predecessor. Whereas Lenin had been a true revolutionary, motivated and inspired by his perceived ability to change his world, Stalin was an opportunistic thug who utilized communism as a tool to bend millions of human beings to his will. According to his daughter Svetlana, he was "a very simple man. Very rude. Very cruel." Asked later in life if she thought of her father she replied, "He broke my life. I want to explain to you. He broke my

* Transcaucasia consisted of the modern nations of Armenia, Azerbaijan, and Georgia.

life twice." "Wherever I go," Svetlana said, "here, or Switzerland, or India, or wherever. Australia. Some island. I always will be a political prisoner of my father's name." Both Lenin and Stalin were butchers; just as shortsighted, obtuse, and cruel as those controlling the systems they claimed to replace in the name of the common man. Both men displayed the traits of autocrats everywhere—a disdain for the common man they claimed to protect and utter contempt for the lives of their fellow countrymen.

Son of an alcoholic cobbler, young Jughashvili entered a seminary to prepare for the priesthood but soon declared himself an atheist and dropped out. Later, as a meteorologist for the Tbilisi Observatory, he vacillated between revolutionary causes, spending years in various prisons and Siberian exile. Having met Lenin at the 1905 Bolshevik Congress, he attached himself to the man and was elected to the Central Committee in 1912. During this time, he began using Stalin as a surname, seeing himself as a "Man of Steel."* Due to a crippled arm, he was unable to fight in the Great War but was a constant advocate for using terror and violence to achieve political ends while staying safely away from danger himself.

Despite no military experience whatsoever, Stalin tried his hand at field command during the Russian Civil War and failed miserably. Though constantly at Lenin's elbow, the two men had many disagreements, most notable was Stalin's desire to force autonomous soviet republics like Georgia into the Russian Soviet Federation. To Lenin, this was tsarist imperialism, while to Stalin this was a means to broaden his scope of control. Stalin was spared the complications of eliminating his competition when Lenin died in 1924. Nevertheless, the father of Russian communism spoke from the grave and very nearly derailed Stalin permanently.

Lenin wrote in his testament that Stalin, "having become Secretary-General, has unlimited authority concentrated in his

---

* From the Russian *stal'*, meaning steel.

hands, and I am not sure whether he will always be capable of using that authority with sufficient caution."

Recognizing the danger, Lenin believed the man had too much power and would be dangerous, so he recommended Stalin's removal from the position of party general secretary, arguing that "Stalin is too coarse and this defect, although quite tolerable in our midst and in dealing among us Communists, becomes intolerable in a Secretary-General. That is why I suggest that the comrades think about a way of removing Stalin from that post and appointing another man in his stead who in all other respects differs from Comrade Stalin."

Despite his character flaws, Stalin possessed animalistic survival instincts and managed to retain his position as the undisputed General Secretary of the Communist Party by 1928. From then on, there was no stopping him, and Russia would be locked into the stifling oppression of Stalinist communism for nearly seven decades. All land was collectivized and controlled by the state; foreign businesses and property were nationalized, as were all indigenous industrial capabilities. Everything passed to the "state" that now unequivocally meant Stalin and his inner circle, who ruthlessly exploited the populace just as viciously as the tsars. Merciless to opposition, real or perceived, Stalin greatly expanded the existing secret police apparatus and the network of forced-labor camps. Over fourteen million would eventually pass through the gulags and labor colonies, of which nearly two million would perish.

Stalin's first ill-conceived "Five Year Plan" for the forced industrialization of Russia had mixed results. State seizure of all farmlands was intended to make production more efficient, yet it had the opposite effect since the incompetent Soviet bureaucracy was unable to realize its goals, and the resulting famine cost another three to seven million dead by 1933. Industrialization faced similar challenges since limited mechanical and educational expertise remained in the country, so the Soviet Union had to rely on foreign, mainly German, assistance. The Treaty of Rapallo had normalized relations between the two countries, which was reaffirmed by the Treaty of Berlin that stated, in part: "The German Government and the Government of the Union of Socialist Soviet Republics will maintain friendly contact in order to promote an understanding with regard to all political and economic questions jointly affecting their two countries."

Germany was offered bases inside the Soviet Union in order to rebuild and rearm its military, far from the prying eyes of international inspectors. Krupp, the great armaments manufacturer, built a facility near the Black Sea, and a school for fighter pilots was established at Lipetsk. Junkers was building aircraft while passing along techniques and designs to the Soviets. German engineers increased Soviet tank production and constructed a naval base at Polyarny. In return for this, the USSR supplied resource-poor Germany with 1.5 billion reichsmarks' worth of raw materials, used to resurrect Germany's armed forces, while Russian scientists and military officers had full access to everything the Germans built or modernized within the USSR.

After Hitler rose to power in January 1933, relations cooled somewhat, with Germany's new chancellor declaring, "We cannot in any way evade the final battle between German race ideals and pan-Slav mass ideals. Here yawns the eternal abyss which no political interests can bridge." Both supplied opposing sides during the Spanish Civil War, and Japan diplomatically recognized the Soviet Union in 1925. Yet tensions over borders, fishing rights in the Sea of Japan, and Sakhalin Island remained fairly constant, so when the Empire invaded Manchuria and created the puppet state of Manchukuo in 1932, Stalin's greatest external fear became a two-front war, with Russia caught between Germany and Japan. Both nations had signed the Anti-Communist International (Comintern) Pact in 1936, and were very public opponents of all that Stalin and his Soviet Union stood for. Italy joined the pact a year later, declaring that the "Communist

International continues constantly to endanger the civilized world in the West and the East, disturbing and destroying peace and order," and the foundations of the Axis alliance were hardened with anti-communism at its base.

Stalin, therefore, was in a difficult place. He controlled the largest nation on Earth, but it still lagged badly behind the East and West in terms of technology and military capability. True, the Red Army could field three hundred divisions—on paper—but it was largely unmechanized, and twenty-four of its twenty-nine marshals, army commanders, and admirals were victims of the Great Purge. Stalin's vulnerability no doubt factored into his thinking when Hitler proposed the 1939 Molotov-Ribbentrop nonaggression pact so essential for Germany's invasion of Poland. Stalin gained half of Poland without firing a shot and, in his mind, had a peace guarantee for ten years, which would permit him to rebuild his military and concentrate on the Far East.

Tsarist Russia, and later the Soviet Union, had a complex history with Japan. Following Russia's defeat in 1905, Imperial Japan sided with the White Russians against the Bolsheviks, and along with the Americans, Canadians, and British they occupied Vladivostok in 1918. Between 1935 and 1939, 108 combat incidents occurred between the Soviets in Mongolia and the Japanese puppet state of Manchukuo. Following Japan's 1937 invasion of China, Moscow sent artillery, tanks, machine guns, and vast amounts of ammunition to the Chinese, along with the Soviet Volunteer Group. During 1938, Japan invaded Soviet territory on the Korean border near Lake Khasan, but were ultimately forced to withdraw even after inflicting heavy casualties on the Russians.

Of greater significance were the little-known battles around the Nomonhan area in Mongolia from May to September 1939. The Japanese claimed the Khalkha River was the demarcation between both territories, while the Soviets insisted the border lay ten miles east of the river in Mongolia. After skirmishing back and forth, the Kwantung Army attacked in force and managed to cross the Khalkha, but were forced back again by a Soviet counterattack. Aware that Germany was going to attack Poland and knowing Stalin wished to end the fighting in the Far East, General Georgy Zhukov mounted a counterattack in August 1939, which annihilated the Japanese 6th Army the day before Hitler invaded Poland.

Japan, shocked by the defeat at Khalkhin Gol and Lake Khasan, signed the Japanese-Soviet Non-Aggression Pact in April 1941. In fact, Stalin stated that all mutual "problems can be solved in a natural way if the Soviets and the Japanese cooperate." Both sides agreed to respect each other's borders, yet Tokyo and Moscow both knew the treaty merely delayed the final reckoning. Japan, after evaluating its performance against an enemy even more careless with soldiers' lives than itself, decided the northern expansion into Mongolia could wait. After Washington's oil embargo, and with the Soviet Union temporarily mollified, the Japanese could now thrust south toward Indochina and the Pacific—and the American navy.

While Plane 8 crossed Honshu, Singapore had fallen and the Japanese were raiding deep inside the Indian Ocean, sinking HMS *Hermes*, a Royal Navy aircraft carrier. The USS *Langley*, America's first carrier now serving as a seaplane tender, sortied from Fremantle, Australia, on February 22, 1942, with thirty-two P-40 fighters of the 13th Pursuit Squadron. She was bound for India by way of Ceylon when Vice Admiral Helfrich, the Dutch officer commanding Allied naval units in Java, ordered her to Tjilatjap on the Java coast. Desperate for air support against the Japanese, Helfrich wanted *Langley*'s planes and pilots. Unfortunately, a Japanese reconnaissance aircraft spotted her south of Java in the Indian Ocean, and on February 27, thirty-one 11th Air Fleet aircraft flew from Bali's Denpasar Airfield and put five bombs into the old flattop. Dead in the water, *Langley* was abandoned and later scuttled. Java surrendered in March, and the Imperial Army now occupied the Dutch East

Indies, providing Tokyo with all the rubber and oil resources needed to fight the war. Bataan fell on April 9, with the remaining American and Filipino defenders retreating to the island fortress of Corregidor at the mouth of Manila Bay.

As for the Soviet Union, Stalin's towering miscalculation of Hitler's intentions and the success of Germany's invasion forced him to temporarily reevaluate his alliances. With no other choice, Stalin sided with the West to stave off the enemy on his doorstep, but this in no way diminished his ambition to create a communist Europe with himself at the center. In the dark days of 1942, this hinged on throwing endless Russian bodies at the Germans and on Lend-Lease materiel supplied by the United States. Despite having stopped the Wehrmacht short of Moscow, the Red Army's January 1942 counteroffensive was a disaster. In attempting to destroy a salient formed by the German Fourth and Ninth Armies, the Russians lost several million soldiers dead, wounded, and missing. This was roughly four times the casualties incurred by the Germans, who remained in place, and news of this military failure reached Moscow about the same time as Plane 8 touched down in Russia.

Stalin's primary concern, as always, was self-preservation, and in 1942 this meant avoiding a two-front war at *all* costs. The Soviet Union might have withstood the German onslaught unaided given German logistical shortcomings and the sheer size of Russia—it was possible, but at great cost, certainly. However, if the Japanese renewed their cherished territorial ambitions in Mongolia and attacked from the east while their nominal Nazi allies assaulted from the west, then the Soviet Union, and Stalin, would certainly have fallen. As Major General A. K. Kazakovtsev, the Soviet Far Eastern Army's chief of operations, stated bluntly, "If the Japanese enter the war on Hitler's side . . . our cause is hopeless."

So when the Americans, who wanted something in return for their Lend-Lease billions, suggested bases east of Lake Baikal, Red Army authorities were "shocked by the idea and literally turned white." Stalin would now openly accept any aid that assisted him in killing Germans, but would also assiduously avoid *any* action giving the Japanese a pretext to annul the nonaggression pact and again invade in the east. This included a declaration of war against Japan, which Washington and Britain greatly desired, and the basing of Allied troops or aircraft in the Soviet Maritime Territory.

This, then, was the situation within the Soviet Union when Plane 8 landed at Unashi airfield some sixty miles east of Vladivostok on the early evening of April 18, 1942. The consternation caused by a lone American bomber suddenly landing in the Soviet Union *after* attacking mainland Japan was a policy shock that went straight to the Kremlin: it became a tense diplomatic and military juggling act, with a lonely American crew caught squarely in the middle.

# 7

## CONSEQUENCES

"You guys stay in the ship," Ed York unclasped the lap belt and tossed the ends off his seat, "and keep me covered." Leaning forward, he also unhooked the khaki M1936 pistol belt, pulled it off his hips, and handed it to Bob Emmens. The crowd of dark-coated men hadn't moved and were simply standing off the right wing staring up at the cockpit.

Tugging open his side window, Emmens felt a wave of cold, fresh air slide past his cheeks and he breathed in deeply. It smelled wonderful after nine hours in the cockpit. York crouched against the yoke and then carefully put his right leg down between the seats, balancing a moment as the blood flowed into his cramped muscles. Nine hours and ten minutes of sitting hurt, and the pilot winced as he clambered past Nolan Herndon, who had appeared once they shut down the engines.

"By the way," Bob called as York squeezed behind the seats toward the forward hatch. "Do you know any Russian?"

"Hell, no."

Unlocking the hatch, York sat and slowly dropped through it feet-first, holding on to the opening as he did so. It wouldn't do to fall on his face in front of the Russians—if, in fact, that's who they were. Navigation was tough without good maps, but they'd planned to fly over the first bay inland from Cape Povorotnyy, and assuming that finger-like spit of land was the cape, then he had turned in over American Bay.* The airfield they needed to know about was ten miles up a river north of the bay, and this place matched the location. If they'd spotted the correct cape . . . and if that was the right bay and river.

If.

Lots of ifs.

Well, he sighed and slowly straightened. Too late now. Walking slowly and deliberately toward the waiting soldiers, or whatever they were, the pilot was careful to keep his hands in plain sight. They didn't seem to be carrying rifles, but each had a black holster attached to their black belts. No one moved, and as he got closer York saw they were running their eyes over his uniform. They were also smiling, but only with their mouths and not their eyes, like true Slavs. Watching from the cockpit, Emmens gripped his pistol as York stopped and began speaking. His arms were moving, and the men up front smiled broadly. Bob figured the pilot was greeting them in Polish, which he spoke, and maybe it was close enough to be understood.[†]

"Ski turned around and smiled," he recalled, "which we took as the 'all clear' signal." Emmens, Herndon, and Sergeant Laban dropped down from the forward hatch, while Pohl came down from the rear hatch and joined them next to the wing. Waving them forward, Ski continued talking as the men clustered closely around him. For a few minutes they gestured, talked, and pointed.

"*Witam,*" Ski kept repeating. "*Jestem przyjacielem.*" Hello. I am a friend.

---

* Named in 1859 for the Russian corvette Amerika.

† Polish, along with Czech and Bulgarian, is a West Slavonic language. Russian belongs to the East Slavonic family with Ukrainian and Belorussian, so they are not close enough to be mutually understood.

Several nodded and smiled again, understanding the intent if not the meaning.

"*Amerykański*," Ski said and pointed to his chest, then at his crew.

More smiles. One of men up front nodded enthusiastically. "*Da . . . Amerikanskiy.*" He waved at those around him. "*Russkiy. My russkiy!*"

Relief seeped through Bob's muscles at that word. Russian. He hadn't really doubted it after seeing the strange letters on their hatbands, but it was still good to hear. No matter what else, they were in Russia.

Suddenly the gathered men snapped to attention and stood rigidly, their long ribbons waving in the breeze. Three new Russians had appeared, obviously higher ranking. Dressed in similar long black overcoats, these men had peaked caps and wore officers' shoulder boards, though Bob didn't know the insignia. One of them waved his hand, then barked something, and the initial crowd quickly dispersed. Short and stocky, the officers were not unfriendly, but neither were they smiling.

"*Amerykański.*" Ski tried Polish again, then French, and got steady blank looks in return. Emmens tried German, which probably wasn't a good idea, and *that* got a reaction. They looked at each other, then at the bomber and one of them pointed out the American markings. Finally, another nodded slightly and pointed back toward a small building behind the bomber to the left. "*Prikhodit'! . . . poydem s nami.*"*

Bob didn't understand the words, but apparently York did and nodded in return. Anyway, the meaning was clear enough. Though they were stiffly polite, no one drew pistols, so the Russians must have decided their new arrivals were not Germans.

"*Prikhodit' . . . Prikhodit'!*"

The sun was "a ball of red on the horizon now," just above the

---

* "Come. Come with us."

mountains to the west. The wide valley was beginning to darken as the steady northern breeze chilled the air. Short grass crunched beneath their boots as they walked, and it was quiet: very unlike an American base. Crossing the flattened landing strip, they walked up to and entered a dirty, white, run-down building. Motioning for them to follow, the senior Russian officer strode into a small, shabby office and pointed at a few chairs. He removed a telephone from its cradle on a surprisingly ornate and well-made wooden desk, then spat out short, terse sentences in rapid-fire Russian. His call completed, the officer slammed the phone down, lit a cigarette, and looked at each American in turn through puffs of smoke.

It was no use trying to communicate, so the pilots discussed their options in low tones. The first priority was hundred-octane fuel for the bomber. Then, no matter what happened, if they could get to the Mitchell, then they could get away. The fighter's sudden appearance was discussed and, in fact, it answered one of the questions regarding Soviet air defenses. But had they been detected by radar, which was supposedly unknown in Russia, or had the pilot simply seen them visually? In any event, if they could get airborne, York was confident that the B-25 could outrun any fabric-covered biplane, and he hadn't seen any anti-aircraft guns on the way in.

Unashi, or anything else built near here, would be ideal for bombing Japan. With a proper runway, this field could support heavy bombers, and the nearby port on American Bay was big enough for logistics. York had jotted down all the distances, and from this part of the Soviet Union most of Japan would be directly threatened: certainly Tokyo, Yokohama, and the other centers of industry. Plane 8 had flown painfully slow to conserve fuel, but from here a fully fueled and combat-loaded B-25 could make the Honshu coast in less than two hours. Tokyo, Nagoya, Osaka, and Kobe were all around six hundred miles from where he now stood, which was less than two and a half hours at tactical airspeeds.

York intended to report to Hap Arnold that if the Soviets

agreed to basing, a wing of medium bombers—or better yet, heavy bombers—operating from the Maritime Territory would be a tactical and strategic nightmare for the Japanese. Such attacks on the Home Islands would be politically untenable, and militarily utterly unacceptable, so Tokyo would have to alter its balance of power in China or the South Pacific to deal with such a threat. It would also blunt the momentum that had swept imperial forces to victory so far in this war, and that, Ski knew, was crucial. The appearance of enemy combat aircraft at Japan's back door would force Tokyo to react to America's actions rather than driving the fight as they were at the moment. The Japanese liked a plan, their own plan, and nothing he had heard about them indicated much skill at adaptation, at least not without time to fully flesh out details. On the other hand, York knew that Americans operated exceptionally well without much structure. In fact, many, himself included, preferred it that way. But the entire discussion was academic unless the Soviets agreed to a basing proposal, and assessing that possibility was the second objective of this mission.

When the telephone rang, it was harsh and startling. The officer picked it up and once again spoke curtly. As the door opened, he replaced the receiver, stood, and straightened his uniform. Nodding toward the door, he shrugged into his greatcoat and motioned for everyone to follow. A steady cold breeze was now blowing, and the sun was completely down behind the mountains, though the relatively flat north-south ridgeline was starkly visible against the darkening sky. "Flanked and rear guarded," Emmens wrote, "we headed across the field toward a larger building." The Mitchell was exactly where they'd left it, and York saw there was no guard posted.

The half-mile walk took about fifteen minutes, and though much bigger, this structure was similarly run-down, and the concrete corners were crumbling. Four pillars extended across the front, and a "wide, red banner, sagging in the middle" was strung up above them. The writing was Cyrillic and meant nothing to them, but the meaning was clear. This was some sort of headquarters building, likely for the entire air base. Several women, shabbily dressed, hunched over and carrying pails, never looked up, though a few men near the entrance saluted the Russian officers and ran their eyes over the Americans. Passing through a large, barren, and unheated lobby, they were led to an office dominated by another huge desk where several Soviet officers waited. Behind the desk was "an obviously higher-ranking individual," who stood, smiled, and waved a hand toward the chairs.

York tried his greetings, but was again met with blank faces. Giving up, the Russians talked among themselves, and both pilots did the same, quietly agreeing to withhold details of the Tokyo raid. If they were permitted to leave, then it didn't matter; and if they weren't, York decided to speak with the American consul first before disclosing any information. There was supposedly a consul at Vladivostok, so if they had to remain a few days, he would insist upon seeing this individual. It would also be good to have someone beyond this base know that the crew of 42-2242 was in the Soviet Union. A pang of uneasiness shot through his stomach at *that* thought. Hap Arnold and Jimmy Doolittle knew Plane 8's objective, but the bomber's vanishing act over Honshu ensured no one knew for certain they had even made it out of Japan, much less to Russia.

At that moment the door opened, and another officer stepped in carrying a huge map. Spread out on the table it was nearly five feet long and was intended to be a map of the world, but as he leaned over, York stifled a laugh. All the Soviet areas were bright red and extended far into the northern hemisphere, while rest of the earth's surface was colored in drab pastels. Not only that, the "red area [was] completely out of proportion to the rest of the world." The senior officer pointed at the map, and began talking very excitedly. He plainly wanted to know from where they had come.

"Well, here goes," Ski muttered, and got up. "Either we make asses of ourselves, in which case they won't believe anything we say from now on, or we make an ass of this guy, who apparently isn't a pilot."

The Russian clapped and smiled. York leaned over the map, took a breath, and "pointed generally in the direction of Alaska." The Russians clustered around, intensely interested, and several nodded as if this made perfect sense. Ski smiled broadly at the ranking officer, who seemed to be buying the explanation, and ran his finger across the Aleutians then down the Kamchatka Peninsula to Petropavlovsk. Still smiling, York met Emmens's eyes.

"If they believe this, they'll believe anything," he said cheerfully, knowing the Russians did not understand English. His finger traced a route across the Sea of Okhotsk past Sakhalin Island to the Maritime Territory and tapped the area around Cape Povorotnyy. Straightening up, he looked at the officer with an expectant "take that" expression, which no one saw but Emmens. The Soviets were nodding, pointing, and jabbering amongst themselves. "I think they believed it all," Bob recorded.

It was patently absurd. The distance York indicated was over three thousand miles, and quite beyond the range of a medium bomber, but only another pilot would know that. A portable gramophone was brought in, and Russian records were loudly played at too high of a RPM setting. Nevertheless, York nodded and smiled after each song. A chess set appeared, and while the Soviets played the three American officers went over their story, which had morphed into a goodwill tour from Alaska, to be followed by a rendezvous with other Army bombers in China. Ski was thinking they might just get away with this when the door suddenly swung open and "in stalked a young, healthy-looking Russian officer." His athleticism, fur cap, and fur-lined jacket marked him as a pilot. In fact, he was quite likely the fighter pilot who had followed them in.

This was trouble.

Smiling and nodding politely to the Americans, he spoke rather brusquely to the other officers, then waved a hand toward Ski and map. Muttering "this guy's no dummy," York bent over the map again, and reenacted the imaginary route from Alaska to Russia. Still smiling slightly, the Soviet officer waited until Ski was finished and, eyes twinkling, he shook his head slowly. Then, very deliberately, put his finger on Tokyo. Trying to keep a straight face, York again traced the preposterous goodwill-tour route, but this time the other pilot laughed out loud "as if he were enjoying a good joke," and tapped Tokyo. Nodding politely to Ski, he said a few things to the other officers, then turned and left.

Sighing, Ski sat down. "I guess that guy wasn't fooled any."

The Russians didn't seem to mind, however, and continued to smile as if they, too, appreciated the attempt. Obviously, the Russians, at least the air force, had heard about the Tokyo raid and knew exactly where Plane 8 had been earlier in the day. The waiting went on until 2100, when a "rather short and stocky officer in a dark blue uniform" entered with a man dressed in a civilian suit. Everyone appeared friendly enough, and to York's surprise the civilian said in slow, precise English, "May I present Colonel Gubanov, commanding officer of the Vladivostok garrison."

The colonel shook hands with each man, then through the interpreter welcomed them to the Soviet Union and asked if they were tired from the long flight. Passing around American cigarettes, Ski took the opportunity to explain that he and his crew were expected in Chungking, and asked whether 100-octane fuel could be obtained so they could be on their way. The colonel's answer was that "such a question will be decided soon." Then he asked how long it had been since the crew had eaten, and all the Americans enthusiastically accepted that invitation. The Russians liked the cigarettes very much, and the colonel began barking orders, which made everyone else scurry from the office.

"A room has been prepared in this building where you will sleep tonight," the interpreter said. "It will take a little time to prepare a meal, but first you must write your full name and rank on a piece of paper."

The room to which they were shown was large enough, with three beds against one wall and two on the other. A bust of Stalin rested on a shelf, and there was a bathroom down the hall, where York and his crew washed up. It was nearly 2200 before the dinner was ready, and now that the adrenaline had worn off, both pilots were at that limp, drained phase after a physically and emotionally exhausting day. Beyond tired, and York's stomach felt like an empty balloon that had shrunk into a tight little ball deep in his gut. They were guided to a central hall downstairs, with two long tables and five waiting Russian officers, including the colonel.

Sitting squarely in the center of the tables were platters of fish, mostly pickled, surrounded by plates covered with heavy black bread, lumps of butter, and red caviar. At each place was a plate of meat, roasted potatoes, and some sort of sliced sausage or bologna. Smaller platters of sardines and cheese were scattered about, and there was lots of alcohol. Wine glasses and decanters, colored liquor bottles, and vodka. Vodka everywhere. Several homely Russian girls poured a half glass of vodka for each man, then moved off to bring more food. At the head of the table, the colonel spoke and the interpreter translated: "A Russian always begins and ends his meal with vodka!" York looked dubiously at the glass. Clear liquor, in his experience, was always the strongest. "Each drink is always to the bottom." The interpreter continued for the colonel. "I toast two great countries, the United States, and the USSR . . . fighting side by side for a great common goal!"

They all raised their glasses to each other, and drank. York, no stranger to strong Polish vodka, was fine for the first two swallows, but the third made his eyes water. "I could have sworn someone had drawn a hot barbed wire across my tonsils," Emmens remembered. The secret seemed to be having a thick piece of black bread ready, and to take a big bite of it before exhaling. Having not eaten all day, the vodka went straight to their heads, but the food helped, and there was lots of it. The wine tasted like kerosene, so Bob stuck to the vodka. Toast after toast rang out: to America and Russia, Stalin and Roosevelt, and death to Germany and Italy.

No one mentioned Japan.

York finally leaned over and whispered to Emmens, "I think we should tell this guy the true story. I'll get him and the interpreter and we'll go upstairs, so don't wonder what's going on if we leave after dinner." Minutes later the three of them quietly left, and Bob was concerned about the Russian's reaction. After drinking and speaking with the colonel, Ski obviously believed if he knew the truth about the raid, he might be more helpful about refueling the bomber and letting them go. Fifteen minutes later, the three men returned and they were all smiling. Calling for more vodka, the colonel was beaming. "On behalf of my government, I congratulate you for the great service you have rendered your country. You are heroes in the eyes of your people." Everyone drank and refilled. Through the interpreter, the colonel continued, "To your magnificent flight today and to the victorious ending of the war for both our great nations!"

As the party broke up, the Americans staggered back to their room. It was cold, but there was a heavy wool blanket on each little bed, and to stretch out, relatively safe and relatively warm, was paradise. What a day. To begin far out to sea on the *Hornet*, bomb Japan, then end it here in a Russian field headquarters full of vodka and caviar was a bit surreal. They still had no answer about the American consul or getting gas, but Bob was literally limp with fatigue and couldn't worry about it now. York was similarly drained, as only responsibility for other lives and combat can do. He'd gotten his bomber and his crew 700 miles over the North Pacific to the Japanese coast, another 170 miles over enemy territory, and the final 530 miles here to Russia. Whatever he could not do now he would take care of in the morning. Falling asleep thinking of his wife, Justine, and his upcoming baby, York's last conscious thought before sleep overwhelmed him was of the other fifteen bombers.

Had they survived Japan and landed safely in China?

In fact, they had not.

Egressing from Japan began well enough. No one was shot down, and with the exception of Brick Holstrom's in the fourth Mitchell, all the bombloads were dropped on mainland targets. The headwind they'd been fighting all the way down Japan turned into a thirty-mile-per-hour tailwind once the bombers cleared Kyushu and turned west for China. This was unexpected and very, very welcome as it extended their range by at least one hundred miles. "We picked up this tailwind for a good five, six hours," Davey Jones recalled, "and that's the only reason we all made it to the Chinese mainland.

China was a problem.

From Manchuria, past the Korean peninsula, and south beyond Shanghai was territory occupied by a million Japanese soldiers, and this included the major cities, railroads, and seaports. Along the most direct route the raiders had to fly to reach Nationalist Chinese, or Kuomintang, airfields, the Japanese held the Yangtze westward to Lake Poyang, some three hundred fifty miles inland from the coast. Additionally, the tenuous alliance formed between Mao Tse-tung's communists and Chiang Kai-shek's Nationalists to fight the Japanese had fallen apart, and both sides were again fighting each other. Then there were innumerable local warlords and bandits scattered throughout the interior who would likely kill anyone not connected with their bands, even more so white-skinned foreigners. However, there was no other alternative. The bombers could not land on an aircraft carrier, and with Stalin's official refusal to use the Soviet Union, that left China.

Several Kuomintang airfields were supposedly supplied with thousands of gallons of high-octane fuel, oil, and ammunition flown in from American bases in India. Doolittle had been told that if they could make it west of the Yangtze into the Anhui or Hubei Provinces, then all would be well. The bombers could either be flown on to India or remain in China as part of a new American bomber wing. Radio homing equipment was to be installed at these airfields, and using the code 57, Doolittle and his raiders would be able to find a place to land.

None of this was true.

Several of the airfields had been bombed by the Japanese, and the supplies brought in from India vanished into Nationalist hands for use after the war. Bad weather prevented the aircraft carrying the radio frequency homing equipment to land, so this was never put in place. Even if the B-25s had landed, those arranging the post-mission logistics were planning from the wrong date. Everything on their end in China was calculated based on an April 19 raid followed by a landing, and a continuation to Chungking the following day. They either didn't realize the launch would occur on the western side of the International Date Line, or they assumed those planning the mission in America did not know a day would be lost in transit. In fact, Davey Jones and his team did know that, and April 18 meant April 18 on the west side of the line. In any event, the supplies that did arrive had already been stolen as corruption and thievery were rampant in China. One estimate stated that for every fourteen thousand tons of Lend-Lease aid sent along the Burma Road into China, only a third of it actually arrived intact.

Approaching the Chinese coast, the American pilots' luck began running out. The weather, so helpful earlier, turned on them, and Doolittle hit a wall of clouds and rain that totally obscured the ground. As darkness fell, he climbed up to eight thousand feet to avoid mountains he could not see and continued west toward the Nationalist airfield at Chuchow. Running out of fuel and now blind except for his instruments, the colonel repeatedly tried to raise the tower but never did. "No answer," he wrote. "This meant that the chance of any of our crews getting to the destination safely was just about nil." Without a homing beacon, he wasn't about to descend on instruments through the mountains, and as his fuel needles sagged toward zero, he decided that bailing out was the only hope for his crew.

Telling the gunner, Sergeant Paul Leonard, to remove the camera film and hold on to it, Doolittle ordered the jump; Sergeant Fred Braemer, the bombardier, would lead off, followed by Lieutenant Hank Potter, Leonard, and Lieutenant Dick Cole, the copilot. Switching on the autopilot, Jimmy then shut off the main fuel valves and, legs aching from sitting for thirteen hours and 2,250 miles, pulled himself to the open hatch and dropped into the wet darkness over China. Lucky to come down in a rice paddy, Doolittle's relief quickly turned to revulsion when he realized he was sitting in human excrement used to fertilize the soil. "I stood up, unhurt and thoroughly disgusted with my situation," he recounted. The next morning, a peasant took him to a Chinese Army outpost, and after a few misunderstandings, the major in charge gave him a warm meal and a bath. Doolittle's crew was rounded up unharmed, and the soldiers helped find what remained of B-25 #40-2344 scattered about on a mountaintop.

"I sat down beside a wing and looked around at the thousands of pieces of shattered metal that had once been a beautiful airplane," Doolittle recalled, describing his utter despondency. "This was my first combat mission. . . . I was sure it was my last. As far as I was concerned, it was a failure, and I felt there could be no future for me in uniform now."

The other fourteen crews that hit Tokyo, Nagoya, and Kobe made similar individual decisions. Bailing out over China hadn't been discussed since the original plan was to arrive over friendly territory during the day, then land at Kuomintang airfields, preferably Chuchow. Trav Hoover, who had followed Doolittle out of Japan and across to China, lost the colonel in the clouds over the coast below Ningbo. Well aware they were over Japanese terrain, Hoover angled off to the southwest toward a line of low mountains to avoid the populated areas, then as he added power and climbed, the left-hand engine coughed.* Almost nothing gets a pilot's attention quicker than an engine sputtering—especially at night, in bad weather, and over enemy territory.

Turning back toward the coast, Hoover ran through his checklist and figured the boost pump had failed. Trying three times to clear the hills, with sixty gallons remaining, he "started to look for a place to land along the coast," Hoover remembered. Circling over a wide, flat rice paddy, he brought the bomber in on a shallow final, left the gear up, and switched off the engines. Splashing down perfectly on the paddy, no one was hurt, and they managed to finally start a fire that ignited the fuel tanks and destroyed the Mitchell. After evading the Japanese, Hoover and his crew were fortunate enough to run across Chinese guerrillas, who had an English-speaking former aeronautical engineering student named Tung Sheng Liu with them who guided the Americans to Chuhsien. After that, they made it to Hengyang, where an American C-47 transport ferried them to Chungking. Lieutenant Bob Gray's crew bailed out successfully but came down in the mountains, and Corporal Leland Faktor was found dead, probably from a secondary fall in the rough terrain. Similarly, Brick Holstrom's crew all made it out and to safety, as did Davey Jones and the crew of the fifth bomber, who were actually the first to arrive at Chuchow.

Dean Hallmark and the *Green Hornet* were not so fortunate.

Out of fuel, both engines quit four miles off the coast south of Ningbo, yet Hallmark managed to ditch, at night, in heavy seas. His seat broke loose on impact, and the pilot was catapulted through the windscreen. Swimming ashore, at dawn on the beach he rejoined his copilot, Lieutenant Bob Meder, and navigator Lieutenant Chase

---

* Siming Mountain range southwest of Ningbo.

Nielson. They discovered the bodies of Sergeant William Dieter and Corporal Donald Fitzmaurice washed up on the sand and buried them above the waterline. Local Chinese aided them, and the three officers attempted to move inland out of the occupied zone but were captured several days later near the village of Shiputzen, fifty miles south of Ningbo. Taken to the infamous Bridge House in Shanghai, the three officers would spend the next six months in the hands of the Kempeitai, the Imperial Army's brutal secret police.

Also out of fuel at the coast, Ted Lawson attempted a tricky nighttime beach landing between Taizhou and Ningbo. The four officers were badly injured, and only the gunner, Sergeant David Thatcher, was unharmed. Local villagers from Haiyou hid them from the Japanese, but their injuries were so severe they were moved forty miles inland to the Linhai Enze Medical Bureau, where the battered fliers were attended to by Doctor Chen Shenyan. Eventually, Lieutenant Thomas White, a Harvard-educated flight surgeon serving as a gunner on the fifteenth bomber, was brought to Linhai, where he had to amputate Lawson's mangled and badly infected left leg.

Lieutenants Harold Watson and Richard Joyce, flying Mitchells 9 and 10 respectively, made it off the *Hornet* and into Tokyo Bay. Watson was to bomb the Tokyo Gas and Electric Company, but instead dropped on the Mazda Electrical Bulb Plant located between the Takioji and Yamanaka residential areas in Shinagawa, just south of downtown Tokyo. Joyce intended to bomb the Japan Special Steel Factory but hit the nearby Toa Seisakusyo factory. His last bomb and the incendiary struck the Japanese Government Railroad Clothing Factory in the center of an immense rail yard and industrial complex.

The eleventh bomber off the carrier was Captain Ross Greening's *Hari Kari-er*, which was headed for Yokohama. Making landfall north of Cape Inubo, Greening recognized this and flew southwest toward Tokyo. "We approached an airfield full of training planes," Greening later wrote. "We looked down and saw the Japanese students and instructors going to their aircraft. Some of them waved to us, completely unaware that we were the enemy."

It was, in fact, the Imperial Japanese Army flying academy, and *Hari Kari-er* flew right over the top of it. Greening wrote of "four Japanese fighters" intercepting them, and that Sergeant Melvin Gardner shot two down and damaged another while the bomber roared south toward Chiba, east of Tokyo Bay. Japanese records do not verify this, and many aircraft have been badly damaged and on fire yet still able to land. Combat is confusing, and if Gardner shot the fighters down, this would not likely be acknowledged by the Japanese in the wake of the embarrassing attack. What is known for certain was that a prototype Ki-61 "Hien" taking off on a test flight from the academy field did intercept the Mitchell and put "a line of ten or fifteen hits on our plane, from the trailing edge of our fight wing up to the prop," according to Greening. The Hein, called a Tony by the Allies, caused a great deal of confusion since it greatly resembled the German Me 109 fighter, and Greening, along with others, believed Nazi pilots were fighting with the Japanese.[*]

Not yet over Tokyo Bay yet but seeing a "concentration of buildings ahead," Ross decided to drop on what he believed to be a refinery, pipelines, and storage tanks. Pulling up to seven hundred feet, he released all three bombs and the incendiary, which resulted in a huge explosion followed by a concussion so bad that he and copilot Kenneth Reddy hit the cockpit ceiling. Dumping the nose, Greening accelerated to three hundred miles per hour and left most of the fighters behind. What he actually hit was a fuel dump on Katori Airfield, under construction for the Imperial Navy, and the damage delayed its completion until 1943.[†] Zipping

---

[*] Originally the Bf 109, the designation was officially changed to Me 109 after Willy Messerschmidt gained a controlling interest in the Bayerische Flugzeugwerke (Bf) in 1938. However, both prefixes continued to be used interchangeably throughout the war.

[†] The main runway is now used by the Nisshinbo Brake Company as a testing facility.

over the mouth of Tokyo Bay, *Hari-Kari-er* strafed three patrol boats, then headed down the east coast of Japan. Encountering the same bad weather over the Chinese coast, Greening tried to climb up through the clouds to get a celestial fix but ran into ice. With the fuel gages reading zero, he ordered a bailout and, like all the others, found himself drifting down through the rainy blackness onto China.

After a cold, wet, miserable night on the hillside, Greening followed a stream downhill through a canyon and, to his delight, found Lieutenant Ken Reddy. They made their way farther down to a small village, and the postmaster agreed to guide them deeper into the interior. By nightfall, they reached a small town called Wei Chou Fu and were put up in a hotel. Passing out from exhaustion, the two pilots were greeted the next morning by the other three members of *Hari-Kari-er*'s crew. Given a Chinese version of an "American" breakfast consisting of fried snake, eggs, and beer, they were loaded into a twenty-year-old Dodge truck and taken on to Chuchow. There they were greeted by Davey Jones, who was wearing Chinese clothing and sporting a Fu Manchu mustache.

Lieutenant William Bower, pilot of the twelfth bomber, *Fickle Finger of Fate*, was there with his crew. Targeted against the Ogura Refinery at Yokohama targets, Bower actually dropped on the Nippon Pipe Factory and Showa Fertilizer Company in the Kawasaki Industrial Area, very close to Dean Hallmark's targets. Bower's bombardier, Sergeant Waldo Bither, amused them with his story of opening his parachute while still inside the *Fickle Finger* and repacking it while the bomber was going down so he could bail out. Later that evening Major Jack Hilger and his crew of the fourteenth Mitchell were safely brought in. Hilger's targets were in Nagoya, some one hundred seventy miles southwest of Tokyo on Ise Bay, and he hit them all. With Nagoya Castle as an unmistakable landmark, Hilger dropped on the Imperial Army 3rd Division barracks and the nearby garrison hospital. He also hit the

Sasashima Freight Yard, followed by the Mitsubishi aircraft plant in the downtown port area.

Lieutenant Don Smith in *TNT* was fifteenth off the *Hornet* and flew in formation with Jack Hilger until the latter peeled away for the castle. Smith's targets were in Kobe, one hundred miles farther southwest past Nagoya, and he dropped all four incendiaries on what he believed to be an aircraft factory, though *TNT* actually hit the Mitsubishi Dockyards and the Central Food Market before scooting southwest for China. Making it to the coast and out of fuel, Smith ditched the bomber offshore south of Ningbo, and his crew made it out safely before *TNT* sank beneath the waves. Sheltered and aided by the Chinese, Smith heard about Ted Lawson's injuries and met up with *Ruptured Duck*'s crew so Lieutenant Thomas White could treat him.

By April 25, seven days after the raid, Lieutenant Bob Gray's *Whiskey Pete* survivors showed up at Chuchow, along with Brick Holstrom's bunch and the crew of Lieutenant Edgar McElroy's *The Avenger*. McElroy, like Hilger and Smith, was able to find his primary target in the Yokosuka Naval Base at the mouth of Tokyo Bay. Crossing Chiba at treetop level, McElroy dashed across the water to drop his payload on the drydock along Yokosuka's western edge. One five-hundred-pounder struck the forward area of the light aircraft carrier *Ryūhō* in Drydock Number 4, killing seven of her crew and delaying her commissioning until November 1942.

On a rainy Sunday, April 26, twenty of the surviving raiders left by train from Chuchow to Kweilin, then the following day by bus to Kiang. From there to Hengyang, where an American C-47 landed. Without the aircraft even shutting down, the ragged, dirty fliers piled aboard and were flown on to Chungking. "When it flew over with our insignia on the side, we all shouted with joy," Lieutenant Ken Reddy recalled. "It was the most beautiful sight we had witnessed in China."

Courtesy of helpful Chinese guerrillas, Doolittle and his crew finally made it into Chuchow shortly after the first group of twenty departed. They had come down farther north than the others, due west of Shanghai along the Zhejiang and Anhui provincial border near Haotianguan. Eventually reunited, the Americans were taken to the provincial governor's house, where Doolittle learned four other crews had been located and escorted to Chuchow. The colonel then sent a telegram to the U.S. embassy in Chungking, which was to be forwarded to Hap Arnold in Washington:

TOKYO SUCCESSFULLY BOMBED. DUE BAD WEATHER ON CHINA COAST BELIEVE ALL AIRPLANES WRECKED. FIVE CREWS FOUND SAFE IN CHINA SO FAR.

By riverboat out of Japanese occupied territory, then by rail, bus, and rickshaw, Doolittle's crew made their way west to Chuchow. It was here, on April 28, that Doolittle was informed that Arnold had promoted him directly to brigadier general, skipping the rank of full colonel entirely. "Since I had been promoted," he wrote, "I tried to see to it that every man on the raid was also promoted." It was here that Doolittle also learned of the beginning of savage Japanese reprisals against the Chinese for aiding the Americans. Tokyo, embarrassed and enraged, commenced Operation Sei-go, eventually a three-month campaign penetrating some two hundred miles inland from the coast. Fifty-three infantry battalions of the Thirteenth Army, elements of the Eleventh Army, and the North China Area Army were to destroy the airfields in the Chekiang and Kiangsi Provinces the Americans planned to use. A carte blanche order was given to ravage the countryside: "Airfields, military installations, and important lines of communication will be totally destroyed."

Lieutenant Harold Watson of the *Whirling Dervish* had been cared for by a man named Ma Eng-lin in the village of Ihwang. Upon hearing of this, Japanese soldiers tied Ma Eng-lin to a chair, soaked the terrified man in kerosene, and forced his wife to set him afire.

Father Wendelin Dunker, a Catholic priest in the village of Ihwang, witnessed the unrestrained brutality firsthand. "They shot any man, woman, child, cow, hog, or just about anything that moved," Dunker recorded. "The big maggot-producing flies were almost as thick as snowflakes in a snow storm. They raped any woman from the ages of 10–65."

Chuchow was especially hard hit. Over a thousand sorties were flown against the town, which killed 10,246 people, and Japanese soldiers burned 62,146 homes, leaving 27,456 Chinese civilians homeless and destitute. Worse still, the Manshu Detachment, also known as Unit 731, was given a free hand to use the current area of operations as a field laboratory for its bacteriological and biological warfare experiments. Headed by Lieutenant General (Doctor) Shiro Ishii, a vehement nationalist, Unit 731 had operated in Manchukuo since the mid-1930s with the full approval of the Imperial General Staff and the cooperation of the Kwantung Army.

Aside from vivisections performed on pregnant women and pressure experiments on living humans, Unit 731 was particularly focused on bacteriological warfare. Rolls and bread were impregnated with typhoid, then distributed to starving Chinese prisoners who were released to inadvertently spread the disease. Wells and other water sources were contaminated with plague, cholera, and anthrax. Typhoid-infected cookies were left by withdrawing Japanese troops, knowing the hungry Chinese would eat anything they found. In total, some 225,000 to 250,000 Chinese were killed or perished from starvation and sickness in retribution for their resistance to Japanese occupation and for the aid provided to the raiders. Doolittle was appalled, and Chiang Kai-shek cabled Franklin Roosevelt directly: "These Japanese troops slaughtered every man, woman and child in those areas."

Arriving in Chungking on May 3, 1942, Doolittle was summoned to Washington immediately and departed China two days later on a DC-3 flown by Captain Moon Chin—a Chinese American born in

Baltimore. From Myitkyina, in the country then called Burma, Doolittle landed in Calcutta, India, where he replaced his ragged uniform with the only outfit he could acquire: an English bush jacket, shorts with silly knee-length socks, and a pith helmet. He "looked ridiculous" but did not want to arrive in torn, oil-stained khakis. Now on a BOAC (British Overseas Airways Company) transport with stops in Persia, Egypt, and Senegal, Doolittle steadily headed west to Brazil, then north to Puerto Rico, and finally, on May 18, 1942, one month after flying off the carrier and bombing Tokyo, he landed in Washington.

Meeting Hap Arnold in his office, they chatted, then met with Army Chief of Staff George C. Marshall. Afterward Arnold, with his customary grin, suggested the pilot visit the officers' uniform clothing store so he'd look more like a general, then go home to his apartment off Rock Creek and wait. Hap called later, then showed up in a staff car with Marshall in the back and, with a twinkle in his eye, told Doolittle, "Jim, we're going to the White House." Surprised and a bit confused, Jimmy thought about that moment and asked, "I'm not a very smart fellow and I don't want to embarrass anyone ... what are we going to do there?"

"The President is going to give you the Medal of Honor," Marshall replied.

Doolittle blinked, shocked. Without thinking, he blurted out, "General, that award should be reserved for those who risk their lives trying to save someone else. Every man on our mission took the same risk I did. I don't think I'm entitled to the Medal of Honor."

Jimmy knew immediately he had said the wrong thing, because both generals flushed, then Marshall growled, "I happen to think you do."

Still desperate to locate his missing crews, Doolittle knew that without Chinese assistance finding them would be next to impossible. Of his seventy-nine fellow raiders, he was aware Ted Lawson had survived but without his left leg, and from Lieutenant Bob

Gray he learned that Leland Faktor died while bailing out. Doolittle was aware of York's mission to the Soviet Union, but nothing had been seen or heard from the bomber since the carrier launch. They were to have refueled in Russia, then come on to Chungking, or at least Chuchow. That should have happened within days of the raid, and the fact that Plane 8 never arrived in China did not bode well.

Also completely unknown at this point were the fates of Lieutenant Dean Hallmark's *Green Hornet* and Lieutenant Bill Farrow's crew of *Bat out of Hell*. Combat pilots are notoriously superstitious, and beginning with the *Hornet's* flight deck, Farrow's mission was under an ominous cloud. Sixteenth and last in line, *Bat out of Hell* was so far aft that her fuselage largely hung over the carrier's stern and the gunner, Sergeant Harold Spatz, had to wait for Farrow to taxi forward in order to access the rear hatch. *Bat* was unchocked and ready to move when *TNT*, the fifteenth bomber, ran up her engines for takeoff, and the prop wash sent Farrow's Mitchell tilting backward, twin tails pointing at the churning sea below. As the nearby sailors scrambled to save the plane, Machinist Mate Bob Wall slipped and tumbled into *Bat's* left propeller.*

Bombardier Jake DeShazer recalled, "I turned around, and here that sailor was, laying right under where the propeller turned. His arm was laying out separate from the rest. . . . [It] had been cut off." When he did finally crawl into the nose compartment, he discovered there was a twelve-inch-wide hole in the glass that meant he'd have to deal with a 160 mile-per-hour draft all the way to Japan and then to China. Farrow launched, and like all the others got his heading from the carrier, then turned west for Japan.

---

* According to the Navy, Wall's arm was still intact but was later amputated. Regardless, he survived and received a medical discharge. The Doolittle raiders later donated $2,700 dollars (about $50,000 in 2023) directly to Wall. Upon receiving the gift, he "broke down in tears."

Following Hilger south of Tokyo, per the original plan Farrow was supposed to turn off for Osaka when Smith headed for Kobe—but he did not. Following Hilger over Nagoya, *Bat* dropped all its incendiaries in one pass before heading across Ise Bay to Yokkaichi on the western shore. Japanese documents, primarily police reports, show that Farrow hit the Toho Gas and Chemical Factory, the Imperial Armory, and the Toho Chemical Plant; all lay along a north-south line from Nagoya Castle to the port area. A combat report from the Yokosuka Land Defense Force, dated April 22, 1942, confirms that at "1427 (Tokyo Time) an aircraft flying extremely low, bearing 225 deg. had approached" Yokkaichi, and "Strafing by enemy" occurred over the rail line leading south out of town. The aircraft then vanished in the direction of Kameyama, to the southwest, then out of Japan and across to China. Encountering the same foul weather, darkness, and low fuel, somewhere east of Nanchang the crew successfully bailed out.

One version of the story states that Farrow and DeShazer found each other and spent the night in a graveyard near a small village. In the morning, they approached the elderly headman, who eventually fed them and agreed to have the pair taken to Chungking. Some word must have reached the village about approaching imperial troops, because the headman hid the Americans in a small hut, which he barred from the outside. A group of soldiers did appear and their officer questioned the old Chinese gentleman, obviously about foreigners who had suddenly appeared, but the man repeatedly shook his head.

Losing patience, the officer resorted to a favorite Japanese punishment and had the old man wrapped in a blanket soaked with kerosene. When Bill Farrow saw this, he knew what was going to happen, and could not let the man die for their sake. Yelling and pounding on the door, he and DeShazer tried to make themselves heard, but to no avail. The officer lit a small stick and thrust it toward the headman's wife, who refused to immolate her husband. Grabbing the woman's small son by the throat, the officer began to strangle the boy with one hand while holding the burning stick in the other. Confronted with such an agonizing choice, the woman moaned and threw the stick on her kerosene-soaked husband, who began screaming as he burned. Laughing and cheering, the soldiers then smashed the man's head in with their rifle butts, and as the noise died down, they heard Farrow yelling from the hut.

Quickly disarmed, bound, blindfolded, and dragged from the village, the two Americans heard rifle shots as the soldiers killed the remaining Chinese. This sounds suspiciously like Wendelin Dunker's eyewitness account in Ihwang, and is not mentioned at all in Sergeant Jake DeShazer's oral history. Forty-seven years later, now a retired reverend and missionary, he recounts spending the night alone in a graveyard and, the next morning, observing a military camp across the road and "a couple of fellows in uniform playing with some children." Joining them, DeShazer told the soldiers he was an American, and one who spoke English said they were Chinese. The men fed him a "mashed up bean" paste with sugar that they called *yōkan* then surrounded him and said "we think you better let us have your gun."* Faced with rifles and bayonets, he handed it over, and the soldier calmly stated, "You are in the hands of the Imperial Japanese Army."

However it happened, all five of *Bat's* crew had been captured immediately and were reunited that very afternoon in the Japanese camp. Taken to Nanchang, they were tossed into a cell with *Bat out of Hell's* other three crew members, who had been captured the night before. Flown to Shanghai, the men were beaten and interrogated, yet all five men refused to give any information, though co-pilot Lieutenant Bob Hite recalled the officer who questioned him already had a list of all eighty Doolittle raiders, knew Doolittle was the commander, and knew that they'd flown off the aircraft carrier

---

* *Yōkan* is a Japanese dish, but DeShazer did not know that at the time, nor was there anything he could have done at that point to escape.

*Hornet.* On April 20, Farrow's crew was flown to Tokyo and handed over to the Kempeitai. Five days later, they were joined by Lieutenants Dean Hallmark, Bob Meder, and Chase Nielson.

For these eight young Americans, the next few months were a nightmare. Subjected to waterboarding, shin kicking, and the "pipe" treatment, each of them firmly resisted and refused to disclose any information other than their names, ranks, and serial numbers.* In the end, it was torture for the sake of torture, as the Japanese had recovered maps, charts, and papers from several of the crashed Mitchells and knew everything about the raid. On May 22, the men were forced to sign papers written in Japanese, which were fictitious confessions about *intentionally* strafing schools, children, and bombing nonmilitary targets. Fed a few ounces of maggoty rice, "soup" made from water used to wash vegetables, and a half cup of water per day, each man steadily lost weight and grew weaker. By June they had been taken by boat back to Shanghai and again lodged in the Bridge House, where they would remain for seventy days.

July 1942 saw the issuance of Secret Order 2190, which stated, in part, "An enemy warplane crew who did not violate wartime international law shall be treated as prisoners of war, and one who acted against the said law shall be punished as a wartime capital crime."

This was laying the legal groundwork, Imperial Japanese style, for Military Order Number 4, issued on August 13, 1942, later known as the "Enemy Airmen's Act." The order read:

> Article I: This law shall apply to all enemy airmen who raid the Japanese homeland, Manchukuo, and the Japanese zones of military operations, and who come within the areas under the jurisdiction of the China Expeditionary Force.

---

* The prisoner squats on his haunches, and a steel or bamboo pipe is placed behind his knees. A guard then jumps on the quadriceps, forcing the body's weight back on the pipe.

Article II: Any individual who commits any or all of the following shall be subject to military punishment:

Section 1. The bombing, strafing, and otherwise attacking of civilians with the objective of cowing, intimidating, killing, or maiming them.

Section 2. The bombing, strafing or otherwise attacking of private properties, whatsoever, with the objectives of destroying or damaging same.

Section 3. The bombing, strafing or otherwise attacking of objectives, other than those of military nature, except in those cases where such an act is unavoidable.

Section 4. In addition to those acts covered in the preceding three sections, all other acts violating the provisions of International Law governing warfare.

Article III: Military punishment shall be the death penalty [or] life imprisonment, or a term of imprisonment for not less than ten years.

Most damning for the captured raiders was the last line, which stated "This military law *shall be applicable to all acts committed prior to the date of its approval.*"

It was, in fact, a retroactive death sentence.

On August 28, the eight men were transferred to Kiangwan Miliary Prison near Shanghai and subjected to an Imperial Army "trial" by the 7330 Noburo Unit Military Tribunal for their alleged crimes. All eight were sentenced to death by firing squad, with an execution date set for October 15, 1942. General Sadamu Shimomura, commander of the Thirteenth Army in China, commuted five of the sentences to life imprisonment with "special treatment," meaning that even in the event of future prisoner of war exchanges, these five Americans were war criminals and were not eligible for repatriation. On the evening of October 14, Lieutenant Dean Hallmark, Lieutenant Bill Farrow, and Sergeant Harold Spatz were told they would be shot the next day, and Sergeant (later captain) Sotojio Tatsuta gave each man several pieces of paper for letters to their families.

Bill Farrow, just twenty-three years old, wrote to his widowed mother in South Carolina: "Don't let this get you down. Just remember that God will make everything right, and that I will see you again it the hereafter." He also wrote to his fiancée and thanked her "for bringing to my life a deep, rich love for a fine girl." Twenty-eight-year-old Dean Hallmark, the former collegiate football star, was so weak from dysentery and beriberi that he couldn't stand, but told his family in Dallas "try to stand up under this and pray." Kansan Harold Spatz, who turned twenty-one in the Bridge House, wrote to his widowed father: "Dad, I want you to know that I love you and may God bless you. I died fighting for my country like a soldier."

Led out to Public Cemetery Number One at 1630 on October 15, the three fliers were made to kneel before wooden crosses constructed a day earlier by a Japanese carpenter. Sotojio Tatsuta told the Americans, "We have been living together under the same roof and on this day you are going to be executed . . . but I feel sorry for you. My sympathies are with you. Men must die sooner or later. Your lives were very short, but your names will remain."

Farrow thanked him and asked that he "tell the folks at home that we died very bravely."

Tatsuta later recounted that "I told them that Christ was born and died on the cross and you on your part must die on the cross . . . you will be honored as Gods." Highly unusual for an imperial soldier, Tatsuta closed with, "you will soon be bound to the crosses and when this is done it is a fact that that man's faith and the cross shall be united. Therefore, have faith."

Clean white blindfolds were wrapped over each man's eyes, and a black mark placed in the center of their foreheads. Six riflemen lined up barely twenty feet away, and their commander, Lieutenant Goro Tashida gave the command: "Prepare!"

Six long Arisaka rifles slowly rose in unison, and two men aimed at each black mark. The lieutenant dropped his arm sharply. "Fire!"

The 7.7 mm bullets shattered each man's forehead, and death was instantaneous. A medical officer checked each body for a pulse, and when none was found the wounds were bandaged and the dead Americans untied and laid in three coffins. These were carried to an altar, and the gathered Japanese saluted. Removed to the nearby Residents Association Crematorium, their ashes were later placed in small wooden boxes on the Kiangwan Prison altar. The remaining five men, Lieutenants Bob Meder, Chase Nielsen, Bob Hite, George Barr, and Corporal Jake DeShazer knew nothing about the execution. Meder, sick with beriberi, dropped from 175 pounds to just over 100 pounds and died in his cell, alone, on December 1, 1943. The last four men would face a total of forty months of mistreatment, occasional torture, and desperate loneliness. They also faced that hollow uncertainty of not knowing one's daily fate, or even if anyone on the outside was aware of their existence.

Ski York and the crew of Plane 8 would have understood that completely. Awakened by the interpreter the morning after their arrival, they were stiff from the iron camp beds, and the scratchy wool blankets did nothing to alleviate their hangovers. The adrenaline had worn off, and the five men were grumpy. "When we went to bed that night," York recalled, "we were fully confident we were going to leave the next morning."

They were informed that "the Colonel and members of his staff will breakfast with you at ten." Believing they would still depart today, Bob Emmens wanted a souvenir, so he swapped pennies, nickels, dimes for kopecks. While dressing, the three officers discussed the plan for the day, with York deciding to press the fuel issue and, if possible, to lift off for China after breakfast. To avoid occupied China, Ski knew they'd have to fly one thousand miles west, almost to the

Mongolian border, before turning south for another nine hundred miles or so to Chungking. There really was no other option. Flying down the coast between Japan and Korea, and then over to China, did not appeal in the slightest. Especially with the Japanese thoroughly stirred up and angry after yesterday's raid. The distances were about the same, either way, and at least via the western route they'd be over Chinese territory for most of it. If, that is, the Russians let them leave and granted overflight permission. If they did not, York intended thank them nicely, take off, and head south over the Sea of Japan. Once out of the Soviet Union, he'd turn west for the Chinese border, which was only a hundred miles away, then to the Mongolian border and south to Chungking.

The "breakfast" turned into a five-hour marathon of vodka, zakuska, pickled fish, caviar, and mounds of black bread. And more vodka. York tried to get an answer regarding fuel, but was told "business must never be discussed over meat and wine. All decisions will be made in due time. First," the colonel beamed, "you must eat and drink heartily." It was hard not to do so. Roast goose, fried potatoes, and an entire young pig were all brought in relays, with endless toasts, cheeses, and pickled vegetables. Somewhere in the melee it was decided to inspect the Mitchell, and the entire party made its way out to the bomber. Ski offered to give them a ride, but fortunately the colonel politely refused.

By 1600 the Americans were all back in their iron beds, heads swimming and bellies churning. A half hour later the interpreter threw open the door, quite excitedly, and blurted out, "You must hurry and get up. You are leaving at once. The airplane is waiting!" Thinking they were now allowed to leave, Ski pulled on his A-2 jacket, then all five headed downstairs and out to a dilapidated school bus. To Bob's surprise and consternation, the bus drove past the Mitchell to a silver DC-3 waiting at the end of the field.

"Where are we going . . . and what about our bags?"

"You will learn everything in due time," replied the colonel, who was apparently coming along. Standard Russian answer. Piling into the plane, York's crew sagged onto the narrow, uncomfortable troop seats, still very much feeling the effects of the huge meal, especially the wine, cognac, and vodka. Lurching into the air, the DC-3 banked slightly and headed north, following a ridgeline up a long valley "containing a fair-sized river."* Over the deep throbbing of the engines, Emmens and York discussed this latest development and arrived at three options. First, they'd been told the American consul was not in Vladivostok, but that they would "see their American friends soon," so perhaps they were being flown to see the consul. That wasn't as good as flying out to China on their own, but if this was the situation, certainly it meant getting back to the United States.

That was another possibility. Both pilots knew there were military flights between the Soviet Union and the United States via Alaska, so they could be on their way to a northern airport and from there back home. They liked this option and decided it was the most likely scenario.

But there was also a third choice: Manchuria and the Japanese. Maybe, in order to mollify Tokyo and prevent a declaration of war, Moscow had agreed to hand Plane 8's crew over to the Imperial Army in Manchuria. The local Soviets had not seemed upset by the presence of the Americans, but the Kremlin might have other notions.

In any event, both pilots were relieved when the DC-3 started a descent about two hours into the flight. They hadn't flown long enough to be close to Manchuria, so this had to be something else. Even through the fading afternoon light, they could see a large air base with many rows of aircraft next to a relatively big town. The Soviet colonel pointed out the window and yelled "Khabarovsk."

---

* The Partizanskaya River flows nearly ninety miles down Golden Valley to Nakhodka Bay.

Bouncing down on the grass, the transport slowed rapidly, and as it taxied past the parked aircraft, Bob was surprised to see they were all dummies. All the operational aircraft must have been sent west to fight the Germans, and that was another point worth noting. The Soviet Maritime Territory, which would bear the brunt of any Japanese onslaught, had been stripped of its defenses, which would also explain the obsolete biplane fighter that escorted them in to land. York doubted that if the Japanese did attack there was much the Russians could do to stop it. Thinking of the lengths Moscow would go to in order to avoid such a conflict brought another chill to his spine.

There were three cars waiting, and the colonel took Ski and climbed in the first, Emmens and Herndon took the second, with Laban and Pohl in the third. Each car had a driver with an armed soldier, and after a short trip to the edge of the airfield, they were led into a dimly lit building and up to an office. Against the far end by a window was the biggest desk York had ever seen, and beside it "stood a hulking, middle-aged Soviet officer." Those with them, including the colonel, snapped to attention and stood rigidly in a line. The American officers straightened up a bit, but did not come to attention, and stared at the Russian. "He had a huge girth," Emmens recalled, "which was all the more accentuated by his shortness of stature and his perfectly round, shiny bald head. The length of his arms gave him the appearance of a gorilla."

He wore a dark green tunic over dark green riding pants with black boots and an officer's sword belt. On the collar, York saw five gold stars arranged on a crimson-red background. Gorilla or not, this was obviously a high-ranking general officer who now held their lives in his hands. "He was an ugly individual with small, beady eyes," Bob wrote. Another interpreter and an expressionless female standing near the desk introduced them to the "commanding general of the Far Eastern Red Army," then bade them take a seat for there were a few questions. In fact, this was General Iosif Rodionovich Apanasenko, a fifty-one-year-old combat veteran of the Russian Imperial Army who had gone over to the Bolsheviks and fought for them during the Civil War.* The general asked about their target and their route into Japan but was most interested in the route out. Had they been detected? Had they been followed by Japanese planes, or been sighted by any Japanese ships on their way across to Russia? He wasn't much interested in where they had come from, or the *Hornet*, or where the other raiders went after Japan, but he asked three times about being followed to the Soviet Union. Now it was quite plain to Ski York that Russian concerns about a Japanese declaration of war were of the utmost importance to Moscow and that this man, who commanded all Soviet Forces in the Far East, had been directed to assess the risk.

After a half hour of back-and-forth statements, Apanasenko made a slow, deliberate statement, his hard little eyes flickering to each American face. When he finished, the general nodded at the woman and she stood.

"The general has asked me to tell you that according to a decision reached between our two governments, and by direction of orders from Moscow, you will be interned in the Soviet Union until such a time as further decisions are made in your case."

Ski York was surprised, but considering the Russian penchant for deception, he realized this should have been expected. The Mitchell had only landed yesterday, so there had been no time for any exchanges between Washington and Moscow; this was strictly a decision made by the Kremlin. Damage control, Russian style. Ski was suddenly quite relieved that both Doolittle and Hap Arnold knew about this mission, not that it would do them much good at the moment, though Soviet uncertainty on that point was probably why his crew was still alive. They could have been simply shot dead and dropped in a ditch, he knew, though Moscow was unsure of who in Washington was aware Plane 8 had landed here. With

---

* Apanasenko would later be killed in June 1943, fighting during the Battle of Kursk.

the Germans on their doorstep, the Japanese in their backyard, and their continued existence dependent on Lend-Lease, the Soviets dared not alienate the United States by executing an Army bomber crew.

The general stood, said something to the interpreter, and with a slight bow turned to his officers and walked toward the door. The interview was clearly at an end, and the woman cleared her throat.

"You will begin internment immediately."

# PART III

Never give in—never, never, never, never, in nothing great or small, large or petty, never give in except to convictions of honour and good sense. Never yield to force.

—WINSTON CHURCHILL

# 8

## QUESTIONS AND ANSWERS

Admiral William Harrison Standley, United States ambassador to the Soviet Union, was the first American to know the fate of Plane 8 and its crew. "I had no official notification of the landing of the American bomber on Soviet territory until April 21st," he wrote in his memoirs. "The Soviet Foreign Office sent me word that the crew would be interned near Khabarovsk."

In fact, they were already there.

As Ski York deduced, the decision had been made by Moscow, not by Washington. Standley, a combat veteran of the Spanish-American War who had commanded the battleships *Virginia* (BB-13) and *California* (BB-44), served as chief of naval operations before retiring in 1937. Recalled to active duty in February 1942, he was immediately sent to Russia as the United States ambassador to the Soviet Union. On April 23, while meeting with Joseph Stalin, the Soviet premier stated that the crew was safe but "they should not have landed on Soviet territory."

Nonetheless, the Russians had officially acknowledged the crew's presence in the Soviet Union, so they could not now simply "disappear" or be handed over to the Japanese. "We'll have to intern them,"

Stalin affirmed, "in accordance with International Law." By April 25, the cat was out of the bag as Soviet newspapers ran a headline declaring AN AMERICAN WARPLANE HAD LANDED IN THE SOVIET MARITIME PROVINCE ON APRIL 18. The bomber had apparently "lost their way after bombing Japan."

Jimmy Doolittle and Hap Arnold knew this was utterly untrue, but said nothing about it because none of the raiders were supposed to have landed in the Soviet Union. In fact, Doolittle expressly ordered them *not* to land in Russia. Ski York, however, had been acting under instructions from Hap Arnold, who was Doolittle's superior officer, chief of the Army Air Forces, and member of the Joint Chiefs of Staff. That this endeavor had been sanctioned by Hap Arnold was the reason for the subterfuge and cover stories up to that point, and for future obfuscation by Jimmy Doolittle, Ed York, and Bob Emmens. To understand this extraordinary mission, one must answer two fundamental questions: why, and how?

The genesis for Plane 8's sub-rosa flight to Russia lies with Doolittle himself, though he had no idea how it would manifest itself during the raid on Japan. In the last paragraph of his February 1942 feasibility study to Hap Arnold, Doolittle writes, "Should the Russians be willing to accept delivery of 18 B-25-B airplanes, on lease lend, at Vladivostok our problems would be greatly simplified" (see appendix one). This suggests that Moscow's approval of bomber deliveries to the Maritime Territory would streamline the flow of Lend-Lease aircraft to the whole of the Soviet Union.

Arnold took it a step further. If the USSR allowed such an influx of materiel directly to their Far East bases, then they would surely accept American basing proposals from which to strike Japan. After all, Tokyo would know about the Lend-Lease routes and would hardly accept Moscow's word that such war materiel would only be used against the Germans. Therefore, if Stalin permitted this, then he was willing to accept war with Japan as a consequence; ergo, he completely sided with the Allied cause, and there was no immediate risk of Soviet duplicity or a separate peace.

But how would Washington know that?

Arnold had the answer.

Bombing Japan in April 1942 had been approved and encouraged by Roosevelt himself, and the president would certainly welcome any action by any ally that would relieve the tenuous American situation in the Pacific. These were the darkest days of the Second World War, and the Axis seemed undefeatable, so desperate measures were definitely within the realm of possibility. Lend-Lease, which was extended to Moscow in October 1941, was the lifeblood of the combined Allied fight, and although prodigiously generous, the United States expected a quid pro quo. From Britain, this included long-term basing rights, among other concessions, but from the Soviet Union, Washington desired active war against Japan. Knowing Moscow was unwilling to do this, the fallback position was passive cooperation in the form of air bases in return for billions of dollars' worth of Lend-Lease credits.

But negotiating is problematic without a clear idea of your adversary's true strengths, weaknesses, and expectations. The best way to assess Soviet intentions and capabilities would be a firsthand analysis of the Maritime Territory. So, Arnold reasoned, if one of the Doolittle bombers landed at a selected airfield east of Vladivostok, the pilots would know immediately if such a place was suitable as a bomber base. Where would Plane 8's high-octane fuel come from, if there was any there to begin with? Could oil be replenished, and how long would this take? Just as critical, what would the Soviet reaction to their presence be? Would they be enthusiastic, or fear the consequences; lend political and military support, or hand the crew to the Japanese—or, worse, make the crew simply disappear? It was a terrible risk Ed York and his crew were taking, but in hindsight their risk was no greater than that of the other raiders who met tragic fates in China. Arnold, and obviously York and Emmens, felt it was a risk worth taking.

This answers the question, why?

As for how, this is at times equally simple and complex.

Once he decided to proceed, Hap Arnold needed the right man to bring it off. Just as he'd chosen Jimmy Doolittle as the man to plan and then eventually lead the mission, Arnold required a similar type of pilot to fly the mission to Russia. Someone experienced and senior enough to accept the added danger, a man capable of a fast, accurate assessment of the previously mentioned factors, and one who could deal with the Russians. Excepting Jack Hilger, Ski York had more B-25 time than anyone else and, like Arnold himself, was a West Pointer, the only one on the raid. York was also the 95th Bombardment Squadron commander, and as the raiders' operations officer he was responsible for the planning, crew training, and oversight of every aspect of the mission.

Given the tensions in the Far East, diplomatic sensitivities, and the need for plausible deniability for Roosevelt, the Army Air Forces, and Hap Arnold, believed a compelling reason would be needed for a bomber to land on Soviet soil. Battle damage was too unpredictable and was not guaranteed to occur. Navigation or instrument error was too sketchy; Japan's landmarks were easy enough for orientation, and there were backups to magnetic dead reckoning such as celestial navigation. Mechanical issues would be noted by the rest of the crew, who were *not* in on the plan, and such problems might be remedied or cause for the mission to be scrapped.

For York, the most obvious solution was fuel.

It couldn't be a self-created leak, because that would force an abort and, again, would be obvious to the crew. How, then, to have a real fuel problem that would permit bombing Japan but be serious enough to force a divert to the Soviet Union? Knowing, as he did, that the forty-eight carburetors on all twenty-four Mitchells (eighteen primaries plus six spares) had been adjusted and bench checked at Eglin Field to run extremely lean at low altitude, York hit on the solution.

Carburetors.

Each Wright-Cyclone engine utilized a floatless Holley 1685 HB-type carburetor that controlled the fuel-air mixture entering the combustion chamber. Essentially, pressurized fuel is suctioned into a low-pressure air chamber created by a shaped venturi, and the ratio of fuel to air, called the mixture, is set in the cockpit. The volume of this mixture flowing out to be burned in the combustion chamber is set by the throttles. A fuel-heavy mixture is rich, and one with more air than fuel is lean. Leaning the mixture saves gas, and as every pound of fuel was precious over the planned route, each Holley carburetor had been painstakingly modified to run "leaner" at low-altitude cruise settings. A leaner mix meant less fuel used per hour, and this was absolutely critical in giving the Mitchells the range to reach safe bases in China.

The modified carburetors produced a cruise fuel flow of about 65 to 70 gallons per hour for each bomber, whereas Plane 8's unmodified engines consumed about 98 gallons per hour. In practical terms, over a nine-hour flight, York's Mitchell would consume roughly 250 gallons more than the other raiders, resulting in a loss of at least 425 miles in range. This became more crucial when the raiders were forced to launch early on April 18 after the task force was detected, and without the Eglin carburetor modifications, none of the bombers would have reached the Chinese coast. Had Ski attempted to follow the other raiders, he would have run out of fuel over the East China Sea.

York, calculating the fuel burn for unmodified engines, figured they could make it to eastern Russia with approximately 150 gallons remaining, so if the tanks were inspected this would bear out their story. No blame could be attached to Washington, or even to himself as the aircraft commander—what choice was there *but* to land in the Soviet Union. In fact, the fuel tanks were inspected by the Russians and were found to contain roughly one hundred gallons. In a May 25 telegram to the U.S. secretary of state, Ambassador Standley made a very emphatic point of declaring the bomber landed "with only enough gasoline left to proceed about 150 miles." Such a detail would not normally be prominently stated in an ambassadorial-level telegram to the secretary of state, so this was obviously included to give credence to the crew's story and to alleviate potential diplomatic tension.

On March 25, twenty-two of the Mitchells departed Eglin for Sacramento, California, for final modifications, and en route they were to verify their performance and fuel numbers. Previously designated the Pacific Air Depot and the Sacramento Air Depot, by 1939 the field had been renamed McClellan, and was one of four primary maintenance, repair, and overhaul facilities in the Army Air Forces. It was the most convenient facility to finish removing any of the remaining lower gun turrets and installing the sixty-gallon-tank fuel cell that could be refilled in flight from five-gallon cans. New glass windows would replace the older Plexiglas type, and the cumbersome, unnecessary 230-pound liaison radios would also be removed. New hydraulic valves would be installed, and the older seat-type parachutes were to be replaced by the newer back-type model. One of the more important modifications was to replace the propeller blades that had been pitted and scratched during the past year. New Hamilton Standard constant-speed props were installed, which meant up to a 20 percent increase in airspeed at any power setting.

Interestingly, the afternoon before the raiders were to depart for Alameda Naval Air Station and the USS *Hornet*, Doolittle and "a couple of pilots" just happened to be in base operations when someone attempted to start the left engine on one of the Mitchells. The civilian mechanic "churned the prop, but couldn't get the engine started," Doolittle wrote. "There was a loud bang and backfiring

with black smoke and flames pouring out of the exhaust stacks."
According to Doolittle's account, he nearly threw the mechanic out
of the cockpit, and was so enraged that he "used some expletives I
hadn't used before and probably haven't since."

Angry, the civilian retorted that he was just following procedures;
anytime carburetors were adjusted or changed, the engines were required to be started and checked. It was also a USAAF regulation
that all equipment changes were to be noted and recorded in the
aircraft logbook—but that wasn't done in this case, nor was there
any accounting for the new carburetors leaving storage and being
installed. Doolittle appropriately, and quite conveniently, went on
record with the base commander, Colonel Clark, formally protesting the action, which, again rather conveniently, was only performed
on a single Mitchell.

Plane 8—Ed York's bomber.

"No mention was made," Ski recounted in a 1943 memorandum
to the assistant chief of air staff, "or notation made, to let us know
that the carburetors had been changed." To this rather implausible declaration, he added another lame statement: "I didn't think it
made any difference."

All the pilots, *especially* Ed York, were aware that fuel was critical,
and without meticulous planning and the modified equipment, no
one was getting safely to China. Also, York was quite likely one of
the pilots with Doolittle in base ops as Plane 8 coughed and backfired. Major Jack Hilger was there, later stating about the engine-
start incident, "I don't know what he told that fellow, but the air
inside that cockpit turned blue." Doolittle, Hilger, and York would
have spent most of their time together ironing out details to ensure
all the aircraft were in perfect shape, so even if Ski wasn't present,
it is utterly inconceivable that any pilot, let alone Doolittle's chief
of operations, would *not* have been told his engines had been tam-
pered with. It is equally implausible that if this truly was an accident that the original carburetors would not have been immediately

reinstalled, especially given that the bombers were departing for Alameda the following day.*

The final nail in this incident's figurative coffin would be Sergeant Ted Laban. As the engineer, he should have been informed at once that the depot maintenance personnel had disassembled his engines, but he was not. In fact, the first Laban knew of it was aboard the *Hornet* when he noticed the carburetor serial numbers did not match the originals recorded in the bomber's maintenance log. Laban duly reported this to York, who now publicly informed his commander. This is patently absurd since Doolittle (and York) had known about the switch since McClellan Field. Now, however, all the raiders knew about it—which was precisely the point of the playacting. It was far too late to do anything about the issue, and the groundwork was successfully laid for York's subsequent divert to the Soviet Union.

This, too, was carefully considered.

First, the target. According to the planning documents and Jimmy Doolittle, Ed York was to lead the third flight of five bombers "to cover the southern part of Tokyo and the north-central part of the Tokyo Bay area." Plane 8 made landfall close enough to Cape Inubo for the pilots to know exactly where they were, and therefore where Tokyo was located. Even if he had been off, as Doolittle was, York was highly experienced and would have turned southwest until he found another landmark. However, this was hardly necessary on a clear day like April 18, 1942, since Mount Fuji would have been visible along the entire shoreline, from Cape Inubo and as far north as the Mito area. The isolated, snowcapped peak would also be recognizable for most of the bomber's course across Japan, until Ski dropped low in the mountains toward the Honshu coast.

Emmens actually noted, "Fujiyama reached skyward to our left," which is exactly where it would be as they headed across Honshu,

---

* Mr. Tony Ritzman, a B-25 engine expert and the owner of Aero Traders in Chino, California, acknowledged that it would take "about two hours per engine" to accomplish this.

whereas if they were heading toward Tokyo, it would be directly off the Mitchell's nose. Equally preposterous is to imagine that Ed York and Bob Emmens inadvertently turned some *thirty degrees* to the northwest, the wrong direction, toward the equally visible Japanese Alps rather than southwest to Tokyo. The only rational conclusion is that this was the correct heading for them to take since Plane 8 never intended to bomb Tokyo, and thus they never flew within fifty miles of the capital. During his 1943 military intelligence debrief, York was pointedly asked if he flew over Tokyo, and contrary to some published accounts of the raid, he confirmed that they did not overfly the city and never got within sight of it.

Where did they intend to drop their bombs, then?

Fuel was extremely critical, so there could be no wasted time flying around looking for a target of opportunity. Because of this and to minimize time over very hostile territory, neither could York deviate much from the straight-line course across Honshu. He would also want to drop his two-thousand-pound bombload as soon as possible to increase his potential airspeed and to reduce fuel consumption. Now, on such a course from Cape Inubo to the Niigata coast, there was only one city with easily identifiable, first-look targets of any military or industrial significance: Utsunomiya.

About sixty miles north of Tokyo on the edge of the Kanto plain, Utsunomiya was a major hub for the Tohoku and Electric main line railroads, as well as an electric-power distribution center for the Tochigi Prefecture. Aside from the rail yards, there was the Kakuwa Manufacturing Company, a major producer of aircraft parts for Nakajima Aircraft; the Nishin Flour Mill; and the Shimozuke Paper Mill. Utsunomiya was an Imperial Army center as well, with one of Japan's five main air arsenals and an air training school. The 44th Division was headquartered just west of the city, along with the 18th Cavalry Regiment, the 20th Field Artillery Regiment, and a garrison hospital.

During another 1943 interview with Army Air Forces intelligence, York actually states that "they flew over the city of Utsunomiya." This extraordinary admission lays to rest once and for all any doubt that Ski ever intended to strike Tokyo. Therefore, there is no alternative explanation for Plane 8 to be sixty miles north of the raiders' primary target and heading in the wrong direction, except that this was planned from the beginning. If the decision to divert to Russia had been "spur of the moment," then how did York identify the city, by name, in an intelligence debriefing after the fact? Obviously, because he planned the strike back in March and, in fact, made a special trip to Washington, D.C., to acquire whatever scanty information the military had on central Honshu.

The Army's military intelligence section (MIS) had the available maps and target-area photos available in early 1942, and this was fairly thin material. It is revealing that York just happened to be in Washington during mid-March when he accidentally encountered Captain Davey Jones, who was the raiders' designated navigation and intelligence officer, and Lieutenant Tom Griffin, navigator for *The Whirling Dervish*. Ski was cordial but never gave a straight answer as to why he was there, much less in the MIS. According to Griffin, Ed York was "evasive."

As Doolittle's operation's officer, Ski had countless details to finalize at Eglin, and at this point in March he was not even *officially* on the raid. York had been "loaned" to Doolittle by Lieutenant Colonel William "Newt" Mills, commander of the 17th Bombardment Group, with the understanding that the pilot would not go on the raid. Mills was anticipating a move to Europe and needed experienced commanders. "You can't have York," Mills was adamant, "because he has just been made group [17th BG] ops officer, and we're going overseas ourselves pretty soon, and I need him." Doolittle strung Mills along all through March at Eglin Field stating "I need an operations officer too. Then he can come back." This edged York closer and closer to the West Coast, where it would be too late to return him.

"Newt, old boy, I am going to need York out in Sacramento for a few days," Doolittle told the other colonel in the third week at Eglin, and he kept up the charade during the raiders' stay at McClellan. But as far as anyone else was concerned, Ski was not going on the raid until he flew Plane 8 to Alameda.

So—why would he be in Washington, specifically in the intelligence section, long before he was a designated pilot? The answer is that he was an official pilot and had been since Hap Arnold decided on the Russia mission. "York would have perfect for a 'Hap' project," his grandson Robert Arnold explained. "He was a fellow West Point graduate with skills, character, and connections." Ski was summoned directly to the chief's office, and it was there the question was put to him—quite likely on the very day he was spotted by Jones and Griffin. Naturally, York accepted, and headed to Army Intelligence in order to begin his own planning. This is circumstantial, as nothing was ever put in writing, but that was not unusual for the time and place. These men all knew one another, or of the others, and Arnold was fond of verbal orders with minimal paperwork. He did the same thing with Doolittle regarding the raid. York was part of the plan from early in March; Hap and Jimmy both knew it, but no one else, including Bob Emmens, was aware of it. No other scenario explains the known facts and subsequent actions.

The story, then, and what Bob Emmens was originally told, was that they had been selected to replace one of two crews that had suffered an accident. On March 10, Lieutenant Richard Joyce landed B-25 #40-2254 at Ellington Field during a cross-country training flight and the nosewheel collapsed. The bomber was damaged, but Joyce was simply reassigned another aircraft and went on to fly the Tokyo mission in the number ten position. On March 23, the final day of training in Florida, #40-2291 stalled on takeoff and crashed. With the airframe damaged beyond repair, the pilot, Lieutenant James P. Bates, and his copilot, Lieutenant Roloson, were scrubbed from the mission. It was Ski York's subsequent phone call to Columbia, South Carolina, that brought Bob Emmens and B-25 #40-2242, soon to be Plane 8, down to Florida. However, the replacement explanation is too thin. Even with the dismissal of the second accident crew, there were still eight additional crews that had completed the entire short-takeoff training, navigation, and bombing course at Eglin.

At this point, Doolittle's number for the raid remained fifteen official mission aircraft, though he knew a sixteenth bomber would be required since York was going to Russia. If only another qualified crew was needed, Doolittle already had them, but he also already knew York had to go on the mission. "I roomed with Doolittle down at Eglin," Ski admitted in his oral history. "So I got to know him pretty well." It was during this time, no doubt, that many of York's mission details were discussed and ironed out, starting with getting him on the lineup.

Flying as a replacement was what Emmens and the ad hoc crew were told, and this is what the copilot would later write in *Guests of the Kremlin*, proving that he, too, had a gift for obfuscation. York, on the other hand, stated, "No, that was not true at all. He [Emmens] was not in on this at all, the planning or anything, until the very last day." What Ski meant by "or anything" is conjecture, and his words could imply either the Eglin short-takeoff training or Plane 8's actual mission to Russia. As the copilot, Bob Emmens eventually had to be told the truth. The engineer and gunner would have no idea in flight of the bomber's position, and Ski could fudge courses and headings to the navigator with no explanation.

But another pilot was something else. He would know exactly where they were and where they were going. Also, if anything happened to York, then the copilot needed to get the Mitchell to the target and on to Russia. This was not a problem as the two men knew each other quite well. Stationed at March Field together, they'd been neighbors as newlyweds, and their wives were good friends. Yet it wasn't until Emmens got to Eglin that York asked, "Would you like to go with me?" This is also quite revealing since Ski was not yet on the raiders' official roster, but he knew, of course, that Plane 8 was flying the mission. In any event, Bob Emmens did not hesitate, and replied, "I have nothing else to do."

Where and how Emmens was informed of the plan will never be known; no records exist, or at least none have been found. Yet Ski would have told him about the Soviet Union, the planned carburetor switch, and their intended target in Japan. At seventeen minutes inland from Cape Inubo, Utsunomiya was ideal for all the reasons York discovered in Washington, and the fuel issue would make the impromptu "decision" to drop on the city perfectly believable.

Unfortunately, they missed it.

Though he could not have known it, and would not have cared if he had, York actually attacked the smaller, but similar, town of Nishi Nasuno twenty-three miles north of Utsunomiya. The error is not surprising—recall Ted Lawson believing he was over Tokyo, when in fact he bombed Kawasaki, and that was on a well-defined, geographically significant bay. Add to this that detailed, accurate maps of Tokyo and the surrounding areas were not available, much less maps for an obscure city deep within rural Japan. Both Utsunomiya and Nishi Nasuno lay within the Nasunogahara alluvial fan, which is dominated by the Kinugawa and Naka Rivers. It was a heavily agricultural area serviced by the Tōhuku Main Line that passed south to north over the plateau. Navigation in 1942 was problematic at best, and ingressing at fifty to a hundred feet aboveground does not give a pilot a usable, comprehensive view for a target area.

As the prefectural capital, Utsunomiya was, and still is, considerably larger than Nishi Nasuno, but this would not have been obvious at such a low altitude. Also, the town of Otawara is less than three miles to the southeast, and even in 1942 it was spreading toward Nishi Nasuno, so at a few hundred feet this easily could have been mistaken for the larger town of Utsunomiya. In any case, there was no time or fuel left for a precise comparison. The only real clue York might have noticed was that instead of the planned eighteen minutes inland, Plane 8 roared over the town twenty-three minutes after landfall at Cape Inubo. Based on the target photos taken by the Mitchell's tail-mounted automatic camera, York entered the area from the southeast and had obviously followed the Naka River through the foothills of Mount Yamizo, believing it to be the Kinugawa River.

This orientation is logical given Emmens's statement about a "single tall radio transmitting pole" directly ahead as they approached a "more thickly populated area." He also describes a "single small airplane" approaching from the right, or northeast, of the bomber, which was in a left turn toward the river. The urban area was undoubtably the town of Otawara, and while the Japanese aircraft never spotted the Mitchell, it was quite likely in the landing pattern for IJAAF Kanemaruhara,* an airfield to the east across the Naka River. Incidentally, Utsunomiya had an army air base, named for the town, in a very similar position across the Kinugawa River.

Given that all the other B-25s crashed or were ditched, Plane 8's film was the only target-area evidence ever recovered, aside from photos snapped from personal cameras. Long buried in the U.S. National Archives, these few frames show an area positively identified by the eminent Japanese historian Makoto Morimoto as within a thousand yards southeast of the Nishi Nasuno train station and rail yard. The town of Otawara and the Sabi River, which runs along its eastern side, can be clearly seen, as can the Nasu Takuyo agricultural school to the bottom right. So, too, can the well-known villa of Field Marshal Oyama, a national hero and founding member of the Imperial Japanese Army, be seen in the foreground a few hundred yards east of the first bomb's explosion.

According to Emmens, their target was a "big factory installation

---

* Imperial Japanese Army Air Force.

with four puffing stacks," and that fits the Kakuwa Manufacturing Company or Shimozuke Paper Mill in Utsunomiya—but this matches nothing in Nishi Nasuno. York was undoubtably surprised not to see the factory he planned to hit, but he believed the town off his nose was Utsunomiya and there was no time to reattack or troll for targets of opportunity. Ski visually acquired the only significant structure in the town, which was the train station and, according to Nolan Herndon, "He [York] designated it as the target."

Impacting 185 yards southeast of the station, the five-hundred-pounder exploded in what was a farmer's field in 1942.* The Imperial Army's 14th Division Headquarters at Utsunomiya investigated the incident and compiled a report dated May 10, 1942, of the Nishi-Nasuno bombing, which reads, in part:

> Damage-Tochigi prefecture: Enemy plane "North American" type appeared around Nishi Nasuno Station at about 13:03 from South, dropped bomb from height of 200–300 meters, flew away towards North. The bomb exploded in a farm field 30 meters south of house belonging to (Mr.) Isamu Yagisawa. Due to the blast door(s) and screen(s) were blown away, but since resident was not at home there is no human / livestock damage. Damage is 100 [JP] Yen: Bomb crater is diameter 9m, depth 2m so the bomb is estimated to be 100 kg class.

Another source states, "First arrival of American aircraft over Tochigi prefecture is 18th April Showa 17 (1942), the so-called Doolittle Raid. One B25 that bombed Tokyo had crossed the prefecture, and on its way dropping [a] bomb in a field nearby Nishi Nasuno Station."

There is no doubt that Plane 8 hit Nishi Nasuno and that this

---

* Today the spot lies under a four-way intersection in a mixed commercial/residential area of the modern city. Ironically, and entirely coincidentally, there is a York-Benimaru supermarket within a mile of the impact site.

was a case of misidentification by a crew that certainly intended to strike Utsunomiya. In *Guests of the Kremlin*, Emmens describes smokestacks and a factory, which was likely their intended target in Utsunomiya, yet there was no such building in Nishi Nasuno. This discrepancy was revealed in three lines of text buried within the June 1943 intelligence debriefing. Nolan Herndon stated, "Well, as the major said, we couldn't see too dog-gone much," which is not likely if you're dropping on a factory with four stacks puffing smoke. But this is consistent with a low-profile target such as a train station, where the only visible clues would be converging tracks and steam rising from any locomotives present. Interestingly, Herndon also said he "saw the blast and the steam and smoke rising."

Steam and smoke. Not a secondary explosion, but "steam and smoke rising," as one would expect from a train station. The Japanese reports state only one bomb impact was witnessed and recorded, yet in all American accounts provided by York and Emmens, the entire load was dropped. Nolan Herndon clearly stated, "We went up to 1,500 feet and dropped the bombs."

Bombs, which would seem to mean all three five-hundred-pounders and the incendiary.

From a tactical standpoint, this makes perfect sense: extra bombs were extra weight, and since there were no other targets of opportunity in the area, York would have wanted to immediately proceed across Honshu as fast as possible to get out of Japan and on to the Soviet Union. There are two solutions to this puzzle.

First, because of the low altitude, the other three bomb fuses did not function, so there were no explosions. In 1942 the area was more forested than it is today, and there was a canal, so if the other bombs were dropped and did not fuse, they may have landed in the water or in the soft dirt of the surrounding fields. In any event, if anything was recovered, it was never reported. Second, there is incontrovertible evidence that Niitsu, a larger town in the Niigata Prefecture on the northwest coast, also suffered an attack. The Im-

perial Army Aeronautical Technical Unit investigated an air raid
that occurred on April 18, 1942, and subsequently filed a report out-
lining an attempt to bomb a bridge over the Agano River about 1.5
miles northeast of Niitsu. An extract from a wartime log available
in the Japanese Center for Asian Historical Records preserves a
telephone message from Niigata Prefecture stating, "aircraft came
from upstream [southeast] of Agano river, dropped bomb and flew
away towards direction of Soviet Union."

One bomb landed on a sandbar in the river, and the other two in
farm fields on the west bank of the river. The bridge was unharmed,
and a nearby farmhouse suffered minor damage from "5 roof tiles
and 3 screen windows."

On that same day, the prefectural governor, Shohei Doi, arrived
to inspect the damage, and the Niitsu town record for April 1942
documents the following:

> On 18th April, at 1:30 P.M. one american [sic] aircraft ar-
> rived and dropped 3 bombs, but damage was very minimal
> at the farmland of Ohaza, Naka-Shinden. No human /
> livestock casualties. At the same time bombs were dropped,
> the aircraft made a strafing as well as dropping incendiaries,
> but it was lucky that all of them fell into Agano River.

The basic problems with the Mitchell continuing on to Niitsu
were fuel consumption due to extra weight and, most important,
rationale. The distances involved are relatively equal. From Utsunomiya, where York believed they were, to the Niigata coast below
Sado Island, was approximately ninety miles, and to the Agano
River bridge the distance was right at eighty miles. This is the same
distance from Nishi Nasuno to the coast, or to the bridge in the
Niigata Prefecture. Interestingly, the bomber was seen over Niitsu
from 1330 to 1340, depending on the source, and this is perfectly
within the nineteen-to-twenty-minute flight time required from

Nishi Nasuno to the Agano River area at the 250 miles per hour York maintained over enemy territory.

Now, if Plane 8 dropped only a single bomb on Nishi Nasuno, then it carried fifteen hundred pounds of ordnance eighty additional miles, which, combined with higher fuel flows for the increased airspeed, would have cost an extra twenty to thirty gallons of gasoline. Not a huge amount, unless you still have five hundred miles to fly across the Sea of Japan to the Soviet Union. Also, flying to Niitsu and then heading directly toward Russia would place the bomber *north* of Sado Island, yet both pilots later emphatically stated they passed *south* of the island on their way across the Sea of Japan.

The final difficulty with this scenario lies with rationale. The real mission was to get to the Soviet Union, so why risk another attack on a city far to the north, expending precious gasoline and critical time to do so? The point had been made by dropping on the first target, so there was no need to hit another. York, in fact, states unequivocally, "We passed within sight of it [Sado Island]—to the southwest of it. As soon as we got down in this flat, we let down near a bay northwest of Central Honshu south of Sado Island, and continued in a northwesterly direction toward Vladivostok." Forty-two years later in his United States Air Force oral history interview, Ski again affirmed that "after we got rid of our bombs, we made a beeline to the northwest." There has never been a mention, from any member of the crew, that Plane 8 struck two targets in Japan—but given the detailed Japanese records compiled from independent sources, this second attack is now a certainty. Only the crew knows why it was never mentioned. Possibly the secrecy surrounding the mission, or a fear of facing questions about bombing unidentified and possibly civilian targets.

There are a few possibilities that must be considered for the Niitsu story.

First, the incident was a product of Japanese propaganda put forward to further stoke war fever, control the populace, and encourage

greater efforts from northern prefectures fairly far removed from the
industrial south. Second, it was an accident. The Imperial Japanese
Army Air Force (JAAF) had at least twelve airfields from which
training was conducted scattered throughout Honshu alone. According to Makoto Morimoto, a piece of metal was recovered with
CHICAGO ACME STEEL stamped onto the surface. While this is no
doubt accurate, by itself it does not guarantee the metal was part of
a bomb delivered from a U.S. aircraft. A significant number of Japanese munitions, including aerial bombs, were made from the millions of tons of American scrap metal, particularly steel, imported
during the previous decade.* On the other hand, if this incident was
an accidental bombing by the JAAF, then they would hardly admit it
given the other events of that day.

The third, and most likely, possibility is that York, a consum-
mately professional military pilot, dropped only a single bomb on
the train station at Nishi Nasuno because he did not see the factory
he planned to hit—obviously because Plane 8 was not over Utsunomiya. This left him with two five-hundred-pounders and the incendiary bomb. His only real option would be to get to the coast
and find a target of opportunity, such as a bridge, or simply release
the remaining weapons over the water. If one takes their planned
egress heading from Utsunomiya to the coast and shifts it north to
commence from Nishi Nasuno, the Mitchell's flight path would be
directly over Niitsu: the same heading and the same distance—310
degrees for approximately 80 miles. After exiting the hills and dropping down on the coastal plain, both pilots and the navigator would
have clearly seen Sado Island, which is forty miles long and barely
twenty miles offshore. The Agano River bridge is practically the first
target of significance as one approaches Niitsu, so upon seeing this
it is logical that the remaining bombs were dropped immediately. A
due west heading for sixteen miles would take the Mitchell over the

* In 1939 alone, 2,000,000 tons of scrap steel and iron were exported to Japan.

Shinano River and out to sea toward the south tip of Sado Island, where they could now pick up their planned route to Russia.

In this context, the final scenario fits the events recorded at Nishi Nasuno and Niigata on April 18, 1942. There were witnesses to both attacks, and the Japanese naval attaché in Niigata clearly reported that military police identified a "two engine, single wing type" bomber with "a circle with star" marking on the underside of the wing and on the fuselage "similar to those insignia found on Imperial Japanese Army soldier's field caps." There were no witnesses from the downtown area, but the Agano River bridge is on the eastern edge of the city, and if Plane 8 dropped back down to fifty feet and turned immediately toward Sado Island, then it would have missed most of the populated area. There were also no photographs of any other targets from the bomber's tail camera, but this is hardly definitive. The film could have run out, or been lost in Russia, or simply not passed on to the American military attaché in Moscow, as was the first batch of pictures from Nishi Nasuno. The fact that York went on to bomb another target near Niitsu on the northwestern coast did not affect the rest of the mission, but it does clear up yet another historical mystery.

One hour out from the Russian coast, Plane 8 would have had less than 250 gallons of gasoline, and when York made landfall an hour later after 470 uneventful miles across the Sea of Japan, there would not have been fuel remaining to loiter anyplace very long, nor did he. "I didn't want to land in Korea," Ski recounted. "I knew Korea was part of Japan in those days. When we made landfall, I just turned up the coast and flew on until our fuel started getting pretty low."

In fact, he flew about twenty miles northwest along the coast, later claiming he wanted to make certain it was Russia, not the Korean Peninsula, but this also is obfuscation. The extreme northern edge of Korea was another seventy to eighty miles farther west—at least another half hour of flying. Also, with Sado Island as an exact landmark, Nolan Herndon was able to precisely calculate the heading to Cape Povorotnyy, the closest piece of Soviet territory they would encounter. The heading difference between Korea and the cape would have been twenty-five to thirty degrees—an error that York, Herndon, or Emmens would not make.

Far more certain is that York had planned on landfall at Cape Povorotnyy, but when he arrived it wasn't clear if the spit of land off his nose was the correct spot, so he turned right, to the northwest. This made perfect sense from the Korean point of view, if one accepts that two pilots and a navigator followed a thirty-degree incorrect heading for eighty miles farther than planned, but that theory holds no water. However, it is logical that from one hundred feet over the water, a pilot getting his first look at such a landmark could not absolutely determine if the rocky shoreline was Cape Povorotnyy or Cape Sysoyeva, thirty-five miles farther west. A pilot *would* turn right, figuring that if it was the latter, the bay he was looking for would quickly appear, and if the former, he would know in twenty miles or so, because there would be no bay.

In this case, it was Cape Povorotnyy.

There was no large bay after York turned right, so he turned around and headed back toward Povorotnyy. But why did this matter? They were plainly not in the area close to Vladivostok, where York later insisted he was heading, so what were they looking for? What bay in that area, sixty-five miles east of Vladivostok, was he trying to locate, and why?

Nakhodka. Also known as American Bay.

In fact, another obscure sentence buried in the U.S. Army intelligence memorandum unambiguously admits that Plane 8 "landed at an airfield on American Bay." York never intended to land near Vladivostok any more than he intended to bomb Tokyo. Short on fuel as they were, Ski would not have flown up and down the coast unless he was looking for a specific area, which he found. York reveals that he landed the bomber "at an airfield on American Bay," which is Nakhodka Bay, "about *forty miles* from Vladivostok." In fact, American Bay is closer to sixty miles east of the city, and the only airfield that fits the description was Unashi Aerodrome, which is eleven miles north of the bay on the Partizanskaya River.* Incidentally, this neatly matches the cryptic description given of a "fair sized river" at the head of a bay, which is not an obvious feature anywhere around Vladivostok. Unashi also would fit York's account of an air*field*, not a runway, in a valley, as would the description of Russians dressed in black coats, with "flat black caps with ribbons in the back and blue lettering on the bands."

This was the uniform of the Russian Naval Infantry, and the field was therefore a Russian naval airfield. Unashi's location makes this a certainty, as it was closer to the Sea of Japan than the bases near Vladivostok. York himself specifies that the Soviet officer who visited them later that night was not an army colonel but rather a "naval colonel." American Bay was selected because from the maps he procured in Washington, from Hap Arnold or Army G-2, York knew there was a base less than fifteen miles up the valley. Had this not been known in advance, there was no reason to turn north, ninety degrees away from Vladivostok, and fly to Unashi. Verifying its condition, its infrastructure or lack thereof, and its suitability for USAAF use against the Japanese islands was a central objective of Plane 8's mission. Unashi was also far enough from Vladivostok and the prying eyes of Soviet officials that Ski believed he could bluff the surprised local Russians into simply refueling the bomber and letting it continue. In any event, he certainly would not have risked fuel at such a critical juncture had he not already known of the airfield.

Unashi is not a place one finds by accident—especially from a few hundred feet up over unfamiliar, marginally mapped terrain. Gasoline was now very short, and a competent pilot would never

---

* This became Zolotaya-Dolina air base from 1951 to 1998.

arbitrarily head off in a random direction hoping to discover a place to land, especially when there were known airfields fifty miles farther near Vladivostok. York explicitly names American Bay, and this is corroborated by Russian historian Boris Egorov, who writes of the incident, "It was only at half past five in the afternoon, after the American warplane had appeared over Unashi military airfield a few dozen kilometers from the port of Nakhodka."

A final photo was taken of York's bomber by the Russians before it was confiscated by the Red Air Force. According to Walter Kurilchyk, an amateur sleuth who made the Mitchell's fate a sixteen-year hobby, "After landing in Russia, it was flown 107 hours. It was used to shuttle mail and military personnel [in Russia]. Then it was overhauled with two new engines and flown [back] to a station in Unashi, in eastern Russia."

As with everything regarding Plane 8's mission, deception and obfuscation were vital components, not only during the original flight but also during the decades following the flight. No one has satisfactorily answered why one of the spare crews that made the trip west to California did not substitute in for Bates and Roloson, nor is there an explanation except that York had to go on the mission. This is also why the sixteenth Mitchell was added at Alameda. Doolittle always said he was not certain how many bombers would fit on the *Hornet's* flight deck, but this is nonsensical. With a doctorate from MIT, Jimmy was quite capable of figuring out the flight deck's available square footage, and since he required 350 feet for his takeoff, he would know how many B-25s could fit in the remaining space, angled outboard and parked staggered nose to tail.* Like York's crew, the sixteenth plane was added, seemingly by chance at

---

* *Hornet's* flight deck was 814' x 86'; therefore, with 350' subtracted out, 39,904 square feet remained. Staggering sixteen bombers was not an issue, thanks to the Navy's expertise in making use of every square inch of available deck space.

the last minute, because Doolittle knew he was one bomber short; York would not be over Tokyo, and Jimmy needed five flights of three aircraft to cover the listed targets.

Deception.

The Mitchell's sudden appearance over the Maritime Territory brings up yet another series of opaque details and obfuscation from this extraordinary flight. These elements are amplified by two contradictory reports later made to Army intelligence and York's own oral history. The first document is the combined debriefing from the *entire* crew under the auspices of the assistant chief of air staff, intelligence, on June 3, 1943 (see appendix one). This lengthy interview was conducted by ten Army officers, the majority with operations or intelligence backgrounds, though two men represented the historical division, so this account was quite obviously being preserved for posterity.

Interestingly, in this document the McClellan carburetor incident was covered first, before any other facet of the crew's mission or internment. York stuck to his story, emphatically making the point that the only reason he had to divert was due to the increased fuel consumption and that the first time he knew about the switch was aboard the *Hornet*. When queried about crossing into Japanese airspace, he disingenuously said, "We made our landfall and should have been in the area of our target in about 20 to 25 minutes . . . we still hadn't spotted Tokyo itself." Which was true; he had not spotted Tokyo because Plane 8 was fifty miles north of the city going in the other direction.

Only York and Emmens were in on the airborne portion of the plan, and they did not reveal anything more than the other three crew members had experienced. In fact, the entire document is a recitation of the party-line story that would be told again and again over the decades. The gunner and engineer would not have been able to piece together what truly happened, and they believed what they were told. In any event, sergeants don't question captains and aircraft commanders, so even if they had doubts nothing would have been said. The navigator, Lieutenant Nolan Herndon, was a different matter. He was not part of Arnold's plan, and was never told about it. Yet he could read a map and was quite aware the pilots were flying nowhere near the planned targets. He would also have known that the tip of Primorsky Krai was not the Muravyov-Amursky Peninsula containing Vladivostok.

What transpired between the navigator and the pilots has never been revealed, but Herndon figured out fairly quickly that York was executing his own plan independent of the raid on Tokyo. Years later, the navigator put the question directly to Jimmy Doolittle, who answered, "I'll tell you one thing, Herndon: I didn't send you there." Lieutenant Tom Griffin also stated in later years, "I guess we will never find out if the State Department or the Secret Service set up 'Ski' York for a special secret mission. It is my belief that his clandestine mission instructions were never put in writing."

The second document is an interview compiled in memorandum form for the Army Air Forces director of intelligence, and the interviewee is Major Edward York—alone (see appendix one). There is no discussion of carburetors or not being able to find Tokyo. In this document, York specifically mentions Utsunomiya, American Bay, and the nearby airfield. Most of this memorandum is an assessment of the Russians, both collectively and individually, the conditions of the country, Stalin, and the crew's itinerary over their eighteen-month internment. This document contains the truth, not the cover story, and deals with some of the questions Ski was sent to answer regarding Soviet ability and capabilities. This needed to be in the official record, and it is quite revealing that the interview is conducted solely with York, and not for one of the lesser departments, but for the director of Army intelligence.

With the luxury of examining all the available documents, and with a combat pilot's experience as to what is probable and improbable, a clear pattern emerges. It is important to note that even if the deception was penetrated, after 1943 it was a moot point. Still, the stories published for public consumption were, in modern eyes, contradictory and woefully unbelievable. In the first interview with military intelligence, York specifically states he landed at a base "40 kilometers north" of Vladivostok, after overflying one field. The only two fields that fit this description within forty kilometers of the city are Uglovoye and Knevichi. Yet this begs the same question, if fuel was so tight, why would he overfly a suitable place to land? He would not, because he was never close to Vladivostok, nor would an American pilot in 1942 measure distance in kilometers.

Deception.

At first it seemed possible that York and Emmens simply misidentified their location. This would be all too easy after their extremely long day and the poor quality of their maps. Yet the subsequent comments by York identifying American Bay and the very vague descriptions of their actual location negate that assertion. Emmens writes that they were flying over an "inlet, or bay," but even with their inaccurate maps the pilots would have been aware of the obvious size difference between this bay and those bordering Vladivostok and the Muravyov-Amursky Peninsula. Nakhodka, or American Bay, is approximately six miles wide and ten miles inland. Ussuriyski Bay, east of Vladivostok, is at least twenty miles wide and thirty miles deep, while Amurskiy Bay to the west is nine miles wide and some twenty miles deep. Even one thousand feet up, York and Emmens would have recognized that they were not close to Vladivostok.

Obfuscation.

Emmens also claimed in *Guests of the Kremlin* that York had never made a simulated carrier takeoff, yet that was not true. "I had done two or three of those short takeoffs," Ski recounted, "and that is enough. You don't have to do 500 to be proficient. It is not all that big a deal to tell the truth." Emmens knew this, of course, but the conversation took place over the bomber's intercom, so the rest of the crew heard it. This also was another layer of the cover story that, if ever repeated, would add substance to York's "last minute" inclusion in the raid.

Deception.

Unquestionably, landing near American Bay *was* the plan, so why was this important to Hap Arnold? Undoubtably, his reasons were based on pressure from Roosevelt regarding a second air front against the Japanese and the level of expected Soviet cooperation. Hap's brother Tom Arnold had worked as a field engineer in the Soviet Union during the 1920s, when Stalin desperately required foreign expertise to build infrastructure—especially airfields. Convinced the Russians would never let him return to the United States, Tom escaped from the Soviet Union one dark winter's night by walking across frozen Lake Ladoga into Finland. What he had seen, and what he knew of Russia, was passed along to his brother, including the existence of aerodromes and rail and port facilities near Vladivostok.

Yet this data was more than fifteen years old by April 1942, and Arnold would need to know the exact field location north of American Bay, and whether there was an actual concrete runway or simply grass. Was there room for additional runways to be built, as well as hangars, with support buildings and billets? What type of roads and/or railways ran into the area from Vostochny Port on American Bay? Were any deep-draft vessels visible in the bay that might give an indication of how deep it was? Were there wharfs and dockyard facilities, and how close was the railhead? Answering these questions was the reason the Mitchell purposely came in over the bay rather than simply hopping the ridgeline into the valley. Both Ed York and Bob Emmens were capable of gathering viable intelligence from a brief look at the area.

The remote location was another consideration in choosing Unashi. Such a base would be easier for the Americans to secure and, if the port was suitable, to resupply without having to depend on Vladivostok. It would also be easier for Plane 8 to fly out of as they planned to do. The sudden appearance of an American bomber would take the Soviets by surprise, so York would have a better chance of capitalizing on the confusion to get fuel and simply depart again from Unashi rather than the center of power in Vladivostok. In fact, this was likely the plan, as Bob Emmens related Ed York wanted to continue on that very night, even after flying nine hours. Both men realized, or had been briefed, that the longer they remained in the Soviet Union the greater the risks—of detainment or even being turned over to the Japanese. A quick drop in, with a fast refueling and departure, stood a good chance of success as long as the local Russians were caught off guard and remained so.

The Soviet reactions at the local level and within the Kremlin would reveal much—and they did. Due to the unexpected internment, whatever York and Emmens learned would not make its way back to Washington soon, but the fact they *were* interned told Arnold, and Roosevelt, part of what they needed to know. There would be no second front against Japan from the Soviet Union because the Russians were more concerned with a Japanese threat to their east than with cooperating in a full Anglo-Soviet alliance to defeat Japan. Stalin's reluctance to openly fight kept the specter of a separate peace with Tokyo alive and well, yet this may have been a blessing in the end. The Americans were forced to assume they would receive no material Allied assistance in the Pacific War, so if victory was to be achieved, then their force of arms would have to do it alone.

There was China, of course, but at the national political level she was an unreliable ally. The courage and fortitude of the Chinese people saved most of the raiders, and the civilians paid for it with their lives, but their leaders were a separate matter—the raid also made that clear. Chiang Kai-shek was not to be trusted, and it was evident that as soon as the conflict was over, China would once again descend into civil war. So, Washington decided to let America's "allies" in the Far East serve a passive but essential role by pinning down a million Japanese soldiers and preying on Tokyo's fear of what China or the Soviet Union *might* do. In the meantime, the United States would leapfrog up the Pacific to Japan's front door, while Tokyo was always forced to look over its shoulder at the Asian continent.

As with Utsunomiya in Japan, without prior knowledge York could not have identified this obscure, specific location off American Bay to Colonel Johnston in 1943. The fact that he did so, expecting that such an intelligence debrief would remain classified, reveals the most significant facet of his assignment: landing at Unashi was preplanned, ergo the entire mission to the Soviet Union was not accidental but undertaken by request. Within the Army Air Forces there was only one man with enough reason to do so and enough authority to make such a request a reality—that man was Hap Arnold.

After the internment surprise, Ed York and his crew were loaded back into the three automobiles they had arrived in, and the little cavalcade moved off into the clear, cold night. Though dark and unlit, by the faint moon and the vehicle's single headlight Emmens saw a run-down industrial town of unpaved streets pocked with holes, clogged with horse-drawn carts, and shabby people "dressed in rags," who stared at them. High fences were everywhere and seemed to be the most substantial construction in the town, though men periodically stopped to urinate against them. If this was the workers' paradise, then what must their hell look like? "Occasionally," he wrote, "we saw a man or a woman gnawing at a three- or four-inch slice of very black bread."

Bob Emmens was uneasy, as was Nolan Herndon. The Russians obviously considered the crew a liability and were not going to release them, and now they were driving off into the night far inside the Soviet Union. They were faced with that hollow, helpless feeling experienced by those who are thousands of miles from safety, deep in a foreign country, and at the mercy of others. Despite the dangers, until now there had been a connection with their lives, their mission, and their own country—Plane 8 itself. The *Hornet*, even while it brought them closer to Japan, was still America, and over Japan the crew had the Mitchell and thus, to some degree, control of their own fate. Even at Unashi the bomber was there, not too far away, and with it the illusion that they could still return to the freedom and safety of the sky. But it was chillingly apparent that this had been an illusion; reality was that there were armed Russians in all three cars and a darkness folding in around the car as Khabarovsk vanished behind them.

"I wish we had been shown some proof that our people in Moscow really did know we were here," Emmens said, taking a deep, steady breath.

Herndon was staring at the last row of unpainted wooden fences and the nearest tower, where a heavily overcoated guard stood, rifle across his chest. "Yeah . . . I do too," he replied quietly. "These people could stop anywhere along here, stand us up against a tree, shoot us, dig a hole . . . and no one would ever know the difference."

# 9

## LOOSE ENDS

While Plane 8 bombed Japan and landed in the Soviet Union, the Imperial Japanese Navy General Staff put its finishing touches on Operation Mo: the conquest of Australian New Guinea and the capture of Port Moresby. This would place most of Australia, including Darwin and Brisbane, within range of Japanese land-based bombers. Another arm of the operation would strike southeast into the Solomon Islands, occupying Tulagi, then establish an airfield on a delphic speck of ground few could name: Guadalcanal.

Once complete, the airfield would allow Japanese aircraft to control the surrounding area for a thousand miles in all directions and open further advances toward Fiji and New Caledonia. If these last islands fell, the sea route to North America would be severed and Australia completely isolated. As York's crew pondered their fate in Khabarovsk, two Japanese submarines put into the Imperial Navy's port in Rabaul, New Britain, to report the area south of New Guinea, named the Coral Sea, free of Allied warships.

They were dead wrong.

Six weeks earlier, while Doolittle and York were working out details of their Tokyo raid, the U.S. Navy Office of Naval Communications had deciphered enough of the Japanese JN-25B code to read 15 percent of the Combined Fleet's encrypted messages. By April, while *Hornet* steamed west toward Japan, American code breakers had divined Port Moresby as the next enemy target, and Admiral Chester Nimitz saw an opportunity. On April 29, he dispatched Task Force 11, commanded by Rear Admiral Aubrey Fitch and centered on the carrier *Lexington*, to the Coral Sea south of the Solomon Islands. Rear Admiral Frank Jack Fletcher's Task Force 17 and the *Yorktown* was already en route, and both planned to rendezvous with Task Force 44, a joint surface battle fleet of three heavy cruisers with three destroyers commanded by Australian Rear Admiral John Crace. Finally, Bull Halsey's Task Force 16, with *Enterprise* and *Hornet*, had safely returned to Pearl Harbor but was immediately refueled and sortied for the Coral Sea to join the other two American carriers.

On May 1, the Imperial Japanese Navy Carrier Strike Force, consisting of the carriers *Zuikaku* and *Shōkaku* and eight warships, departed Truk for the Coral Sea. On May 3 the Japanese captured Tulagi, which was undefended, and began converting it into a seaplane base while, some twenty miles across Savo Sound, they began building a runway on Guadalcanal that would shape the course of the Pacific war. The following day eleven Japanese transports carrying a five-thousand-man invasion force left Rabaul headed for Port Moresby via the Solomon Sea. By now, with the exception of Halsey's two carriers, the Allied task forces had rendezvoused and steamed farther west into the Coral Sea. After some near misses, the first battle fought entirely beyond visual range of its opponents was joined in earnest on May 7, and both fleets would claw at each other until the next afternoon.

By evening on May 8, a mortally wounded *Lexington* was scuttled, sinking in over fourteen thousand feet to rest on the floor of the Coral Sea. *Yorktown* was badly damaged, but limped back to Pearl Harbor trailing oil and rounded Hospital Point for Drydock Number One on May 27, 1942. The Japanese lost the light carrier

*Shōhō*, and both sides more or less broke even on aircraft and air-crew losses. Though they could replace aircraft, the Japanese had never considered it possible to lose so many trained pilots and did not have an adequate replacement training system in place—nor would they. *Zuikaku* had lost fully half of her air group and steamed for Japan in an attempt to replenish her aviators. *Shōkaku* was so critically damaged that she also headed slowly home, barely making it into Kure. Though the Japanese arguably won a tactical victory, the Port Moresby invasion force was ordered back to Rabaul without landing its troops. That, plus two fleet carriers put out of service for Yamamoto's next operation, gave the Americans a resounding strategic victory.

York and his crew departed Khabarovsk on April 29, the same day Nimitz sent his carriers into the Coral Sea. While the great sea battle raged 4,500 miles to the south, the five Americans began a painfully slow, 4,700-mile trek across the Soviet Union via the Trans-Siberian Railway. Hunched down in unheated, dirty, and sparsely furnished cars, they had little to do all day except watch Russia unfold before them, drink rough potato vodka, and play chess. During their two days at Khabarovsk, York gave considerable thought to swimming across the Amur River into China at night. It was only 600–1,000 yards wide and appeared slow-moving. Fast or slow, wide or narrow, Ski reckoned he'd have a better chance now before he became physically weaker and geographically deeper into the Soviet Union. The thought was intoxicating: he could have his crew on "friendly" territory in a matter of hours. Surely, the Chinese would allow contact with the U.S. ambassador, and surely the Chinese were cleaner. Well, he didn't know about that, but they certainly would smell better than the Russians. At any rate, he could be in China quickly, since Khabarovsk was less than five miles from the provincial border at Heilongjiang.

But they were closely watched. Not exactly prisoners, but hardly free. York got the impression from his escort, a Russian lieutenant, that if the Americans escaped or caused trouble of any sort, then their escorts would bear the brunt of it. In point of fact, there was no way to escape, and as the Trans-Siberian railcars shuffled away from Khabarovsk late in the evening of April 29, the whole crew was aboard. Heading northwest to Tynda, this was the beginning of an arc around Manchuria and Mongolia, then past Lake Baikal to Bratsk. The railroad was single-track, the unheated cars unfurnished, and the monotonous boredom was stupefying. Playing chess, writing letters they hoped to send, and talking, Plane 8's crew was somewhere between Krasnoyarsk and Novosibirsk above the Mongolian border when *Lexington* went down in the Coral Sea.

"Everyone we saw, on and off the train, was in rags," Emmens recalled. "Everyone . . . in every station we passed seemed to be a pauper." Each day the train lumbered westward with the Americans receiving a valuable look at Russia's interior, and visible proof of communism's reality. Times were hard due to the war, but these people looked as if they had always lived this way. Stopping in Omsk near the Kazakhstan border, Bob Emmens especially noted the children begging pitifully for food. "Bands of them dressed in absolute tatters, no shoes, and covered with filth." Armed soldiers on the platforms swiped at them with their rifle butts.

The Russian officers accompanying the crew warned them explicitly about giving food away to anyone as there were not enough soldiers to deal with an angry, desperate mob. "It is bad . . . very dangerous. It must only be given to those who deserve to have it." York took that to mean those in combat deserved food, yet the Russians with them certainly were not fighting, and they ate heartily at every meal. Black bread, red caviar, and vodka—though sometimes there was some type of dubiously canned meat. Doubts grew as the miles passed by. Obviously, they were not going to be quietly shot someplace and left to rot in a ditch, yet the Soviets were notoriously fond of imprisoning those they did not murder but could not keep in plain sight. Once the train turned west after Tynda, York breathed a bit easier knowing they were not heading for Siberia.

He had been assured the U.S. government was aware of their location; after all, Washington had agreed to the internment. York was also told they would be able to meet with Americans from the embassy once their final destination was reached, but he did not believe either statement. "Very quickly," Ski recalled, "I made up my mind that whatever they told you, if anything, wouldn't be necessarily true or correct. It is just a way of life to those people."

The Russian lieutenant was fond of exhorting the virtues of the Soviet Union, despite the daily visual contradictions the Americans observed. He picked up newspapers at each station, and would practice his English by translating stories from *Ivestia*, *Red Star*, and *Pravda* to his captive audience. The articles were all variations on the same theme: the unconquerable Red Army was destroying the Hitlerite rat invaders on all fronts and driving them out of Russia through a series of brilliant campaigns.

The truth was drastically different.

Stalin believed the German halt before Christmas was due to his prowess and the skill of his fighting men rather than bad weather and overstretched logistics. As the ground dried and the weather warmed, 765,000 Russians began an offensive from their bridgehead at Izium on the Donets River in Ukraine. Marshal Simyon Timoshenko drove far enough west to create a salient between the German 6th and 17th Armies south of Kharkov, but he overestimated his capabilities while underestimating his enemy. Friedrich Paulus let the Russians lunge, then closed in around their flanks with a massive air, artillery, and armored counterattack that cut off the Soviet 9th, 57th, and 6th Armies. As York's crew trundled west toward the Urals, 170,958 Red Army soldiers were killed, went missing, or became prisoners of war, while another 106,232 were wounded in action. Three complete Russian field armies were annihilated, leaving the Germans free to advance toward the Caucasus and its desperately needed oil fields. Only one final obstacle stood in their way: a city on the Volga River called Stalingrad.

Ed York knew nothing of this, nor, in all likelihood, did his escorts. By mid-May the train was approaching Yekaterinburg in the Urals, where Tsar Nicholas and his family were murdered in 1918. Here at last the Americans were told they were headed to Kuybyshev, 480 miles away on the west side of the mountains, where Stalin evacuated his government during October 1941. This seemed to be good news, as the remaining foreign embassies, including that of the United States, had also relocated to the city. The Russian officer said he would contact the U.S. embassy, and Plane 8's crew was hopeful that this would get them off the train and finally back in American hands.

Pulling into Kuybyshev at 0530 on May 18, York asked to leave the train and go see the defense attaché at the embassy, but the lieutenant refused. "It is unwise and unsafe for you to go into towns. You see, we have many Japs in our country and we must protect you from them." That wasn't quite believable, but the crew was certain that if they couldn't get to the embassy, at least the Russians would bring the attaché to the train. They put on what clean clothes were available, shined their shoes, and made a list of things that were running short of, like soap, toothpaste, and shaving cream. The men also carefully put together the letters they'd written so the embassy could send them home to their loved ones. Then they waited.

And waited.

All day the train sat on the siding and the Americans watched the crowded platform. As with every other station, this one was "crowded with the poorest, hungriest, and saddest looking people we'd ever seen," Emmens recalled. No one ever came from the embassy, and about ten hours after he'd left, the lieutenant reappeared, stinking of vodka and flushed from a hot steam bath. Both pilots cornered him and asked if he'd contacted the embassy. "No," he seemed surprised by their anger. "Why should I?"

At sunset the train lurched forward, and after crossing the Volga River made its way west out of Kuybyshev. This incident hardened York's feelings toward the Russians, and from then on he took whatever they said with less than a grain of salt. "They can be friendly, even generous," he recounted. "But don't take that to mean they wouldn't turn on you and stab you in the back or cut your throat. I wouldn't trust any one of them as an individual or collectively. You have to make up your mind that that is the way it is."

All night long they continued west, and during the following late afternoon the Americans were told they would be arriving at their destination in about an hour. Crossing the Sura River, the train pulled into Penza on May 19, 1942, and stopped. There was no station. Their car, the last on the train, was disconnected and tugged onto a siding, where four dilapidated automobiles and a half dozen Soviet officers waited. The newcomers smiled and everyone shook hands while the crew's baggage was transferred to the vehicles. York was told they would be going to a "pleasant village which contains rest homes where Soviet officers are assigned for rest periods." Pleasant. Both pilots doubted that, given what they'd seen so far, but there was no discussion or choice in the matter. Ski asked the name of the place, and a Soviet captain answered, "Okhuna . . . a small village about fifteen kilometers from the city of Penza."

And that was that.

It was a small village—about five hundred people. Living far below the poverty level, the villagers were all emaciated from hunger or malnutrition, and "rags constituted their clothing." For the next two and a half months, York and his men would be generally confined to a three-building compound surrounded, as always, by a high, sturdy fence. The house had been whitewashed, so it appeared in better condition than it was, and the bedrooms were large with a large open porch on three sides. The inside was unpainted but boasted the mandatory busts of Lenin and Stalin, and the food was a vast improvement. Unlimited black bread, of course, but also fresh vegetables, butter, and meat—and vodka. Lots of vodka. Several women cooked and cleaned, and the crew watched Russian movies and learned local folk dances and a game called "Garrotky."*

There had still been no word about contact with the embassy. However, on June 3 their Russian escorts were quite excited that the commander of the Volga Military District was paying a call the following day.† Accompanied by two colonels, Lieutenant General Stepan Kalinin arrived at 1230 on June 9, 1942. Shaking hands with each American, he seemed cordial enough, and his chief concern was their treatment. Ski told him through the interpreter that the quarters were fine, but they weren't allowed outside the compound except to visit the bathhouse. Kalinin apologized and quietly berated the escort, who then told York they would certainly be permitted to swim in a nearby river if they wished.‡ He also told Ski that he would be happy to convey any messages to the U.S. embassy. Cheered considerably, but always cautious, York and Emmens hoped to speak to another American and at last have their families informed. Embassy officers would also hopefully know about the other raiders, and certainly tell them what was happening in the world beyond Russia.

The day after York was told of the upcoming visit by General Kalinin, a battle was joined six thousand miles away in the Central Pacific that altered the Pacific War. Admiral Yamamoto had conceived an operation that he believed, and certainly hoped, would finish off the U.S. Pacific Fleet. Time, he well knew, was running out for Japan's su-

---

* Gorodki. This is an old Russian folk sport, much like combining horseshoes with bowling. From forty-three feet, clubs are pitched at targets made from stacked or arranged wooden pins. Whoever knocks them down with the fewest throws wins the game.

† Emmens incorrectly states the "Penza Military District," but here was no such administrative area in 1942 Soviet Russia. Of the sixteen districts, Penza was included within the Volga area of responsibility.

‡ The Sura River.

premacy in the Pacific, and the admiral needed to decide the matter now before America's vast military production capability mirrored its rage. The Battle of the Coral Sea had cracked the Imperial Navy's cult of invincibility, but it was the audacious and embarrassing Doolittle Raid that worried him the most since it conclusively revealed the Home Island's vulnerability to air attack. If the Americans could do this now, five months after Pearl Harbor, what would they do once their shipyards and factories reached full capacity?

Thus, Operation MI was born. The plan centered on taking Midway Island, which would extend Japan's defensive perimeter and, more important, lure the U.S. Pacific Fleet into battle, where this time it would be destroyed. With no navy to protect the West Coast, Washington would have to consider a negotiated peace, and Japan would be safe to consolidate its newly acquired resource-rich territorial gains. With America neutralized, Tokyo could concentrate on subduing China and, perhaps, the Far East Soviet Union. But the admiral's plan, like most imperial plans, had an overarching flaw: it would work only if the enemy did exactly what was expected, and this was a dangerous assumption when dealing with Americans.

Yamamoto, who, from his time in the United States should have known better, underestimated his opponent and had not absorbed the lessons from Wake Island and the Coral Sea. Also, he knew the *Saratoga* was in California but incorrectly believed the *Yorktown* had been sunk in the Coral Sea, so he would have planned to face only *Enterprise* and *Hornet*. He did not order the surviving aircraft from *Shōkaku* and *Zuikaku* to combine and sail with the latter, and with four of his six fleet carriers remaining, the admiral considered the risk justifiable.* Nor did Yamamoto know that Admiral Nimitz had three thousand workers swarm aboard *Yorktown* upon her arrival at Pearl Harbor and that she was back at sea in seventy-two hours. Most

---

* Imperial doctrine was to keep aircraft organic to each carrier, while the Americans regarded air groups as interchangeable between carriers.

damning, he did not suspect that the JN-25B code had been compromised. Nimitz and Rear Admiral Ray Spruance, who commanded Task Force 16, made an educated tactical guess and placed *Enterprise* and *Hornet* northeast of Midway to ambush the Combined Fleet. Joined by *Yorktown*, the three American carriers watched and waited.

Yamamoto's First Mobile Striking Force, again commanded by Admiral Nagumo, appeared northwest of Midway as expected and launched a 108-aircraft strike that was detected on the island's radar at 0535 on the morning of June 4, 1942. Of the available Marine fighters, only two remained flyable after trying to blunt the attack, yet the Japanese assault did not neutralize the island's runway or defenses. A second strike was called for, which was unexpected, thus forcing Nagumo to adjust his plan. Little did he know, the Americans had launched an attack from *Enterprise* and *Hornet*, and they were now searching for the Japanese carriers northwest of Midway. Rearming his reserve aircraft with bombs, Nagumo was informed at 0740 that a scout plane had just sighted the U.S. fleet. The admiral countermanded his original rearming order and switched back to torpedoes in order to attack the American warships.

Launched piecemeal in order to catch the Japanese unawares, the U.S. strike did not assemble for a coordinated assault. This was expeditious, but forced each of the three torpedo squadrons to attack individually, and they were annihilated. Only seven of thirty-one Devastator torpedo bombers survived, and there were no hits on the Japanese carriers. However, their sacrifice accomplished three critical items. First, the enemy carriers could not recover or launch while under attack; second, due to Nagumo's dithering, explosive ordnance was stacked haphazardly about and completely exposed. Fuel lines snaked across each flight deck, also terribly vulnerable to any sort of attack. Finally, the combat air patrol (CAP) protecting the carriers was not well controlled, so the Zero fighters were now all down at low altitude, out of fuel and ammunition.

When the dive-bomber squadrons from all three American

carriers suddenly appeared overhead, there was little the Japanese could do to prevent an attack. Within six minutes *Kaga*, *Akagi*, and *Sōryū* were afire and burning out of control. Only *Hiryū* remained undamaged, and she immediately launched a twenty-four-aircraft strike that followed the U.S. aircraft back to the *Yorktown*. Sixteen of *Hiryū*'s aircraft were shot down by anti-aircraft fire and the CAP's Wildcat fighters, but three managed to hit the big carrier, which left her drifting and ablaze. But U.S. Navy damage control was second to none, and she had partial power restored by the time *Hiryū*'s second wave of sixteen aircraft appeared.

Though they lost nearly half the strike force, the Japanese got two torpedoes into *Yorktown*, which again left her adrift. Later that day, *Hiryū*'s luck finally ran out as twenty-four U.S. dive-bombers from *Enterprise* and *Yorktown* put four bombs into the flattop causing her to sink within hours. The following day, *Yorktown* was under tow and despite her horrific damage, looked to be clear of the battle when she was spotted by *I-168* and took a pair of Long Lance torpedoes. The valiant veteran hung on through the night but rolled over and sank at 0530 on Sunday, June 7, 1942.

In the end, the Imperial Navy lost 3,057 men, including 110 aviators and over 700 highly trained mechanics and technicians that could not be easily replaced from a largely rural, agrarian population. Four of her six fleet carriers were gone forever, as well as a heavy cruiser and 248 combat aircraft. The U.S. Navy lost *Yorktown*, the destroyer *Hammann*, 157 aircraft, and 307 men killed in action. The Battle of Midway represents one of those points in any conflict that are termed pivotal, though an analysis of why is largely beyond the scope of this work.* Nonetheless, the battle's ramifications reverberated through the next twelve to eighteen months, because the Japanese no longer had the same options after losing four fleet carriers in a single battle.

---

\* Reference Parshall and Tully's *Shattered Sword* for the authoritative analysis of the battle.

Also, an oft overlooked facet of the loss was that the Imperial Navy concealed the disaster from the Imperial Army, which continued to plan and operate assuming the full weight of naval support was available. This would, especially in the upcoming Solomon Islands campaign, cost them dearly.

York's crew certainly did not know about the victory, but the rest of the world found out on the same Sunday that *Yorktown* sank. The *Los Angeles Examiner* headline proclaimed:

## US FLEET CHASING JAPS
## TO STRIKE KNOCKOUT BLOW!

Several articles followed, but the most realistic appraisal read:

> Whatever the eventual result may show in terms of respective losses in the opposing forces, one thing was certain. That is that for the time being, at least, the United States retains a firm grip on its westernmost stronghold in the mid-Pacific, Midway Island, 1,149 miles northwest of Hawaii.

Even with the journalistic hyperbole, the event was noted by the Soviets with intense interest and included in their calculus regarding the crew of Plane 8. If the Japanese were truly unstoppable, and if they had inflicted a crippling loss at Midway, Stalin might have been more inclined to deal with Tokyo. However, the irrefutable fact that the Empire had been knocked back on its heels may have saved the lives of York and his crew—or, at the least, encouraged Moscow to consider shortening their internment.

Three days following General Kalinin's visit, the Russian lieutenant hurried in and informed them that "People from your embassy in Moscow are on their way to see you!" Tremendously excited, York and his crew again cleaned up, shined shoes, and got their letters together. Maybe this was it. Maybe they were coming to take the crew to the embassy. The two pilots desperately wanted news of their babies; if they had been born, and were their wives all right? They all discussed the possibilities at length, and York reminded them all of the disappointment at Kuybyshev when no one showed up. It could happen again.

But it did not.

Three cars arrived bearing General Kalinin, several Soviet officers, and two Americans: Lieutenant Colonel Joseph A. "Mike" Michela, who was the embassy's military attaché, and Edward "Eddie" Page, the State Department's second secretary. The new arrivals brought cigarettes, clean shirts, socks, and soap. Page, who was fluent in Russian, also gave York an English-Russian dictionary. After the preliminary greetings and hand shaking all around, the two pilots were able to get Michela and Page alone, where the attaché immediately asked, "How long have you been here?" York was surprised at the question, and the colonel informed them that the embassy had been kept informed, Russian-style, of the crew's whereabouts. This meant he was told after they had been moved each time, but not before. Emmens and York were relieved to know that Michela knew of their presence in late April and that Ambassador Standley had promptly informed Washington. This *was* good news, and the pilots breathed easier knowing their families had not been living with uncertainty for two months. Both men were also told they were now fathers— York had a daughter and Emmens a son—and that their wives were just fine. The day was shaping up to be the best they'd had in the Soviet Union until the subject of going home was raised.

"Well ... getting out is not so easy. You see, these people are worried about a war in the east right now, and they are afraid that the Japs might be offended if you are released." York's suspicions were confirmed, and he asked about a possible solution. This time Page replied with, "I think we may be able to have you out of the country inside of two or three weeks." This wasn't great news, but at least it was light at the end of the tunnel. Unfortunately, lights in tunnels are often oncoming trains.

This light certainly was.

Barbarossa and the ensuing actions on the Eastern Front had drained Germany's fifty-six-million-barrel oil reserve to a dangerous level. Romania, Berlin's main source of imported oil, produced only eight million barrels annually, and the balance of the demand was being met by the production of synthetic oil from coal. In desperation, the Eastern Front's strategic objective now became what should have been Barbarossa's main focus: seizure of the Soviet Union's primary sources of oil deep within the Caucasus. These were Maikop, Grozny, and Baku, which itself was capable of 176 million barrels per year. Capture and operation of this field would be sufficient to maintain Germany's military machine on all fronts against all foes. "If I do not get the oil," Hitler stated, "then I must end this war."

Taking Moscow, or even the defeat of the Red Army, were no longer priorities, and Case Blue, the offensive into the southern Russia and the Caucasus, commenced on June 28, some six weeks after York's men arrived in Penza. The German Army Group South lunged southwest, and by July 5 the Fourth Panzer Army crossed the Don and was battling for Voronezh, just 266 miles southwest of Penza and Plane 8's crew. Capturing Voronezh would anchor the German north flank along the river and permit a drive into the Caucasus without threat of a Soviet counteroffensive. Unfortunately for the Germans, even this short advance had already outrun their logistical support, and fuel was extremely limited. Infuriated by this, Hitler dismissed Field Marshal Fedor von Bock, then split Army Group South into two new entities. Army Group A and the

First Panzer Army were to advance southwest for the Caucasian oil fields, while Army Group B would wheel east and cut the Russian supply lines at Stalingrad, near the confluence of the Don and Volga Rivers.

Despite capturing the plans for Case Blue in June, Stalin refused to initially consider this offensive was anything but a ruse. Moscow, he fervently believed, was still Hitler's main objective. Nevertheless, the chaos and indecision within the Red Army and Soviet command structure caused by the German move meant that the fate of Plane 8's crew was further delayed throughout the summer of 1942. Despite the German logistical woes, by the first week in August Army Group A was closing in on the oil field at Maikop, and 350 miles to the northeast the German 6th Army was less than sixty miles from Stalingrad. Once again, the situation looked bleak for the Soviet Union, and once again Stalin felt he could not afford Japan as another enemy at this point in the war. Fortunately, some seven thousand miles southeast of Stalingrad, another offensive was about to commence. This, too, would have profound consequences for the course of the war, and for five lonely Americans stranded in the Soviet Union.

Eight months to the day after Pearl Harbor, the heavy cruiser USS *Quincy* opened fire with her nine eight-inch guns from the Sealark Channel off the north coast of Guadalcanal in the Solomon Islands. On August 7, 1942, Operation Watchtower, the first American counteroffensive of the war, began with *Quincy's* shore bombardment and airstrikes from the carriers *Enterprise*, *Wasp*, and *Saratoga*. As they watched, a tepid breeze carried the island's stink of decaying coconuts, rotting vegetation, and dead fish to the 19,105 officers and men of the 1st Marine Division crammed into transports idling offshore. Except for the native Melanesians or a few planters and missionaries, no one had any use for Guadalcanal until a month earlier. On July 5, an Imperial Navy captain named Tei Monzen landed with 2,500 men of the 11th and 13th Construction Units to build an airfield on the only feature that made Guadalcanal valuable: a flat, central plain big enough for the 3,600-foot-long runway the Japanese planned.

Wearing new sage-green battle dress but armed with the same Springfield rifles their fathers carried during the Great War, the U.S. Marines clambered over their transport's sides and down to the Higgins boats bobbing below. At 0919, Lieutenant Colonel Bill Maxwell became the first American in forty-four years to lead an amphibious assault as his 1st Battalion, 5th Marines waded through the surf onto a stretch of beach near the mouth of the Tenaru River. The Japanese responded by dispatching a cruiser task force into the Sealark Channel around Savo Island to destroy the Allied surface ships gathered there and isolate the enemy beachhead. They were successful, and the American-Australian task force pulled out after losing four heavy cruisers and 1,077 men: the Marines were now alone on Guadalcanal—temporarily. This began a six-month cycle of hell on earth for the 1st and 2nd U.S. Marine Divisions, the 25th and Americal Divisions of the U.S. Army, and roughly thirty thousand men from the Imperial Japanese 17th Army.

Four days after the landings on Guadalcanal, York's crew was moved away from Penza, and thus from the Germans along the Don River. Four days northeast by rail though Kazan brought the men to the Kama River, where they took a ferry to a small village called Okhansk, about thirty-five miles southwest of Perm. York and Emmens discussed trying to escape but discounted it for the time being since they were too deep in Russia and had no idea where the Germans might be. The same week the crew arrived at Okhansk, the German 6th Army chased the Soviet 62nd and 64th Armies into Stalingrad, where they were stopped cold. Stukas, FW-190 fighters, and Ju-88 medium bombers of General Wolfram von Richthofen's Luftflotte 4 dropped one thousand tons of bombs in two days but could not dislodge the Russians.* Important only to the Germans as flank security for their thrust into the Caucasus, this battle would eventually involve nearly two million men on both sides. Through the long, dark autumn and winter of 1942, the immediate course of the Pacific War literally hung on the outcome of Guadalcanal, while the fate of Plane 8's crew was intertwined with the battle raging in Stalingrad.

For Ed York, the frustration mounted. He would not hear again from the U.S. embassy until September, and even suffering from scurvy and dysentery, they were permitted only a single visit by the embassy's physician. Playing volleyball and swimming, the men tried to remain as fit as possible, while the two pilots threw themselves into studying Russian and were rapidly becoming conversational. They were assigned several women to cook and clean, and one in particular, Zietseva, spoke English and helped with learning her language. In fact, she spoke English better than she should have and tried to seduce Bob Emmens, so it was quite likely she was an NVKD plant.

On September 15, a clean white river yacht showed up on the bank near their house, and among the Soviet officers were a pair of civilians and two Americans in uniform. Joseph Michela, now a brigadier general, was one of them. Eddie Page was there, and the second civilian was no less than Ambassador Standley. Surprisingly, the other officer was an Army pilot wearing the two stars of a major general. After a short tour they swapped news; York was congratulated on his promotion to major, and the general, whose name was Follett Bradley, informed them that none of the Doolittle raiders had been shot down over Japan. He said the Japanese "got one or two of the crews," but he did not know which ones were captured.

Bradley was unusual. Class of 1910 from the U.S. Naval Academy, he opted for a cross commission two years later into the Army

---

* Wolfram was a cousin of Manfred von Richthofen, the Red Baron of Great War fame.

Field Artillery. Bradley then earned his wings in 1916, and though he flew as a pilot during the Great War, he also fought during the Aisne Offensive as an artillery officer. Bradley had been in Russia since August waiting to meet Stalin on behalf of President Roosevelt—and Hap Arnold. Once alone with the pilots, Bradley informed them he was on a "special mission," as he put it, to conduct a survey of Far East airfields and secure Stalin's permission for a joint U.S.-USSR theater of operations. In effect, he was finishing what York started. The war was going badly enough for Moscow that this option was being seriously considered. Yet the Russians, always negotiators, wanted American and British intervention, specifically fighter aircraft, in the Caucasus to protect his oil fields. Stalin also wanted a second front opened in Europe immediately, which was not going to happen since the Americans were set to launch Operation Torch, the invasion of French North Africa, in early November.

With this news, the Russian treatment of his crew made sense to Ed York. Beyond the situation with the Japanese, he and his men were still a card Stalin could play, albeit a small card, to pressure Washington into meeting Moscow's demands. The visitors also filled them in on the Pacific War, specifically Guadalcanal. There had been several large naval battles, and the Marines were clinging to the island by their fingernails. As pilots, York and Emmens were keenly interested in the ragtag "Cactus" Air Force composed of Army and Marine fighter planes that were holding the Japanese at bay. More than ever, the two pilots felt frustrated at being kept out of the war.

Though it has never been recorded, undoubtedly York and Emmens passed along to Bradley and Standley the results of their own survey of the Soviet Far East. It is also logical to assume that procuring York's information was the reason the general made the difficult, dangerous, and uncomfortable trip into the Urals.* The same

* Incidentally, the diaries both Emmens and York had kept disappeared, so the possibility exists that these were given to Bradley, who passed them on to military intelligence.

was true for Standley; ambassadors rarely, if ever, stray far from the centers of power, and to make such an excursion during wartime is highly unusual and bespeaks of a highly significant reason for doing so. Collecting York's information, which was still the only current intelligence regarding the Maritime Territory and its suitability for military operations, would have been important enough to dictate such a journey.

The New Year arrived with no end in sight for York's crew. Drinking homemade vodka and listening to music from Moscow, the Americans ushered in 1943 by singing "Auld Lang Syne" to the Russians. Yet if the Americans stranded in Okhansk had little optimism for the coming year, there was some evidence that the winds of war were shifting, and the first week in February brought new hope to the Allies.

At Stalingrad, the Red Army had gradually sandwiched the 265,000-man German 6th Army into a pocket between the Don and Volga Rivers. Paulus recognized the danger and asked for permission to withdraw, but Hitler refused. Hermann Göring promised that his Luftwaffe could provide an "air bridge" of supplies but managed less than 15 percent of what was required. A breakout effort was initiated by Field Marshal von Manstein, but after getting to within thirty miles of the besieged 6th Army, this also failed. Retreating into the ruined city, the starving Germans held out until February 2, when their pocket collapsed under renewed Russian attacks. Only 91,000 Germans, Italians, Romanians, and Croatians remained to surrender and they, in company with twenty-two general officers, were herded off into captivity.*

This battle halted German offensives in the east and, in conjunction with Rommel's defeat in North Africa, ended the myth of the Wehrmacht's invincibility. The other significant outcome to the bat-

---

* Only 5,000–6,000 of these men survived over a decade of imprisonment, and returned to Germany in 1955.

tle was that the Soviet Union would hold out, against most expectations, and would not initiate a separate peace with Hitler. Tokyo, in particular, noted the battle's conclusion with trepidation. A Russia frightened and surrounded was one thing, but a triumphant and reenergized Red Army was something else entirely.

However, the Empire had other reasons to be concerned in February 1943. At three minutes past midnight on February 7, the last 1,796 emaciated Japanese soldiers were pulled aboard destroyers idling off Cape Esperance on Guadalcanal's northwestern tip. During the six-month-and-two-day campaign, the Imperial 17th Army put nearly 36,000 men ashore; 10,652 were evacuated, leaving 14,800 killed or missing and another 9,000 dead from starvation or disease. The Combined Fleet lost two battleships, a light carrier, and at least 1,000 highly trained aviators. American ground losses stood at 1,207 Marines killed, with 2,894 wounded, and the Army suffered 1,860 dead or wounded. In addition to 420 naval aviators lost, eight cruisers and fifteen destroyers went down, and the bitter fight claimed the carriers *Wasp* and *Hornet*. Launching Doolittle's raiders and surviving Midway, *Hornet* sank in October 1942, north of Guadalcanal off Santa Cruz, while York's crew languished 7,300 miles away in Okhansk.

Just as Stalingrad signaled the end of large-scale German offensive capabilities, Guadalcanal marked the furthest point of imperial expansion in the Pacific. Nevertheless, the Axis was far from beaten. German U-boats would sink five hundred thousand tons of shipping during the opening months of 1943, while the Wehrmacht still had 3 million men under arms, and the Imperial Japanese Army could field twenty-five divisions, another million men, from China. Two bloody years of fighting remained, though the Japanese would remain defensive behind their contracting perimeter as the full weight of American military might was brought to bear. The profound consequences of both battles had smaller, yet intensely personal, ramifications for the men of Plane 8. Japan's defeat removed the threat against the Far East Soviet Union, so an emboldened Stalin now felt he had little to fear from the Japanese and potentially much to gain by remaining with the Allies.

"Christ Bob," Ski York told Emmens, "do you realize that our future is not tied up with the war with the Germans but with the Japs?" True enough, since just six weeks after the American victory at Guadalcanal, "two well dressed, smart looking Russian officers" stepped in through the back door of the crew's house in Okhansk. A major and a captain, both from Moscow, had been sent to move York's men. By now both Bob and Ski were quite conversant in Russian, and after introductions the Soviet major asked when they could be ready to leave. Ski blinked and immediately replied, "One hour." The Russians laughed, but then realized he was deadly serious, and in an hour they were all on the road to Molotov.* Both Soviet officers were courteous, and even showed some humor, which was unexpected. They were "the healthiest Russian specimens we had seen since we had been in the country," Emmens wrote.

Put up in a hotel in Molotov, the crew was fitted with Soviet uniforms and taken to see the Kirov Ballet perform *Swan Lake*. From Molotov, they were flown to Ufa, then Chkalov, about seventy miles north of the Kazakh border.† Remaining here for two days, the five Americans then boarded a train with the Russian major, who was quite firm about placing them in very specific sleeping compartments. Strangely, Ed York was placed in one alone. "This was against all their practices," Ski stated, and he was immediately suspicious. More so when he discovered he was not alone. Several big pieces of luggage were tucked under the lower berth, and a leather satchel lay open on top revealing Maxwell House coffee, butter, and a tin of real American Spam—all in plain sight.

As the train pulled out heading south, a stocky Russian a few

---

* Known today as Perm, the city name was Molotov from 1940 to 1957.
† Chkalov is Orenburg.

years older than Ski appeared, and the two men introduced themselves. His name, he said, was Kolya, and he was an importer of goods to Russia, but based in Ashkhabad, the capital of Soviet Turkmenistan. Thus began a very odd nine-day trip through Tajikistan and Uzbekistan, always heading south. When Ed learned their destination was Ashkhabad, he was convinced that this "was a put-up job, completely." Kolya had an abundance of food, as if it was planned for two, and the pilot ate pickled sturgeon, caviar, various meats, and bread. Of course, the Russian also had vodka—enough for two for the entire trip. The Soviet officers, who brought along food for the other crew members, "never expressed any curiosity about the fact that I was eating all this good food that belonged to this so-called civilian. Well," York added, "of course it was all laid on."

Kolya spoke no English, he claimed, but after ten months of speaking Russian twelve hours a day, Ski was quite fluent. Emmens was fairly proficient, but growing up speaking Polish had given Ski an ear for the Slavonic languages that Bob did not possess. Over the course of the trip, York told Kolya who they were, not that he didn't know anyway, and the man confided that he was actually Caucasian, not Russian, and so he was sympathetic. "I know some of these smugglers near the border. Maybe I can help you."

After learning of the Axis defeats at Stalingrad and on Guadalcanal, York was certain Stalin wanted them out of Russia. Obviously, there remained some lingering doubt in Moscow about the Japanese; otherwise, the crew would have been released outright. It was, Ski knew, a very Russian solution: oblique and deceptive, yet to them quite practical. There was no other reason to send the crew 1,400 miles south and put them in a town eighteen miles from a border through which they could leave Russia. York was positive of it: "If you were running Russia and you had five people that you didn't want to leave, they certainly wouldn't leave." Stalin wanted them gone, but he wanted to be able to claim they escaped; therefore, he was not to blame. The staff officers were sent to ensure this, and Kolya, who was very likely NKVD, was the facilitator. "This [Kolya] was no peasant," Ski said, emphatically. "I don't know what his true function was . . . it just didn't smack right. I made up my mind right then and there that we eventually were getting out of the country. I wasn't put in that compartment by accident, and he wasn't either. He was doing his job."

Ashkhabad was the modern reincarnation of the ancient Silk Road city of Konjikala, which was sacked by the Mongols during the thirteenth century. Russian communists took it over in 1917 because of its proximity to the British installations in Iran, and the city subsequently passed to the newly established Turkmen Soviet Socialist Republic in 1924. Operation Countenance, a 1941 joint Anglo-Soviet invasion of neutral Iran, overwhelmed the country in four days to prevent Reza Pahlavi, the self-proclaimed shah, from allying his nation with the Axis. By taking Iran, the Allies now had access to virtually unlimited oil and a secure supply route for Lend-Lease goods up from the Persian Gulf to the Soviet border.* In partitioning the country, Moscow took the northern part, which included Lend-Lease termini along the Caspian—and the city of Meshed. Moscow's British allies took the south of the country but maintained a presence throughout northern Iran, including a consulate at Meshed—just 130 miles southeast from Ashkhabad.

Upon arrival in the city during early April, the Soviet major took the crew to their quarters, and even his face fell when he saw the shabby mud brick house surrounded by a mud fence they were to inhabit. He left the following day, and the Americans never saw him again.† Under very loose supervision, the crew could basically come and go as they pleased. As York put it later, "They [Moscow] prob-

---

* Forty-five percent (8 million tons) of all Lend-Lease goods to the Soviet Union passed through Iran's "Persian Corridor."

† The major eventually fled the Soviet Union after the war and made it to West

ably said, 'we are going to look the other way, and if they [Plane 8's crew] are too stupid to get out under these conditions, let them rot here." Giving credence to that, Kolya showed up several days later, and during the next five weeks there were many dinners and clandestine meetings. He finally confided to the pilots, "I can help you and I will." He knew a smuggler who ran jewelry and drugs over the Kopet Dag mountains into the Soviet Union and who sometimes took people out. On May 20, Ski was to meet the man, Abdul Arram, and Bob Emmens recalled the night clearly. "It was the twentieth of May . . . on the eighteenth my son had his first birthday. I wondered what he looked like."

Just past midnight on Monday, May 25, the five Americans clambered into the back of a truck, and Arram drove to the border.* They crossed by foot to avoid the Russian checkpoints, then met the truck that took them to Meshed. Rather, to within four miles of the city, where they were dumped and left to make their own entrance. Leaving the other three men concealed in a bomb crater outside the city, the pilots slipped past a final checkpoint and, using a diagram carefully drawn by Kolya, found their way to the British consulate. The Iranian guards let them through a gate in the high whitewashed wall and escorted them in, where the Americans stopped cold.

It was astonishing. A sandy path led through a "rolling stretch of green lawn, beautifully kept," lined by flowers, and at the far end was a swimming pool! A pet gazelle was grazing in the center of the lawn. "It looked like the Garden of Eden to us," Emmens recalled. On a slip of paper that he passed to the guard, York wrote:

---

Germany. He listed Ed York as a reference for his asylum claim. His fate is unknown.

* The price for all five men was two hundred and fifty dollars—the entire cash supply they could muster. Most of it had been won playing poker on the *Hornet* prior to the mission.

Major E. J. York
and
Lieutenant R. G. Emmens
U.S. Army Air Forces

The man left, and within a minute a young Englishman emerged, holding the paper and staring at them with astonishment. Quite surprisingly, he knew all about them. "This is the most amazing coincidence," the man sputtered. "I was on the staff of the British Embassy in Moscow in 1942." Sending a truck back for the others, the crew was reunited within an hour, and as reality set in, they slowly relaxed. For the first time in thirteen months, the weary Americans had a hot bath and a real bed with sheets and pillows. Later they talked about the mission, their internment, and, most of all, of going home. Bob Emmens remembered thinking of those they'd encountered during their amazing odyssey: "they seemed unreal, like characters out of a fiction book. I felt as though I had just awakened from a bad dream . . . or rather, a nightmare." But nightmares fade with the light of day—or in the case of Plane 8's crew, in that singular, warm glow that comes with finally returning home.

# EPILOGUE

Thirty thousand rubles a month.

Despite receiving billions of dollars' worth of Lend-Lease aid, Moscow sent Secretary of the Treasury Henry Morgenthau a monthly thirty-thousand-ruble bill for the upkeep of Plane 8's crew. Any angst over such outrageous behavior, and the bills themselves, was forgotten when Washington received news that Ed York and his crew were safe in Meshed. It was decided to get the crew as close to the Afghan border as possible, and from there to Karachi in northern India, where the American military could take over. The British kept them in Meshed for six days, claiming "we will have to fatten you up a little bit before you can go any-place," which was appropriate given their loss of weight; York himself came out of Russia down from his normal 180 pounds to 130 pounds. From there, all five men were sent on to Quetta, which was the headquarters for the British Indian Army's Baluchistan District, North Western Army.* Their hospitality was superb,

---

* This is now Pakistan, which became independent in 1947 as part of the British Commonwealth, then a fully independent republic in 1956.

and once in Quetta, a brigadier was personally assigned to further "fatten them up" and get them down to Karachi.

After three days of eating and sleeping, the British general arranged for a two-day train ride to take them the 350 miles south to Karachi. Ed York promptly made a phone call to the 10th Air Force Headquarters at Karachi and discovered an old friend, Colonel Ivan McElroy, commanded the 80th Fighter Group. Sent on ahead of the P-40Ns they would employ, McElroy told York he would fly up himself and pick up the crew. He did just that, landing a C-47 at 0900 the following morning in Quetta. The British general smiled and shook his head. "I shouldn't be surprised. The way you people do things I shouldn't be surprised."

From there, things happened fast. Assigned travel Priority 2, just below the White House or diplomatic priority, York's men began a seven-day westward odyssey that took them over the Gulf of Oman to Arabia, then Aden, followed by Khartoum in the Sudan. Due to the fighting in North Africa, they flew the equatorial route to Nigeria, then fifteen hundred miles into the South Atlantic to Ascension Island. From there, they went to Natal at the far eastern tip of Brazil and eventually north to Puerto Rico. After this they traveled to Miami, where the crew called their families before being taken up the East Coast. On June 29, 1943, a little over fourteen months after flying off the *Hornet*, Major Ed York and his crew stepped off an American DC-3 at Andrews Field outside Washington, D.C.

They were home.

The final nineteen days and 11,888 miles of their extraordinary mission was over. Next came a week of debriefings at a Virginia safe house, where "they worked on us for a long time," York recalled. Their firsthand assessment of the inner workings of the Soviet Union, with all the propaganda stripped away, was still quite useful. "The Russians are anything but our allies," Emmens told the intelligence officers conducting the debriefing. York agreed. "They understand force and resolve . . . they understand that. You can't sweet talk them." Emmens was quite blunt. The Russians were "a nation of slaves ruled by abject fear and terror of what fate will be given them by the ruling few," and much worse off than they ever had been under the tsarist monarchy.

Jimmy Doolittle, a major general now commanding the Northwest African Strategic Air Force, was thrilled to get five more of his boys back from the raid and into the war. After the debriefings, York's crew, like the others who returned, was sent in all directions to meet the needs of a military with more than two years of fighting remaining. Thirteen more raiders would perish during the war, and the fate of those still missing from China haunted those who had survived.

However, they could take solace in knowing that their attack on Tokyo was the catalyst for Yamamoto's Midway operations, and entering that battle in some haste cost the Japanese dearly. Had the threat to the Home Islands not been so glaringly and unmistakably revealed by the raid, then perhaps more time and care would have been exercised. Perhaps Yamamoto would have delayed Operation MI until he had *Shōkaku* and *Zuikaku* fully operational, or at least combined his available air groups on the latter, which would have given him five fleet carriers at Midway instead of four. As tantalizing as it is to discuss such possibilities, there is no rewriting historical facts, and those are obvious. Fearful of their vulnerability, the Japanese moved hastily to destroy the threat of the American Navy and to invade the Solomons and were themselves ultimately destroyed by losses, both human and material, they could not replace.

Plane 8's deviation over Japan, and its subsequent mission to the Soviet Union, was always occluded until now. Even if Plane 8 itself was not overtly successful, Stalin's actions regarding the crew did reveal his intentions, his priorities, and ultimately the course his Soviet Union would pursue. In refusing to release York and his men, the Russian leader revealed that his ongoing dread of Japan was initially greater than his desire to remain an ally of the United States and Britain—at least until the Japanese defeat at Guadalcanal. Also, the fear that Stalin would initiate a separate peace with Tokyo may have been the principal motivation behind extending aid to Russia, as a Moscow dependent on America was one that could not back out as it had in 1918. This was, in Washington's calculus, one way to occupy a future enemy while disposing of a current foe.

Awareness of cultural Russian duplicity would, to some degree, be used as a road map during the upcoming forty-five-year Cold War, since Roosevelt, so shrewd in other ways, was proved incorrect in his belief that the dangers of communism could be softened through cooperation and diplomacy. Subsequent American leaders would at least have Russia's Second World War actions, including the internment of York's crew, as a template for decisions. Some remembered this and never trusted Soviet leaders, no matter what they professed; some, regrettably, did not.

In the final analysis, the war was won by the Allies, and Japan was defeated by the United States without any involvement from the USSR. Fascist Italy's and Nazi Germany's defeat was inevitable, but in fairness certainly would have been longer and bloodier without the Soviet Union. However, Russia could not have won without America and Lend-Lease, as Stalin himself admitted during the November 1943, Tehran Conference: "I want to tell you what, from the Russian point of view, the president and the United States have done for victory in this war," Stalin said. "The most important things in this war are the machines. . . . The United States is a country of machines. Without the machines we received through Lend-Lease, we would have lost the war."

From October 1, 1941, to May 31, 1945, the United States delivered to the Soviet Union 427,284 trucks; 13,303 combat vehicles; 35,170 motorcycles; 2,670,371 tons of petroleum products (gasoline and oil), or 57.8 percent of the Red Air Force's total aviation fuel requirements, which included nearly 90 percent of all high-octane fuel used. Additionally, American factories provided 4,478,116 tons of foodstuffs; 1,911 steam locomotives; 66 diesel locomotives; and over 10,000 rail cars. U.S. industry provided almost two-thirds of all the Allied military equipment produced during the Second World War: 297,000 aircraft; 193,000 artillery pieces; 86,000 tanks; and two million utility army trucks. When Washington permitted the Red Army to march first into Berlin, the Russians did so on 10 million pairs of American boots with Chevrolet trucks made in Detroit. It is no exaggeration to say that American production, coupled with the tenacity and vengeful ferociousness of her fighting men, decided the ultimate outcome of the Second World War.

America launched more vessels in 1941 than Japan did during the entire conflict, and her shipyards turned out tonnage so fast that by the autumn of 1943, all Allied shipping sunk since 1939 had been replaced. In 1944 alone, the United States built more aircraft than the Japanese had since 1939, and by the war's end, more than half of all industrial production *in the world* took place in the United States. In four years, American industry, already the world's largest, had doubled in size. As Ed York, Bob Emmens, and Plane 8's crew returned home, much of this was now evident; one *Essex*-class fleet carrier was completed every sixty days, and nine *Independence*-class light carriers would be commissioned by the end of the war.* During the three years following the Battle of Midway, the Japanese constructed six aircraft carriers, while America built fifteen powerful fleet carriers and sixty-four escort carriers during the same period. To be sure, York's men returned to a much different United States from the one they left, but it was a country contending with hard fights in all corners of the globe and, in the summer of 1943, with much still to do if the world was to be free.

---

* Long-hull *Essex*-class carriers were over sixty feet longer than the *Hornet* and carried at least twenty-five more aircraft. Bigger, faster, and more heavily armored than the *Shōkaku*-class Japanese carriers, they also were radar-equipped and mounted twelve five-inch guns, plus eighty-seven anti-aircraft guns of various calibers.

◇ ◇ ◇

On Christmas Day 1944, strange fighter planes roared over eastern China and attacked the city of Nanjing. The Americans were back. They now intended to bomb both Japan and occupied China in the same sort of ruthless, dedicated campaign used in Europe. Just a month prior, as Operation San Antonio 1 commenced in earnest, U.S. heavy bombers appeared over Tokyo for the first time since Doolittle and his raiders in 1942. Over one hundred B-29 Superfortresses smashed the Nakajima Aircraft Company's engine factory in Musashino, less than ten miles from the Toyama Military Academy, where Jimmy's bombs impacted thirty-one months earlier.

Six months later, in June 1945, four filthy, emaciated American fliers were abruptly and inexplicably moved seven hundred miles north from their miserable Shanghai prison to Peking. They had no way of knowing that the Japanese had been inexorably pushed 3,500 miles back across the Pacific. That same June, Okinawa had fallen, placing American military might barely three hundred miles south of Doolittle's exit point at Yakushima, and less than a thousand miles from the Imperial Palace in Tokyo.

By this time, word had reached Washington about a "Kill All" order circulated among Japanese POW camps during early 1944. Document 2701 stated in Section 2, "The Method," that "whether they [prisoners of war] are destroyed individually or in groups, or however it is done, with mass bombing, poisonous smoke, poisons, drowning, decapitation, or what, dispose of them as the situation dictates." To prevent this, American Office of Strategic Services (OSS) agents had been infiltrating occupied China to locate prison camps holding Allied military and civilian personnel. A team had located such a facility in the spring of 1945, at Fengtai, outside Peking, and on August 9, the same day the second atomic bomb was dropped on Nagasaki, a six-man OSS team parachuted into China.

Taking full advantage of Japanese confusion and indecision, the

American commander, Major Ray Nichol, brazenly confronted a nervous imperial general and demanded that all prisoners be released immediately. Through the Swiss consul and two British-educated Japanese intelligence officers, Nichol and his men were quartered in Peking's Grand Hotel, and the following morning discovered that all POWs had been released with no incident—except four fliers in "special" confinement at a nearby military prison.

Fortunately, these men were known to Commander Winfield Scott Cunningham and Marine Major P. S. Devereaux, prisoners for over four years since Wake Island surrendered. When told, Nichol demanded their presence, and the Japanese, who clearly intended to keep the existence of these men secret until they could be quietly killed for their role in bombing Tokyo, were stunned. In the end, the general ordered their immediate release, and four bearded, starving Americans found themselves blinking in the bright light of the Peking Grand Hotel lobby on August 20, 1945. Using a portable transmitter, Major Nichol sent the following telegram to the stately, white-columned building at 2430 E Street, Northwest, on Washington, D.C.'s Navy Hill, which served as OSS headquarters. The message read:

> FOUR DOOLITTLE RAIDERS LOCATED IN MILITARY PRISON
> PEKING. NAMES ARE LT. GEORGE BARR, LT. ROBERT HITE,
> LT CHASE NEILSEN, AND CORPORAL JACOB DE SHAZER.
> BARR IN POOR CONDITON. OTHERS WEAK. WILL EVACUATE
> THESE MEN FIRST.

Two raiders had drowned off the Chinese coast, and one died during the bailout. Four more succumbed to disease and privation while prisoners of war, and three were executed by the Japanese. After returning to combat in Europe, another four became prisoners of the Germans, while thirteen additional raiders died in other theaters where America was committed. After York's crew returned,

Jimmy Doolittle still waited another two years and four months for any word of the missing fliers, and now his final four boys were coming home. Lieutenant George Barr was the last to return after a series of bizarre incidents, and Doolittle personally made certain he was reunited with his family. He also informed Barr that the raiders never held the long-promised party they'd arranged while aboard the *Hornet* "because you and the rest of the fellows couldn't make it."

But they did make it to the McFadden-Deauville Hotel in Miami on December 14, 1945. Most of the men had not seen each other since that fateful April morning forty-three months and twenty-six days earlier when they struck that first hard blow into the Empire's black heart. For three days they relaxed, drank, caught up, and drank some more. Two years later they repeated the performance, so much so that the night watchman formally complained to the hotel manager:

> The Doolittle boys added some gray hairs to my head. This has been the worst night since I worked here. They were completely out of control.
>
> I let them make a lot of noise, but when about 15 of them went into the pool at 1:00 A.M., including Doolittle, I told them there was no swimming allowed there at night. They were in the pool until 2:30 A.M.
>
> I went up twice more without results. They were running around the halls in their bathing suits and were noisy until 5 A.M. Yes, it was a rough night.

At checkout, the hotel manager showed Doolittle the report, then with a broad smile requested that all the raiders autograph it. He also stated "that as far as he was concerned, we had earned the right to make all the noise we wanted to in his hotel."

Ed York and the others from Plane 8 were there and would return every year they could, though through the decades both pilots continued their enigmatic evasions whenever asked about the Soviet Union. They had given their word to say nothing, and they would keep it. The crew members all survived the war and would go on to accomplish other things in life. Gunner Dave Pohl was accepted as an aviation cadet, becoming a commissioned officer and pilot on August 4, 1945—just two days before the first atomic bomb was dropped on Hiroshima. A B-17 pilot, he rose to become an aircraft commander before retiring in 1947 as a first lieutenant. Earning a bachelor's degree in business administration, he retired in San Diego after working for Shell Oil. Dave Pohl died on February 18, 1999, and his ashes were scattered over the Pacific.

Ted Laban served as a flight engineer on B-29 Superfortresses and B-26 Marauders. Retiring as a master sergeant in 1956, Laban married and received a degree in electrical engineering. Working as a research engineer, Ted passed away on September 16, 1998, in Hot Springs, Arkansas.

Nolan Herndon retired as a major in 1945, married Julia Crouch, and moved to Edgefield, South Carolina, where he became a whole-sale grocer. Always convinced that York and Emmens were on a mission beyond bombing Japan, he continued to assert this theory until his death in Columbia, South Carolina, on October 7, 2007.

As it turned out, Nolan Herndon was correct all along.

Bob Emmens came home and met his son Thomas, then went on to command the 494th Bomb Squadron and later became the vice commander of the 334th Bombardment Group. Entering the world of military intelligence, he was appointed military attaché to Romania from 1944 to 1948. With tours at the Pentagon and in Austria, his final full-duty station was, ironically, as air attaché to Japan. Michael Emmens, Bob's younger son, told the author that "my dad ended up realizing that the people of Japan were not the enemy during World War II, but it was the government." Retiring in 1964 as a colonel, Bob returned to his birthplace in Medford, Oregon, where he died of cancer on April 2, 1992.

Ed York returned to San Antonio to meet his daughter, Tekla Ann, called Tina, and in 1944 was flying B-17s with the Fifteenth Air Force in Italy. After sixteen combat missions, much to his disgust, Ski was grounded due to a new policy prohibiting internees and escaped prisoners of war from returning to combat. After the war, he also entered military intelligence and was assigned to Poland, then Denmark, as the air attaché. Ski York retired as a colonel in 1968 and passed away in San Antonio during August of 1984, without ever divulging the request made by Hap Arnold or the true purpose of Plane 8's flight to Russia.

On each anniversary of the day they flew off the *Hornet*, the raiders tried to gather together over the next seventy-one years, and each time there were fewer men present. Every reunion closed with the toast "Gentlemen, to our good friends who have gone," which ended the final meeting in April 2013, at Fort Walton Beach, Florida. Remaining from the eighty men who began the journey were three raiders: Lieutenant Colonel Richard E. Cole, Doolittle's copilot; Lieutenant Colonel Edward Saylor, who was a twenty-two-year-old sergeant and the engineer-gunner on Lieutenant Don Smith's *TNT*; and Staff Sergeant David Thatcher of Ted Lawson's *Ruptured Duck*. On April 9, 2019, at 103 years of age, the final raider, Dick Cole, joined his brothers who had gone on before and who had been patiently awaiting him for nearly seventy-seven years.

With the story of Plane 8's recondite mission to the Soviet Union finally explained, the last of the mysteries surrounding the Doolittle Raid have been answered. There was no "last-minute" decision to divert to Russia, and now we know that the mission was orchestrated to provide current intelligence on a particular Soviet airfield within bombing range of Japan. Another purpose was to objectively assess infrastructure and capabilities while subjectively assessing Russian willingness to engage the Japanese. This was accomplished through the addition of Ed York to the raid and through a carefully arranged carburetor swap that created a plausible reason for flying to the Soviet Union instead of China. Obviously, internment was not foreseen, but the details of that are also clear, as are those of the "escape" from Russia, which was clearly arranged by Moscow. As Ski York himself said, "If Uncle Joe [Stalin] didn't want us to get out of there, we would still be there."

One facet of this mission still remains elusive: did Plane 8 bomb Niitsu on the coast of the Niigata Prefecture after Nishi Nasuno? Again, no word has ever been written, or any hint ever dropped to confirm this, and both military and aviation logic shun the notion that York held on to his remaining bombs until reaching the coast. That Nolan Herndon, who was not reticent regarding his alternative theories of the mission, never spoke of attacking two geographically separated targets appears highly conclusive. Yet the Japanese reports have been verified, and the Agano River bridge was bombed on the same day of the Doolittle raid. Perhaps the elusive clue to this final mystery is still there waiting to be discovered. Perhaps not.

In the final analysis, Plane 8's legacy is more complex.

The horrible chances these men took provided valuable, indirect intelligence of Joseph Stalin's priorities and mind-set, as well as a window into Soviet strategic intentions. This extraordinary mission categorically reveals a tale of personal fortitude and courage and of returning home with honor. This is no literary catchphrase; if one returns from active combat to positive judgments from peers, loved ones, and a grateful nation, then this is enough of an accomplishment for a lifetime. Ed York, Bob Emmens, Nolan Herndon, Ted Laban, and David Pohl did just that.

The others who could make it home from war eventually did so. Those who gave their futures and their lives for our freedom, both during the raid and on other Second World War battlefields, will always remain as they are remembered: young, brave, and full of hope for a better world. They knew the appalling risks and the possible, even likely, consequences, yet they went anyway. Why some lived and others died is the ultimate question, and for that there never has been, nor will there be, an answer. A twitch of the controls, a few more gallons of gas, or a decision to bail out now instead of a minute from now—was it fate or destiny, luck or God? This will never be known. What is known, and occasionally forgotten at our peril, is that a world that creates men like those of Plane 8 is a world that will never surrender to tyranny.

# Appendix 1

# DEBRIEFING EXCERPTS

## 1. INTERVIEW WITH B-25 CREW THAT BOMBED TOKYO AND WAS INTERNED BY THE RUSSIANS

JUNE 3, 1943
ASSISTANT CHIEF OF AIR STAFF, INTELLIGENCE

CREW MEMBERS
Major Edward J. York-021151
First Lt. Robert C. Emmens-024104
2nd Lt. Nolan A. Herndon-0419328
S/Sgt. David W. Pohl-6152141
Sgt. Theodore H. Laban-6559855

**Major York:** In my opinion, the reason that we used more gasoline than we should have was that our two carburetors were especially adjusted and special carburetors were installed at Elgin Field, where we had been training, by factory experts there that they had to do the work. (We moved at Sacramento to the air depot.) When we got to Sacramento, Colonel Doolittle gave orders that no parts would be removed from any of the airplanes without his special permission. The day before we left, we found a bunch of carburetors had been taken off, but it was too late to do anything about it.

**Q: Who took them off?**
A: People at Sacramento.

**Q: Under whose supervision?**
A: Colonel Doolittle's. They were supposed to ask for his permission to change anything, or do any work. They were there for that work—and the Colonel outlined everything that was supposed to be done. There was no statement made on the card covering the work which should be done. They just removed the carburetors. We just happened to find out, by looking the engine over and checking the serial numbers, that they were different. No mention was made, or notation made, to let us know that the carburetors had been changed. We accidentally found out about it. I didn't think it made any difference. I talked to the Colonel about it. He asked me how I felt about it and I said, "All right." We figured, on the carrier, that the auxiliary gasoline should last through Japan and that we would have to go on the main tanks sometime after that. About forty-five minutes before we got there, we had to go on the main tanks. At that time I had already started worrying about my gasoline holding out to get to the final destination. We checked on the consumption and found we used approximately 98 gallons an hour instead of the 72 to 75 we were supposed to use.

**Q: What was your destination?**
A: China.
**Major York:** So I made up my mind when we spotted Japan (I knew the time we had been running on the main tanks) that I wasn't going to try to go to China. I figured I wouldn't get to within 300 miles of shore.

Q: Was there anything else of any note on the trip over on the carrier that you think you ought to bring up? Did you check your armament and everything daily—and your engine?

A: Not daily. We ran the engines up once every three days, I believe it was, to just warm them up and make sure they were functioning properly. Our turret wasn't functioning when we took off, but shortly after it was.

Sgt. Pohl: In the machine guns we found that practically all of the machine guns, after we got aboard the ship, had these weak firing pin springs. There had been cases before when we found the firing springs weren't strong enough—you fired three or four hundred rounds and they would lose all their punch, and start misfiring all the time. We took as many as we could get from the crew on the Hornet—but we didn't have enough to go around. We took all the ones that hadn't fired—that were giving trouble on the Hornet—but we didn't get them all fixed. All that should have been done.

Q: Then you found out your carburetors were maladjusted, wasn't there anyone that could have fixed them up?

Major York: No. Civilian experts from the factory had done the work at Eglin Field.

Q: None of them went along?

A: No. They didn't go to Sacramento. We ran a consumption test from Eglin Field to Sacramento. We knew what they were supposed to burn. We had no chance of running a consumption test at Sacramento.

Q: Now—can you give a brief, detailed description of your plane's action from the time you took off, including your briefing, and give anything that might be of interest during the early morning hours? Start when you found out you were going to take off then instead of later on.

**A:** There wasn't any briefing the day we took off. Of course, he had been briefed continuously all the time on the carrier—targets, and terrain, and all sorts of things. The original plan was for the Colonel to take off two hours before dark and drop incendiaries on Tokyo and light it up so we would be guided in. The rest of them were to take off just before dark and make their attack at night. However, that morning was when we first found out we were going to take off—at breakfast—when an order came for all crews to man their airplanes. There wasn't any time then to get further instructions. So we all ran up on deck, got in our planes and prepared to take off.

**Q: What were your specific targets?**
**A:** I had an aircraft plant in Tokyo. I don't remember the name.

**Q: Could you point it out on a map?**
**A:** I think so if I saw a map. (Looking at map) It was in the vicinity of 341—331 to be exact. Aircraft engine factory #331. On the way in we saw a fairly large freighter, and just before we made our landfall we saw several small boats—tenders I would call them.

**Q: Did you come in directly from the east?**
**A:** We came in from the east, yes. We made our landfall and should have been in the area of our target in about 20 to 25 minutes after making our landfall. After flying for about 30 minutes after our landfall was made, we still hadn't spotted Tokyo itself; so I started looking for any suitable target; something that was worthwhile bombing. Looking back at it now, it must have been just north of Tokyo, or possibly northwest. At any rate, about thirty-five or forty minutes after landfall, we came across a factory, with the main building about four stories high. There was a power plant, and about three or four tall stacks, and railroad yards, and we decided to bomb it. I pulled up to 1,500 feet. I had

been down practically on the ground at the time. We dropped the bombs there, and they said one had hit practically in the middle of the large building. The crew saw smoke and steam rising. I, myself, didn't see it. I lowered away immediately and sneaked around.

Q: Was it outside the suburbs of the city?

A: It was outside because we didn't see the large settlement that you would expect to see in a city of that size. I must have been in this area here. (Due north of Tokyo.)

Q: How far from the coast were you?

A: We had been flying for about 35 minutes. I would say we weren't going too fast at that time. I would say it was about a hundred miles from our landfall. Now the land here comes out like this (map) so we were approximately in this area here. (Approximately in the area of Kawagos.)

Q: Did you meet any fighter interference or any antiaircraft?

A: No. We saw enemy airplanes, however. But we saw a formation of nine we judged to be at about 10,000 feet when we were right down on the ground. They were fighters ... and they evidently did not see us; because they made no attempt to attack us.

Q: Did you fly over Tokyo itself?

A: No.

Q: You never did see Tokyo?

A: No.

Q: Did you see any other large Japanese city that you recognized?

A: No. We saw several cities coming across—none that I knew the names of.

Q: You had a camera?
A: Yes.

Q: Did you get any pictures?
A: I don't know. It was taken out at the Military Attaché's Office in Russia and brought back here, I suppose.

Q: You never found out whether you got any pictures?
A: No.

Q: About in what order were you?
A: I was number eight. We also saw three other airplanes besides these nine. They were painted yellow. I think they must have been trainers.

Q: Did you see any of our airplanes on the way in?
A: No. Shortly after we took off the only airplane that was in sight was slowly pulling away from us.

Q: Major, you don't happen to know the type of Zero, or fighter?
A: No. They were too high. They must have been at 10,000 feet or more and we were practically on the ground.

Q: Did you notice whether they had square wing tips?
A: No.

Q: Were you flying over relatively flat country when you dropped your bombs?
A: It was before we reached the mountains to the northwest of Tokyo.

Q: Do you remember this river (map)?
A: We flew over a river, or a large stream. I am not sure whether that was it or not.

Q: Do you remember having seen this lake (map)? Northeast of
  Tokyo?
A: I don't think we were that far.

Q: Would you say you were more than halfway between the landfall and the mountains when you dropped your bombs?
A: Yes, I think so—because the way we figured it, we should have
  been here in about twenty-five minutes after hitting the shore.

Q: Where do you think you hit the shore?
A: Well, I assume it was at this point. (Point[s] to the southeast of
  Yokahora.)

Q: But instead you must have hit it slightly northeast of Tokyo?
A: Yes.

Q: Then what did you do after dropping your bombs?
A: We turned to the northwest with the idea of hitting shore someplace north of Vladivostok.

Q: Did you pass over Sado Island?
A: No. We passed within sight of it—to the southwest of it. As
  soon as we got down in this flat, we let down near a bay northwest of Central Honshu south of Sado Island and continued in a
  northwesterly direction toward Vladivostok.

Q: Where did you first note land along in here—do you have any
  idea?
A: We knew we were along the coast north of here someplace so I
  turned and followed the coastline. This was very inaccurate on
  your maps. We figured we would recognize this large inlet east of
  Vladivostok. We turned inland there as I didn't want to go right
  over the city itself. We turned inland and the second airdrome we

came to I circled and landed. That is the second airdrome north of Vladivostok. It was 40 kilometers north of Vladivostok.

**Q: When did you elect to do this rather than continue to China?**
**A:** As soon as we spotted the shore and figured what gas we had left and the distance we had to go to China.

**Q: What about your incendiary bombs—did you drop them in the same place?**
**A:** All in the same place.

**Q: You didn't use any rounds at all?**
**A:** No. Just to test the guns on the way in.

**Q: No strafing?**
**A:** No.

# TOKYO RAID-CREW 8

**MEMORANDUM FOR LT. COLONEL J. E. JOHNSTON**
**SUBJECT: Interview with Major Edward J. York, A.C. (Pilot)**

## INTRODUCTORY

1. The above-named men constituted one of the crews under Major General Doolittle when attacking Japan Proper. Their story will be told in narrative.

## NARRATIVE

2. They left San Francisco on April 2, 1942, on the Hornet. On their return to the United States, they arrived at Miami, Florida, on May 29, 1943.

3. On April 18, 1942, they left the Hornet 750 miles off shore and

crossed Honshu, the main island of the Japanese group, from southeast to northwest, making but one crossing of the island.

4. Each plane in the raid had a definite objective. For this ship, the objective was an airplane factory in Tokyo. However, they were unable to locate it. Instead, they flew over the city of Utsunomiya, which is about fifty miles north of Tokyo. This is a factory city of some 400,000. They bombed factory installations having four tall smoke stacks—power plants, railroad yards, etc., causing substantial damage.

5. From Utsunomiya, they crossed the island and came out about half-way between Sado Island and Nodo Peninsula, on the western central coast of Honshu. While crossing Honshu, they flew at an average height of fifty feet above the ground, except where they were forced to fly over a target.

6. Observations over Honshu: In crossing Honshu, they saw two or three airfields empty. Also, they saw new airfield construction on the central western coast of Honshu. They saw certain Japanese planes in the air. However, the Jap pilots did not see them. They encountered no cross-radio interception. They crossed the island from 12:30 to 1:00 P.M. Many people were seen working in the rice paddies. Many of them waved—others ran away because of fright. This was the normal fright that the peasants have for their own planes. So far as they were able to observe, the people over the country-side had no warning of our raid—life seemed to be functioning normally. At one point, the fliers saw a large group gathered on a beach—the group waved to them. At no point, however, did they see any troops.

7. When bombing, our fliers rose from fifty feet to 1500 feet, prior to dropping bombs. They could see the fire, steam and smoke rising from the bomb explosions. Their speed at the time of dropping bombs was about 300 miles per hour. The average

speed was about 160 miles per hour—except while they were over the island, when they traveled at 250 miles per hour.

8. The planes left the deck of the Hornet at seven-minute intervals. The pilots were ordered not to circle or leave in formation. In order to save gas, each plane went on its mission alone.

## BRIEFING

9. Before departure from the Hornet, each crew was briefed by General Doolittle, personally. Also briefing was conducted while crossing the Pacific, in classes.

## KITS

10. The fliers were supplied with the following items:

Five (5) first-aid kits

Two (2) paper maps

Four (4) cans of C ration

Three (3) containers of meat and vegetable

One (1) container of coffee, sugar, candy and three (3) biscuits

Four (4) containers of water

One (1) pint of whisky

One (1) bottle of iodine, for water as well as injuries

One (1) morphine set, including two (2) needles and five (5) doses

One (1) dozen caffeine capsules

One (1) rubber float capable of supporting five (5)

Five (5) individual life vests

Five (5) parachutes

Five (5) knives

Five (5) pistols

One (1) detachable machine gun, which was used in the nose of the plane, but which could be detached and carried by one man

One (1) large compass.

Each individual was provided with:

One (1) first-aid kit containing One (1) canteen of water but
no food

One (1) pistol

One (1) knife

One (1) pocket compass

One (1) parachute, which did not have the special seat
provided in recent models.

## MISSION

11. The mission of this crew was to fly to Tokyo and bomb certain industrial objectives. Then they were instructed to fly to Chuchow, China, in the Province of Chekiang. At that point they were to be picked up and taken to Chung-king—then to be returned to the United States.

## SHORT OF GAS

12. Due to a shortage of gas, they crossed the Japan Sea and headed for Vladivostok, where they landed at an airfield on American Bay, about forty miles from Vladivostok, proper.

## ITINERARY

13. They landed and remained there that night (April 18, 1842). The next morning they flew to Khabarousk, Siberia, where they were interned. Their ship was held at their first point of landing. They flew to Khabarousk in a Russian D.C.3. At Khabarousk they remained two days.

14. Then they were moved to Penza by railroad. At Penza they were held 2–2½ months.

15. Next, they were moved to Ohansk, at the foot of the Ural Mountains, where they were kept from August 11, 1942 to March 25, 1943. There were very few persons at Ohansk who had ever seen another white person, other than Russians.

16. Their following move was by automobile to Molotov—about eighty miles distant, where they remained two or three days. They then were flown to Chkalovsk, in Russia (formerly Orenburg).

17. From Chkalovsk, they were taken by train to Ashkhabad, where they arrived on April 8, 1943.

18. At Ashkhabad, they were able to contact a Persian smuggler, who agreed to take them across the line to Persia for $250 (in United States money). They were taken from Ashkhabad in a truck to a point near the Russian-Persian boundary. At this point, a second man picked them up at the side of the road, and took them over hilly country into Meshed, Persia, where they, at once, went to place themselves in the hands of the British Consul.

19. The British Consul at Meshed furnished them with truck transportation southeasterly to Zahidan, Persia. The British Consul at Zahidan then took them to the Baluchistan (under Indian jurisdiction) border, from where they continued to Quetta, Baluchistan. It was through the influence of the British Consul that they encountered no difficulty in crossing into territory under Indian jurisdiction, as they had no cards of identification or food cards.

20. The British authorities at Quetta notified the American Consul at Karachi, on the northwestern coast of India proper. A plane was sent from Karachi to Quetta to return them to Karachi.

21. From Karachi, they were flown in an American air transport service plane to Aden, southwest Arabia; then to Khartoum, Egypt; then across Africa to Accra, on the Gold Coast (Gulf of Guinea—central western coast of Africa): then across the Atlantic to Natal, Brazil; then to Bellum, Puerto Rico and Miami, Florida.

## RUSSIAN EXPERIENCE

22. At their first landing in Russia, the local Russian Commander did not know their identity. The fliers did not disclose the fact

until the Russians had received a report from Japan concerning the bombing. When they were accused of being one of the crews, they were forced to admit their identity.

23. They explained their need for gas and their desire to leave for a rendezvous next morning. At first the local Russian Commander gave his consent to their departure, as requested, and promised to see that they received gas. However, when morning arrived, the consent was canceled.

24. At Khabarousk, their point of internment, the members of the crew were taken before the staff of the Russian Far Eastern Army. Through an interpreter, they were asked to identify themselves. Very few questions were asked. The Russian officers seemed to be very pleased over the news of their raid on Japan. They were asked if they had been directed to land on Russia. They stated that they had been forced to do so because of gas shortage and had thought they would have no difficulty in getting gas to continue their journey to their rendezvous in China.

## INTERNED

25. The official action of the Russian Army Board was to intern them. They were taken fifteen miles out of town where they remained two days, being guarded constantly with no one permitted to see them.

26. They asked for permission to communicate with the United States Consul, but permission was refused. Similarly, when they first landed near Vladivostok, they had also asked for the United States Consul, with the Russian Commander stating that he would see if it might be possible. Later, he completely ignored the request.

27. When at Khabarousk, the internees were told that they would be taken to Kuibyshev. On their way to Penza, they went through Kuibyshev, remaining there one and one-half days. However, they were not allowed off the train. Their objections were of no

avail. En route to Penza, they were on the train for twenty days. Their food consisted of sausage, bread, tea and salmon eggs. This was considered a better standard than the average Russian was receiving. On the train they were in a car by themselves, with one guard who had a Tommy-gun and two armed guards outside, on either end of the car. The official explanation given to them for such close guarding was that they were being protected from spies, saboteurs, etc.

## Appendix 2

# JAMES H. DOOLITTLE—
# FLIGHT/MISSION REPORT

CHUNKING, CHINA
MAY 4, 1942.

Take off at 8:20 A.M. ship time.

Take-off was easy. Night take-off would have been possible and practicable.

Circled carrier to get exact heading and check compass. Wind was from around 300°.

About a half hour after take-off was joined by AC 40-2292, Lt. Hoover, pilot, the second plane to take off.

About an hour out passed a Japanese camouflaged naval surface vessel of about 6,000 tons. Took it to be a light cruiser.

About two hours out passed a multi-motored land plane headed directly for our flotilla and flying at about 3,000 ft.—2 miles away.

Passed and endeavored to avoid various civil and naval craft until land fall was made north of Inubo Shuma.

Was somewhat north of desired course but decided to take advantage of error and approach from a northerly direction, thus avoiding anticipated strong opposition to the west.

Many flying fields and the air full of planes north of Tokyo. Mostly small biplanes apparently primary or basic trainers.

Encountered nine fighters in three flights of three. This was about ten miles north of the outskirts of Tokyo proper.

All this time had been flying as low as the terrain would permit.

Continued low flying due south over the outskirts of and toward the east center of Tokyo.

Pulled up to 1,200 ft., changed course to the southwest and incendiary-bombed highly inflammable section. Dropped first bomb at 1:30 (ship time).

Anti-aircraft very active but only one near hit.

Lowered away to housetops and slid over western outskirts into low haze and smoke.

Turned south and out to sea.

Fewer airports on west side but many army posts.

A consensus on the part of crew members is that the upper turret on the B-25B, while far better than the lower turret, is entirely unsatisfactory. Two 24-volt generators went out shortly before take-off and a third plane had trouble with the turret's electrical system thus putting three out of sixteen turrets out of action at a time too late to make repairs. Far more trouble is experienced with the Azimuth motor than with the altitude motor. This is probably due to the fact that the Azimuth motor is used much more than the altitude motor particularly while the gunner is searching for enemy aircraft. The control of the turret is entirely unsatisfactory. It is our understanding that this will be corrected, in part at least, with the new control to be installed. The telescopic sight is unsatisfactory in that it collects dust and moisture and the cone of vision is too small. It is our understanding that this also is being corrected in future sights.

The 30-caliber nose gun installation is entirely unsatisfactory. It is impossible to quickly shift from one position to another under actual combat conditions, particularly if the gun has been fired and the adaptor warmed up and expanded. The glass molding for the nose gun is not strong enough and cracks after a few rounds are fired. It is strongly recommended, in this type of installation, that two 50-caliber hand-operated guns be located low in the nose with an angular movement of about 60° down from the horizontal and 30° to port and starboard. These guns would be operated by the bombardier after he had dropped his bombs. They should lock in the upper forward position (with the line of fire parallel to the longitudinal axis of the airplane) and in that position be operable by the pilot. Had we had such an installation we could have done a great deal more damage. A similar set of guns located near the position of the present rear turret would provide some protection aft and be cleaner and lighter than the present turret in addition to being simpler and more effective.

Passed over small aircraft factory with a dozen or more newly completed planes on the line. No bombs left. Decided not to machine gun for reasons of personal security.

Had seen five barrage balloons over east central Tokyo and what appeared to be more in the distance.

Passed on out to sea flying low.

Was soon joined again by Hoover who followed us to the Chinese coast.

Navigator plotted perfect course to pass north of Yaki Shima.

Saw three large naval vessels just before passing west end of Japan. One was flatter than the others and may have been a converted carrier.

Passed innumerable fishing and small patrol boats.

Made land fall somewhat north of course on China coast.

Tried to reach Chuchow on 4495 but couldn't raise.

It had been clear over Tokyo but became overcast before reaching Yaki Shima.

Ceiling lowered on coast until low islands and hills were in it at about 600'. Just getting dark and couldn't live under overcast so pulled up to 6,000 and then 8,000 ft. in it. On instruments from then on though occasionally saw dim lights on ground through almost solid overcast. These lights seemed more often on our right and pulled us still farther off course.

Directed rear g to go aft and secure films from camera (unfortunately they were jerked out of his shirt front where he had put them, when his chute opened.)

Decided to abandon ship. Sgt. Braemer, Lt. Potter, Sgt. Leonard and Lt. Cole jumped in order. Left ship on A.F.C.E., shut off both gas cocks and I left. Should have put flaps down. This would have slowed down landing speed, reduced impact and shortened glide.

All hands collected and ship located by late afternoon of 19th.

Requested General Ho Yang Ling, Director of the Branch Government of Western Chekiang Province to have a lookout kept along the seacoast from Hang Chow bay to Wen Chow bay and also have all sampans and junks along the coast keep a lookout for planes that went down at sea, or just reached shore.

Early morning of 20th four planes and crews, in addition to ours, had been located and I wired General Arnold, through the Embassy at Chunking, "Tokyo successfully bombed. Due bad weather on China Coast believe all airplanes wrecked. Five crews found safe in China so far."

Wired again on the 27th giving more details.

Discussed possibility of purchasing three prisoners on the seacoast from Puppet Government and endeavoring to take out the three in the lake area by force. Believe this desire was made clear to General Ku Cho-tung (who spoke little English) and know it was made clear to English-speaking members of his staff. This was at Shangjao. They agreed to try purchase of three but recommended against force due to large Japanese concentration.

Left airplane about 9:20 (ship time) after 13 hours in the air. Still had enough gas for half hour flight but right front tank was showing empty. Had transferred once as right engine used more fuel.

Had covered about 2,250 miles, mostly at low speed, cruising but about an hour at moderate high speed which more than doubled the consumption for this time.

Bad luck:

(1) Early take-off due to naval contact with surface and aircraft.

(2) Clear over Tokyo.

(3) Foul over China.

Good luck:

(1) A 25 m/h tail wind over most of the last 1,200 miles.

Take-off should have been made three hours before daylight, but we didn't know how easy it would be and the Navy didn't want to light up.

Dawn take-off, closer in, would have been better as things turned out. However, due to the bad weather it is questionable if even daylight landing could have been made at Chuchow without radio aid.

Still feel that original plan of having one plane take off three hours before dusk and others just at dusk was best all-around plan for average conditions.

Should have kept accurate chronological record.

Should have all crew members instructed in exact method of leaving ship under various conditions.

J. H. DOOLITTLE
Airplane AC 40-2344—B-25B

# ACKNOWLEDGMENTS

To make history come alive requires an effort far beyond the plain recitation of facts and long-past events. In fact, adhering to such a formula nearly guarantees to discourage the love of history and put a reader to sleep.

Fortunately, I have always had the invaluable assistance of wonderful people with firsthand knowledge of each story I write. Those who can add personal anecdotes or supply expert knowledge and provide those small details that differentiate readable works from nonfiction doorstops. Mr. Robert Arnold, grandson of Hap Arnold, and Mr. Michael Emmens, son of Robert Emmens, were two such individuals, who willingly gave their time and shared their memories of the central characters in this story. Gentlemen, my profound thanks.

Research is the cornerstone of any serious work of nonfiction, and though I do most of this myself, it was not possible in this case with regard to the Japanese point of view; specifically, the actual results of each of the Doolittle raiders' attacks. It is no exaggeration to state this book could not have been written as it is without the superlative contribution of Mr. Makoto Morimoto. A peerless researcher who has devoted years to separating truth from error on numerous battlefields, he was forthcoming with his meticulous research, maps, and invaluable expertise concerning the April 1942 attack on Japan. He worked tirelessly to obtain the necessary permission from the National Institute of Defense Studies for the inclusion of several key, original documents never published outside Japan. Through him, I have been able to correct over eighty years of inaccuracies and lay to rest several enduring controversies. Mr. Makoto was intensely interested in verifying Plane 8's actual flight path and targets over Japan, and through our collaborative efforts we have also solved those riddles, so to this generous man I pass my most sincere gratitude.

As he did when I wrote *Vengeance* using his lovely P-38F Lightning, Mr. Bill Klaers, president and CEO of the National Museum of World War II Aviation, permitted me the use of his B-25J *In The Mood*. Without his kind indulgence, the actual flight details, the smell, feel, and personality of the bomber that are so dear to aviation enthusiasts, would have been impossible to write. Thanks, Bill, for continuing to allow me to run up my tab! Tony Ritzman of Aero Trader was also kind enough to answer my technical questions regarding the B-25, and piston engines in particular.

I continue to be indebted to the following people, who kindly respond to my ongoing pesky questions: Dr. Daniel Haulman, USAF Historical Research Agency/RSO; Dr. John Terrino, USAF AETC ACSC/DEA; Dr. Jennifer Bryan, Special Collections and Archives Department, Nimitz Library; Ms. Ruth Kindreich, USAFA Library; Ms. Patrizia Nava, curator of aviation archives, the University of Texas at Dallas; and Ms. Tammy Horton, USAF AETC AFHRA/RS.

With deep appreciation, I thank my agent, Robert Gottlieb of Trident Media, New York, for his tireless efforts in matching my works with top publishers. To Charles Spicer of St. Martin's Press and his talented crew who cut and polish my manuscripts into a form fit for public consumption, I pass a resounding "thank you!"

These books would truly not be possible without your unstinting efforts and skills.

As always, my final thanks are reserved for my family, especially my parents Dan and DeVelva, for their unflagging support, and to Ken and Jen Wyatt for donating the peace and quiet of their beautiful ski chalet when I needed to escape. Most of all for Beth, Tiffany, Dana, and James, who tolerate my surliness and forgive my absences without complaint.

# SOURCES

**Bibliography**

Agawa, H. (1979). *The Reluctant Admiral*. Tokyo: Kodansha International.

Arnold, R. H. (1979). *A Rock and a Fortress*. Sarasota, FL: Blue Horizons Press.

Baime, A. (2014). *The Arsenal of Democracy*. New York: Houghton Mifflin Harcourt.

Barnett, C. (1987). *The Audit of War: The Illusion and Reality of Britain as a Great Power*. Bournemouth, UK: Papermac.

Barnhart, M. A. (1987). *Japan Prepares for Total War*. Ithaca, NY: Cornell University Press.

Bell, P. M. H. (1974). *A Certain Eventuality: Britain and the Fall of France*. Bournemouth, UK: Saxon House.

Bellamy, C. (2007). *Absolute War: Soviet Russia in the Second World War*. London: Pan Books.

Broadberry, S., and M. Harrison. (1998). *The Economics of World War II*. Cambridge: Cambridge University Press.

Brown, D. (1977). *Aircraft Carriers*. New York: Arco Publishing.

Butow, R. J. (1961). *Tojo and the Coming of War*. Princeton, NJ.: Princeton University Press.

Caceres, M. V. (2018). *Rising Sun in the Southern Land: Destruction and*

*Resistance in Sulu and Tawi-Tawi Archipelago (1941–1945)*. Manila: University of Santo Tomas.

Cardozier, V. (1995). *The Mobilization of the United States in World War II: How the Government, Military and Industry Prepared for War*. Jefferson, NC: McFarland.

Cohen, S. (2004). *Destination: Tokyo*. Missoula, MT: Pictorial Histories Publishing.

Collection, T. W. (2020). *USS Hornet: Chronological Pictorial History Volume I and II*. Alameda, CA: Hornet Press.

Cook, H. T. (1992). *Japan at War: An Oral History*. New York: New Press.

Dalleck, R. (1995). *Franklin D. Roosevelt and American Foreign Policy, 1932–1945*. Oxford, UK: Oxford University Press.

Deane, J. R. (1973). *The Strange Alliance: The Story of Our Efforts at Wartime Cooperation with Russia*. Bloomington: Indiana University Press.

Doolittle, G. J. (1991). *I Could Never Be So Lucky Again*. New York: Bantam Books.

Edgerton, R. (1997). *Warriors of the Rising Sun: A History of the Japanese Military*. Boulder, CO: Westview Press.

Elphick, P. (2001). *Liberty: The Ships That Won the War*. Chatham, NY: Chatham.

Emmens, R. (1949). *Guests of the Kremlin*. New York: Macmillan.

Frank, R. (1990). *Guadalcanal*. New York: Penguin Books.

Freeman, R. (2019). *Atlantic Nightmare*. Armonk, NY: M. E. Sharpe.

Fullilove, M. (2013). *Rendezvous with Destiny: How Franklin D. Roosevelt and Five Extraordinary Men Took America into the War and into the World*. New York: Penguin Press.

Galeotti, M. (2020). *A Short History of Russia*. Ontario: Hanover Square Press.

Glines, C. V. (1991). *The Doolittle Raid: America's Daring First Strike Against Japan*. Atglen, PA: Schiffer Publishing.

———(n.d.). *Four Came Home*. Missoula, MT: Pictorial Histories Publishing.

Gordon, J. S. (2004). *An Empire of Wealth*. New York: HarperCollins.

Greening, C. R. (2001). *Not As Briefed: From the Doolittle Raid to a German Stalag.* Pullman, WA: Washington University Press.

Grehan, J. and A. Nicoll. (2020). *The Doolittle Raid: The First Air Attack Against Japan April 1942.* Yorkshire, UK: Air World Books.

Groom, W. (2005). *1942: The Year That Tried Men's Souls.* New York: Grove Press.

Hampton, D. (2014). *Lords of the Sky.* New York: William Morrow.

———(2020). *Operation Vengeance: The Astonishing Aerial Ambush That Changed World War II.* New York: HarperCollins.

Handel, M. (ed.), (1990). *Intelligence and Military Operations.* London: Routledge.

Harries, M. (1991). *Soldiers of the Sun: The Rise and Fall of the Imperial Japanese Army.* New York: Random House.

Hashimoto, T. (1999). *Shogun Midowei Kaisen (Witnesses to the Midway Battle).* Tokyo: Toshio Optical Human Corporation.

Hata, I. et al. (2001). *Japanese Army Fighter Aces (1931–1945).* Mechanicsburg, PA: Stackpole Books.

Hattori, T. (1953). *The Complete History of the Greater East Asia War.* Tokyo: Masu Shobo.

Hayashi, S. (1959). *Kogun: The Japanese Army in the Pacific War.* Quantico, VA: Marine Corps Association.

Herman, A. (2013). *Freedom's Forge.* New York: Random House.

Hiroyuki, O. (1979). *The Reluctant Admiral: Yamamoto and the Imperial Navy.* Tokyo: Kodansha International.

Holland, J. (2015). *The Rise of Germany, 1939–1941.* Vol. 1 of *The War in the West.* New York: Grove Press.

———(2017). *The Allies Strike Back, 1941–1943.* Vol. 2 of *The War in the West.* New York: Atlantic Monthly Press.

Hopps, J. D. (2005). *Calculated Risk: The Extraordinary Life of Jimmy Doolittle—Aviation Pioneer and World War II Hero.* Solana Beach, CA: Santa Monica Press.

Hota, E. (2013). *Japan 1941.* New York: Alfred A. Knopf.

House, D. G. (1995). *When Titans Clashed: How the Red Army Stopped Hitler.* Lawrence: University of Kansas Press.

Hoyt, E. P. (1986). *Japan's War: The Great Pacific Conquest*. New York: McGraw Hill.

Jones, R. H. (1969). *The Roads to Russia*. Norman: University of Oklahoma Press.

Keegan, J. (1992). *The Face of Battle*. London: Penguin Books.

Klingaman, W. K. (2019). *The Darkest Year: The American Home Front, 1941–1942*. New York: St. Martin's Press.

Kusaka, R. (1952). *Rengo Kantai (Combined Fleet)*. Tokyo: Mainichi Newspaper Company.

Kyvig, D. E. (2002). *Daily Life in the United States, 1920–1940*. Chicago: Ivan R. Dee.

Lamont-Brown, R. (1998). *Kempeitai: Japan's Dreaded Military Police*. Phoenix Mill, UK: Sutton.

Lawson, C. T. (2003). *Thirty Seconds Over Tokyo*. Sterling, VA: Brassey's.

Liverpool, L. R. (2008). *The Knights of Bushido*. New York: Skyhorse Publishing.

Manchester, W. (1978). *American Caesar*. New York: Little, Brown.

Millett, W. M. (2000). *A War to Be Won: Fighting the Second World War*. Cambridge, MA: Belknap-Harvard.

Milward, A. S. (1979). *War, Economy and Society, 1939–1945*. Berkeley: University of California Press.

Montefiore, S. S. (2003). *Stalin: The Court of the Red Tsar*. New York: Vintage Books.

Moorhouse, R. (2014). *The Devil's Alliance: Hitler's Pact with Stalin, 1939–1941*. London: Bodley Head.

Morison, S. E. (1958). *Breaking the Bismarcks Barrier*. Vol. 6 of *History of United States Naval Operations in World War II*. Edison, NJ: Castle Books.

———(2001). *Coral Sea, Midway and Submarine Actions, May 1942–August 1942*. Vol. 4 of *History of United States Naval Operations in World War II*. Edison, NJ: Castle Books.

———(2001). *The Rising Sun in the Pacific, 1931–April 1942*. Vol. 3 of *History of United States Naval Operations in World War II*. Edison, NJ: Castle Books.

Nelson, C. (2002). *The First Heroes: The Extraordinary Story of the Doolittle Raid—America's First World War II Victory*. New York: Penguin Books.

Ness, L. (2014). *Rikugun: Guide to Japanese Ground Forces, 1937–1945*. Solihul, UK: Helion and Company.

Nolta, G. (2018). *The Doolittle Raiders: What Heroes Do After a War*. Atglen, PA: Schiffer.

Pope, S., and E.-A. Wheal (eds.) (1989). *The Macmillan Dictionary of the Second World War*. London: Macmillan.

Rose, L. A. (1995). *The Ship That Held the Line: The USS Hornet and the First Year of the Pacific War*. Annapolis, MD: Bluejacket Books.

Ruhle, W. A. (2015). *With Paulus at Stalingrad*. Barnsley, UK: Pen and Sword.

Scott, J. M. (2015). *Target Tokyo: Jimmy Doolittle and the Raid That Avenged Pearl Harbor*. New York: W. W. Norton.

Sebag-Montefiore, H. (2007). *Dunkirk: Fight to the Last Man*. New York: Penguin Books.

Slavinsky, B. (1995). *The Japanese-Soviet Neutrality Pact: A Diplomatic History, 1941–1945*. London: Routledge Curzon.

Spector, R. H. (1985). *Eagle Against the Sun: The American War with Japan*. New York: Vintage Books.

Standley, W. H. (1955). *Admiral Ambassador to Russia*. Chicago: Henry Regnery Company.

Survey, U. S. (1946). *The Campaigns of the Pacific War*. Naval Analysis Division, U.S. Government Printing Office.

*The New Yorker* Magazine (Finder, H., ed.) (2014). *The 40s: The Story of a Decade*. New York: Random House.

Tillman, B. (2010). *Whirlwind: The Air War Against Japan, 1942–1945*. New York: Simon & Schuster.

Toland, J. (1961). *Not in Shame*. New York: Random House.

———(1961). *The Rising Sun: The Decline and Fall of the Japanese Empire, 1936–1945*. New York: Random House.

Toll, I. W. (2020). *Twilight of the Gods*. New York: W. W. Norton.

Tully, J. P. (2005). *Shattered Sword: The Untold Story of the Battle of Midway*. Sterling, VA: Potomac Books.

USS *Hornet* Deck Log. (1942). United States Navy.

Wagner, R. (ed.) (1973). *The Soviet Air Force in World War II*. Garden City, NY: Doubleday.

Walling, M. G. (2012). *Forgotten Sacrifice: The Arctic Convoys of World War II*. Oxford, UK: Osprey.

Willmott, H. P. (1992). *The Great Crusade*. Sterling, VA: Potomac Books.

## Interviews and Oral Histories

Arnold, R. (2021, August 30). Hap Arnold. (D. Hampton, interviewer)

Arnold, R. (2022, January 3). (D. Hampton, interviewer)

Arnold, R. (2022, January 13). (D. Hampton, interviewer)

Arnold, R. (2022, January 14). (D. Hampton, interviewer)

Arnold, R. (2023, February 28). (D. Hampton, interviewer)

Arnold, R. (2023, March 4). (D. Hampton, interviewer)

DeShazer, R. J. (1989, October 10). USAF Oral History. (D. J. Hasdorf, interviewer)

Emmens, C. R. (1982, July 8–9). USAF Oral History. (D. J. Hasdorf, interviewer)

Emmens, M. (2021, May 21). (D. Hampton, interviewer)

Emmens, M. (2021, July 19). (D. Hampton, interviewer)

Emmens, M. (2022, January 3). (D. Hampton, interviewer)

Emmens, M. (2022, January 14). (D. Hampton, interviewer)

Emmens, M. (2022, February 21). (D. Hampton, interviewer)

Emmens, M. (2022, June 1). (D. Hampton, interviewer)

Jones, M. G. (1987, June 13–14). USAF Oral History. (D. J. Hasdorf, interviewer)

Hoppes, M. J. (2021, August 18). (D. Hampton, interviewer)

York, E. H. (1943, June 3). B-25 Crew Interned by the Russians. (C. W. Burgess, interviewer)

York, M. E. (1943). Tokyo Raid-Crew 8; Memorandum for Lt. Colonel J. E. Johnston. (M. H. Stebbins, interviewer)

York, C. E. (1984, July 23). USAF Oral History. (D. J. Hasdorf, interviewer)

# ABOUT THE AUTHOR

**Lieutenant Colonel (Ret.) Dan Hampton** flew 151 combat missions during his twenty years (1986–2006) in the United States Air Force. For his actions during the Iraq War, Kosovo conflict, and the first Gulf War, Hampton received four Distinguished Flying Crosses with Valor, a Purple Heart, eight Air Medals with Valor, and numerous other decorations. An alumnus of Exeter College, Oxford, he also holds degrees from Dartmouth and Texas A&M, and is a graduate of the elite USAF Weapons School. As a frequent guest on CNN, Fox News, and MSNBC, he discusses foreign affairs and geopolitics, and he has also appeared as an analyst on *The O'Reilly Factor*, *The Sean Hannity Show*, *Tucker Carlson Tonight*, and *Anderson Cooper 360°*. He is the national bestselling author of *Viper Pilot*, *Lords of the Sky*, *The Hunter Killers*, *The Flight*, *Chasing the Demon*, *Operation Vengeance*, *Valor*, and a novel, *The Mercenary*.

U. S. NAVAL AIR STATION
N. O. B. NORFOLK, VIRGINIA

**RECEIVED**

URGENT URGENT

HEADING:

HM NR 23 L Z SNUO 071930 / 142 RAFT P GR 6

INFO:

FROM: M. Robert
SECNAV

TO:
ALNAV

URGENT

EXECUTE WPL FORTY SIX AGAINST JAPAN

SE/2005 DEC7TH

| CAPT | EXEC | COMM | GGD | COO | OPER | SO | A&R | ORD | AERO | PERS | DISB | MED | EXP | PWD |
|---|---|---|---|---|---|---|---|---|---|---|---|---|---|---|
| X | X | X | 1517 | X | X | | | | | | | | | FAOOD |

---

# Los Angeles Times

# TOKYO BOMBED!

## Jobs for Women Worrying Olson

## R.A.F. Hurls 600 Bombers Against Nazis

### American Army Primed for Offensive

## Raiding Craft Unidentified

### Jap Control to Be Stricter

Losses of Man Power Total 60,000 in Bataan

U.S. Big Guns Silence Japs

IN THE 'TIMES' TODAY

America Calls Leahy Home From Vichy Ambassadorship